CARVING HISTORY

The Life & Works of Andrew Currie

Bob Johnstone

Carving History: The Life & Works of Andrew Currie
Copyright © 2012 Bob Johnstone

ISBN-13: 978-1479295616

ISBN-10: 1479295612

Cover credits:

Design by Lee Noel; back cover photos courtesy of John Reiach, Walter McLaren and Tom Little Collection (Melrose Historical Association)

For my great-great grandchildren,
if any

CONTENTS

FAMILY TREE I: CURRIES

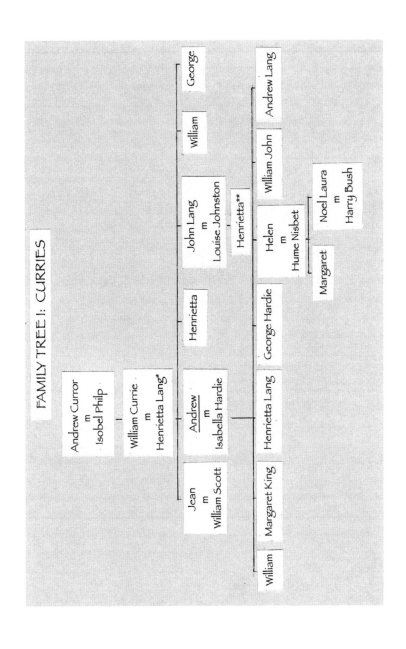

Andrew Curror
m
Isobel Philp

William Currie
m
Henrietta Lang*

Andrew
m
Isabella Hardie

Jean
m
William Scott

Henrietta

John Lang
m
Louise Johnston

William

George

Henrietta**

William
Margaret King

Henrietta Lang

George Hardie

Helen
m
Hume Nisbet

William John

Andrew Lang

Margaret

Noel Laura
m
Harry Bush

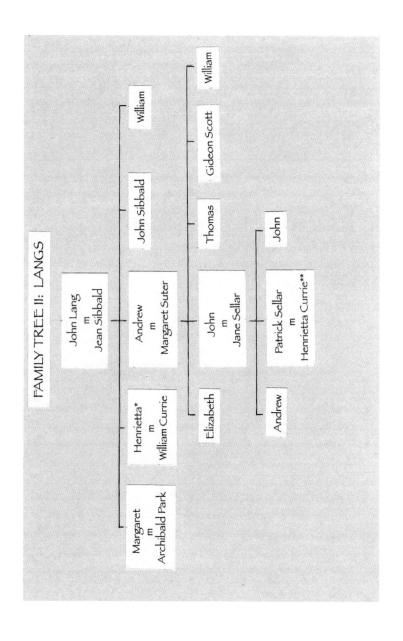

FAMILY TREE II: LANGS

John Lang
m
Jean Sibbald

Margaret
m
Archibald Park

Henrietta*
m
William Currie

Andrew
m
Margaret Suter

John Sibbald

William

Elizabeth

John
m
Jane Sellar

Thomas

Gideon Scott

William

Andrew

Patrick Sellar
m
Henrietta Currie**

John

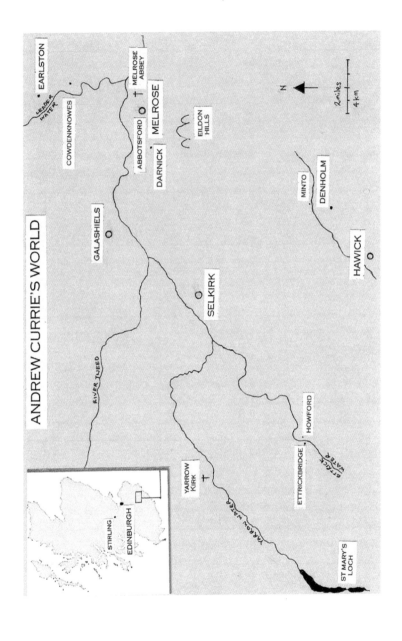

PREFACE

Andrew Currie (1812~1891) was more than just a gifted carver of large-scale monuments in stone and finely-wrought furniture in wood. He was also an enthusiastic antiquary, an oral historian, and a lively writer who penned eminently readable stories of life in the Borders of his youth.

The son of an insolvent Selkirkshire sheep farmer, Andrew Currie was obliged against his will to take up a trade. He worked as a millwright until his mid forties, when his health broke. Only then did he become a sculptor, which had long been his dream.

Despite his late start and the fact that he was completely self-taught, Andrew Currie managed to win prestigious public commissions in competition with much better-qualified rivals. He was, by all accounts, quite a character.

He was also, as it happens, my great-great-grandfather.

*

The chain of events that led me to start work on this book began innocuously enough, with a request from one of my sons. He asked me to put together a family tree for him. This task I immediately passed on to my eldest brother who, being older, is better-versed in such matters than me. He duly obliged, but there was something lacking in the bare framework of names and dates he drew up. Wouldn't it be nice, I thought, to try and put some flesh on the bones: but where to begin? The only ancestor of ours who had been even remotely famous was Andrew Currie.

2 Carving History

He was, we knew, a sculptor with several well-known statues to his credit. Most notably, the monument to the Ettrick Shepherd at St Mary's Loch, the memorial to Mungo Park in Selkirk, the figure of King Robert the Bruce on the Esplanade at Stirling Castle, and two of the character statues on the Scott Monument in Edinburgh. I remember as a boy my mother proudly pointing the latter out to me as we walked past them on Princes Street. There were also some carvings at a Catholic church in Galashiels. And that was about the size of it. But at least it was something to go on. So, sitting at my desk from my home in Melbourne, I began Googling.

A challenge soon formulated itself: to what extent was it possible, using the nternet, to resurrect someone from the mists of time? Of course, to have any chance of success, it had to be a person who was noticed by his contemporaries, as Andrew Currie had been, mainly because of the public monuments he carved. Sure enough, in databases I discovered contemporary newspaper reports about him and his work. In recent years, entire libraries of long-forgotten texts have been digitized and put online. Thanks to them, the quest has been a lot less quixotic than it might otherwise have been.

After a few happy hours - it may well have been days - of digging up bits and pieces here and there, it occurred to me that I did not know even the` basic facts about Andrew Currie's life; in particular, when and where he had been born. So I bit the bullet, paid seven pounds to a government-run website called Scotland's People, and downloaded a handwritten page from the records of the parish of Yarrow in Selkirkshire. From this I learned that Andrew Currie was born on 6th November 1812. It being mid 2011, that meant his bicentennial would fall the following year. This seemed somehow propitious. I also discovered that his parents' names were William Currie and Henrietta Lang; and that William had been a tenant farmer at Howford, a new name to me. So I plugged "Currie" and "Howford" and "Yarrow" into the search engine and hit return. The first result that popped up read as follows:

John Lang Currie — Australian Dictionary of Biography

This came as a smack in the gob, the first of many. Unbeknownst to me, or for that matter anyone else in our branch of the family, we had Australian relatives! John Lang Currie, it turned out, was Andrew's younger brother. In 1841 he had emigrated to Victoria, where he became an immensely successful sheep farmer. When JLC died in 1898 he left a fortune of half a million pounds — serious money in those days (and nothing to sneeze at now). So I was not, as I had fondly imagined, the first in the family to make it as far as the antipodes.

According to his entry in the dictionary, John Lang Currie had had children. So his descendants were probably still out there somewhere. It didn't take me long to discover that at least one set of distant cousins - more than one, as I later learned - were living right here in Victoria. I emailed them, asking if they had any Andrew-Currie-related materials. The initial reply was dubious, its between-the-lines message: don't get your hopes up.

By a curious coincidence, at exactly this time, I came across an exchange of letters about Andrew Currie that *The Scotsman* had published in 1920. One correspondent mentioned that Andrew had been working on memoirs; the other replied he feared that "these [memoirs] are now widely scattered, if they are still extant. I have seen portions in the possession of descendants in Scotland, but the main pile is likely to be in Australia." The idea that memoirs existed was new and exciting. They would surely give at least some sense of the person who had written them. But even if they were in Australia, what were the chances ever finding these memoirs? Not good, I reckoned, real needle-in-a-haystack stuff.

The very next day, I received a series of emails from one of my newfound cousins. Attached to them were scans of documents, contracts and letters, a detailed appreciation from a contemporary magazine of the life of Andrew Currie, and - most remarkable of all - the frontispiece of a diary written in Andrew's own hand. Of all the places in the world that they could have been, the memoirs had turned up right here in Victoria, about a two-and-a-half-hour drive from where we live!

4 Carving History

Up to that point, I had been contemplating a website that would pull together photographs of all of Andrew's known works, plus whatever biographical information I could glean. Now I realized that with memoirs, the project could be much bigger. The idea that became this book began to form.

My cousin kindly allowed me to copy what turned out to be four handwritten exercise books of reminiscences and diaries. Transcribing them was intensely exciting: I felt that Andrew Currie was talking directly to me, telling me stories about his life and times, stories that had lain forgotten in a trunk for many decades. They were, I thought, remarkably well-written, by a man who had obviously had a sharp eye, a lively mind and a fine, self-deprecatory sense of humour. And, as the first page of the reminiscences made clear, Andrew wanted what he had written to be read: "... in hope that there may yet be some passages that may prove instructive to others, especially to those of my own children after me ... ."

So, in addition to photographs of his works, I now understood that his writings must be published, too, so that other family members, scholars and who knew who else might enjoy them. Plus, it might also be possible to compose a short biography of the man based on the memoirs.

*

A brief life of Andrew Currie forms the first part of this book. Having written it, I must confess that getting to know the old boy after all these years has been a great pleasure. It has also been gratifying to learn a little about my roots. Though my father was born in Selkirk and my mother's people (including my grandmother, Agnes Currie) were from Galashiels, I myself have never lived in the Borders.

At the same time, I am acutely aware that there are many gaps in the biography. All sorts of questions remain. How, for instance, was Andrew's father William cheated out of his inheritance? This unfortunate occurrence is what led to his insolvency, thus to Andrew being apprenticed as a tradesman instead of going to university or art school as he might otherwise well have done.

As a young journeyman Andrew worked at Chatham Dockyard in Kent. While in England he almost certainly visited the British Museum - in his writings he refers several times to artifacts there - as you might expect of someone who was passionately interested in sculpture and antiquity. Where else did he go? We will probably never know.

An acquaintance records that Andrew met his hero Sir Walter Scott several times. What did they talk about? We have no idea. Even more frustrating is the nature of the relationship between Andrew and his sometime patron, the writer's grandson-in-law James Hope-Scott. Circumstantial evidence points to Hope-Scott having been instrumental in Andrew's conversion to Catholicism, but was he really?

What follows falls far short of a resurrection. But at least it's a start.

* * *

PART I: BORDER LIFE

One

Born Not Made

For such a secluded spot, it was quite a crowd. On Thursday 28 June 1860, despite weather that was according to the organizer "unpropitious" - meaning that the rain, as is not uncommon in the Scottish Borders, was bucketing down - some two thousand souls had showed up. The occasion was the inauguration of a memorial statue erected to honour a local literary celebrity. To wit, the humbly-born, self-educated poet, novelist and satirist James Hogg, aka the Ettrick Shepherd, author most famously of *Confessions of a Justified Sinner*, who had died twenty-five years earlier, aged 65.

From towns and villages all around they flocked, congregating at a grassy knoll on a triangular patch of ground just off the road, about thirteen miles southwest of Selkirk, where St Mary's Loch meets the Loch of the Lowes. The nobs traveled down from the capital by the first train. They were met at Selkirk railway station, opened just four years earlier, then whisked off by horse-drawn omnibuses. Plough-men and servant-girls dressed in their Sunday best came on foot. Jovial youths brought with them fishing rods and creels (Hogg had been a keen angler). An enthusiastic young photographer lugged his huge camera "across weary hills" in order to record the scene.[1]

---

[1] Seven years later Robert Clapperton would open Scotland's first photographic studio in Selkirk. His nephew Thomas Clapperton (1879~1962) would become a successful sculptor

Inauguration of the Monument to James Hogg, the Ettrick Shepherd, St Mary's Loch, 28 June 1860
Robert Clapperton © Clapperton Trust

whose works include the bronze figures and reliefs that adorn the foot of Andrew Currie's monument to Mungo Park.

The hoi polloi were instructed to assemble at a rendezvous across the road from the knoll, Tibbie Shiel's Inn. This had been a frequent haunt in bygone days of the Shepherd and his fancy Edinburgh writer friends. Tibbie herself, then in her late seventies, was on hand in her old-fashioned widow's cap, dispensing drinks and pithy opinions about the bard, whose death mask hung on her wall. "Aye, Hogg was a gey sensible man," she liked to tell customers, "for a' the nonsense that he wrat."

The festivities began at one o'clock. A procession wound its way from the inn, crossed the bridge between the two lochs, then headed up to the still-shrouded statue. Shepherds had gathered at nearby Crosscleuch farm. Now, providing authenticity, with dogs at heel and sticks in hand they strode forward, their simple black-and-white check plaids flung over one shoulder in the manner that Hogg had made famous. Some carried banners, including one that bore a crude likeness of Hector, Hogg's favourite collie.

The herdsmen were led by the imposing six-foot figure of Donald Bain, gallant piper of the Highland Brigade. A few years earlier, during the Crimean War, Bain had won fame - and been wounded - skirling the regimental colours up the heights at the Battle of Alma. His martial bearing, piercing eye and flowing beard belied a mischievous nature. While the hero was in hospital recovering from his wound, a would-be usurper found mice in the bag of his pipes. It was assumed that Bain was to blame.

Behind the shepherds trotted members of the Shepherd's family, including his three daughters, Margaret, Mary and Jessie; son-in-law, William Garden; and nephew, Robert. The bard's wife, Margaret Hogg, was not present, but would come later to inspect the monument to her husband. Ahead of the relatives, adding a splash of colour and historical pomp to the ceremony, strutted the Albany Herald. This antique functionary, as the wide-eyed wonder of the shepherds plainly told, was "altogether a sight not to be seen in the [Ettrick] Forest every day."

The Herald was attired in the costume of his sixteenth-century predecessors: a sleeveless blue satin tunic called a tabard, black velvet hat with feathers, and black hose with knee-britches. On his breast this striking individual wore his badge, a saltire (diagonal St Andrew's cross) encircled with a golden coronet of four fleurs-de-lys ("one and two halves visible") and surmounted by the crown of Scotland. The badge was suspended on a chain whose enormous links were "only a little smaller than the anchor-chain of a man-of-war." Across his chest the Herald sported the national ribbon and other decorations "too numerous to mention."

The cavalcade arrived at the foot of the monument. Robed in dripping wet canvas this was, for the moment, "as melancholy-looking an object as one could wish to see." The crowd arranged itself in front of a wooden platform that had presciently been provided with an awning to keep off the rain. Onto it climbed the dignitaries, family representatives, members of the monument committee, and several reporters from local newspapers.

The Reverend James Russell, minister of the local parish of Yarrow, initiated proceedings with a prayer. Then, acting as master of ceremonies, the Albany Herald stepped forward to announce that the inaugural ceremony had officially begun. The sculptor uncovered the statue. A burst of loud cheering erupted from the spectators. As if on cue the rain stopped, the clouds began to lift, and within minutes of Henry Glassford Bell beginning his inaugural address, the sun was shining brightly.

Sheriff-Substitute of Glasgow and a renowned public speaker, Bell was also a patron of the fine arts who had known the Shepherd well. He had, he recalled, "listened, many a time and oft," to the bard "warbling his wild, fresh, moorland ditties." Bell's commanding presence and sonorous voice held the audience entranced for over an hour. He eventually concluded with "an elegant panegyric on the poet's genius." His auld acquaintance was "a true poet - not equal to Burns, because no national poet was ever equal to him - but justly entitled to take rank in the second place, and worthily taking up the harp which he found lying on the grave of that immortal man."

Then it was time to eat. For the throng on the green, dinner - or as they say in England, lunch - was al fresco. For almost two hundred ladies and gentlemen, including local bigwigs and the subscribers who had paid for the monument, a banquet was served in a spacious marquee that had been erected for the day near

Tibbie Shiel's Inn. The County Hotel, Selkirk, provided tables and chairs. The sponsor of this munificence, Mr Scott, a wealthy Edinburgh lawyer who formerly had entertained the Shepherd in his home and latterly had acted as trustee to his children, was unavoidably absent.

Scott had been keen that the Hogg monument should be built upon his recently-acquired property of Chapelhope. His offer came as a happy solution to the vexed question of finding a suitable site on which to rear the statue. Ettrick had been the obvious choice, being both the poet's birthplace and "the scene of his interment" in the kirk yard. However, the valley was initially deemed too out-of-the-way for the proposed memorial. In its stead, a prominent spot was selected at Mount Benger, overlooking the farm where the Shepherd had lived at the height of his fame. This site proved impossible to obtain. Consideration next shifted to Edinburgh, where Hogg's writings had been published in magazine and book form. There, as a national bard, he would be worthily associated with his friends and contemporaries, like Sir Walter Scott and Professor John Wilson. The Calton Hill was first proposed, then a site was granted near the Scott Monument in Princess Street Gardens.

"Our citizens must understand that the monument will be worthy of a conspicuous and honorable position," opined a contributor to the *Caledonian Mercury and Daily Express*, "not less on account of the subject than on its merit as a work of art." But the notion of accommodating in such august surroundings the statue of a man of lamentably vulgar tendencies may have given the Edinburgh elite second thoughts. William Wordsworth, who had thrown off an extemporary elegy on the poet's death lauding Hogg as "the mighty minstrel," sniffed privately that while the Shepherd was "undoubtedly a man of original genius," he also had "coarse manners and low and offensive opinions." Besides, Borderers baulked at the prospect of the monument to their man being erected anywhere but Ettrick. With the capital ruled out, Selkirk was suggested as the next best thing. But the subscribers grumbled about "adding to the adornments of a provincial town." Selkirk was already well-endowed with statuary, having put up monuments to two of its favourite sons, Walter Scott and Mungo Park. Ultimately, the site at

Chapelhope was settled upon, an outcome that had fortuitously been predicted in print many years previously by Hogg's crony Wilson:

> "My beloved Shepherd, some half century hence, your effigy will be seen on some bonny green knowe in the forest, with its honest face looking across St Mary's Loch ..."

After dinner, "speeches appropriate to the occasion were delivered." The curtain walls of the marquee were raised to enable the throng outside the tent to hear the fine rhetoric. The first speaker was James Pillans, an eminent educational reformer who had held the chair of humanity and laws at Edinburgh University since 1820. On formal occasions such as this Pillans wore a blue coat with brass buttons, and a top hat made from white beaver fur. Despite his advanced age - he was now over eighty - the professor was still remarkably hale. Disdaining spectacles, he read his text with the aid of a huge magnifying glass.

Pillans was followed by the Hon. William Napier, standing in for his brother Francis Napier, Lord Lieutenant of Selkirkshire, who had his seat at nearby Thirlestane Castle. The Rev. Henry Scott Riddell, a fellow poet and lyricist, best-known for his version of the popular Border ballad, *The Dowie Dens o' Yarrow*, who was like Hogg the son of a shepherd, said a few words. Mr William Pagan of Clayton sang a song, *Love is Like a Dizziness*. Then another reverend, Charles Rogers, stood up to present a history of the enterprise.

Rogers was the commissioner of the statue, organizer of the event, and author of a six-volume compilation, *The Modern Scottish Minstrel*. In the summer of 1858 he had sent out a circular letter "to personal friends of the bard and known admirers of his genius," proposing to erect a monument to the author of such celebrated odes as *Kilmeny* ("Bonnie Kilmeny gaed up the glen"). His purpose was to determine whether in the event of a public appeal the proposal would be adequately supported. The response was uniformly favourable. The Duke of Buccleuch led the way, tendering a contribution of ten pounds.

Who would be a suitable artist to carve the statue? John Steell, the preeminent Scottish sculptor of the day, who had done such a wonderful job with the marble representation of Sir Walter Scott that sits in his eponymous monument in Edinburgh, was well beyond their budget. Handyside Ritchie, the Edinburgh-based mason who had carved the statue of Scott that stands in the centre of Selkirk (and whom Rogers had recently commissioned for another monument nearby), would have been a better bet. After some deliberation, however, it was resolved to entrust the execution to a little-known local artist named Andrew Currie.

This was an inspired choice, for several reasons. Like Hogg, Currie was "a native of the [Ettrick] Forest." In his youth he had been personally acquainted with the Shepherd. The sculptor was eager to do the job, confessing that he had long cherished the idea of constructing a statute to honour the bard's memory. He also had form, in the shape of Selkirk's memorial to the explorer Mungo Park, which had been unveiled to public acclaim earlier that year. Accordingly, in September 1859, Rogers commissioned Andrew Currie to prepare a design and submit an estimate. The sculptor was required to fashion a clay model, which "the ingenious artist accomplished in a very admirable manner." With the preliminaries satisfactorily completed, fund-raising began in earnest.

In a few months, upwards of £300 had been subscribed. Most of the money was raised locally. Contributions were also received from England and America. A remittance of £50 arrived from Australia, sent by "a native of the Border." The target required to complete the structure was £500. In the event, Rogers reported, the entire amount raised was £404.[2] (The reverend gentleman would later indignantly deny scurrilous reports in a Glasgow newspaper alleging that he had creamed 25 percent off the monument fund as commission.)

Though substantial, the figure would not stretch to the cost of purchasing a stone. Happily, the Duke of Buccleuch, the noble magnate who owned much of the surrounding country - both the Shepherd and the sculptor's father had been

---

[2] According to a letter Rogers wrote on 16 July 1860, "[a]fter deducting all expenses ... there will be a balance for Mr Currie of about £345 ...". Using the National Archives calculator, this would be worth about £14,900 in 2005 money.

tenants on his farms - stepped in with a solution to the problem. In addition to a "handsome pecuniary contribution," his grace gifted a massive block of sandstone from his personal quarry, at Whita Hill near Langholm, to be converted into the figure of the bard. The duke gave particular instructions that a stone "without flaw or blemish should be secured." It took four months for quarrymen to disintegrate a suitable chunk. Their first three attempts were found to have flaws thus deemed unsuitable. It was only on the fourth go that they managed to hew an unblemished block. The stone was roughly fashioned into some semblance of the intended figure in the bed of the quarry, then transferred - initially by horse-drawn wagon, an epic journey full of incident and mishap that will be described later - to the sculptor's workshop in Darnick, about thirty miles distant. Eight months later, at the beginning of June, the monument was completed and transported to its final destination upon the slight incline between the two lochs.

The bard is represented larger than life, in meditative mood, seated cross-legged on a moss-covered oak-root, a relic of the old Forest. His head, topped with an unruly quiff, inclines slightly downwards, as if surveying the scenery. A shepherd's plaid is draped gracefully across his torso, from right shoulder to left thigh. His coat is buttoned up to the collar, to keep out the cold. His right hand plants his shepherd's staff firmly in the ground. Beneath his left hand is a manuscript inscribed with a slightly modified version of the last line of his epic 1813 poem, *The Queen's Wake*, whose unexpected popular success had briefly placed Hogg alongside Byron and Scott as one of the most admired British poets of the day:

He taught the wandering winds to sing.

At Hogg's feet lies his favorite dog, Hector. The collie's head is erect, scanning the hills behind, checking to make sure that none of his master's flock has wandered off during the Shepherd's poetic reverie. The bard had been especially attached to Hector. He was a small dog with a rough, shaggy coat which, unusually for a collie, was coloured red. "A shepherd may be a very able, trusty and good shepherd, without a sweetheart better perhaps than with one," Hogg wrote. "But what is he without his dog?"

The ensemble sits on a massive tapered pedestal about ten feet tall. A wreath of oak leaves and acorns surrounds its entablature, a finely-wrought ram's head projecting from each of the four bevelled corners. All four sides of the pedestal contain panels. The front one displays a harp surmounted by a miniature head of Mary Queen of Scots, whose return to Scotland in 1561 is the subject of Hogg's epic. (The "Wake" of the title means a poetic contest, held to welcome back the queen.) The panel is adorned with a delicate wreath of forest flowers, including "the briar rose and heather bell" which, together with the harp, are mentioned in the poem. Underneath, in small letters, the inscription reads:

JAMES HOGG

THE ETTRICK SHEPHERD

Born 1770 Died 1835

On the side panels are engraved passages from *The Queen's Wake*, most aptly:

Oft had he viewed, as morning rose,

The bosom of the lonely Lowes;

Oft thrilled his heart at close of even

To see the dappled vales of heaven,

With many a mountain, moor, and tree

Asleep upon the Saint Mary.

The dignified figure was intended to represent the bard in his prime, "at that period of his life when he was in full bodily vigour and in the zenith of his fame." The sculptor, it was agreed by many of Hogg's former intimates and at least one of his daughters, had well and truly captured the poet's features.[3] "None who remember the Shepherd in his vigour - his manly lith and limb - can doubt the fidelity of the likeness," enthused the Rev. Russell.

It fell to the minister to round out the afternoon's entertainment. His task was to propose a toast to the health of the monument's creator, Andrew Currie. The man of the moment was a diffident, dreamy-looking 48-year-old with "well-formed features of a slightly Jewish cast," a reference perhaps to a prominent, somewhat aquiline nose. His long face was framed by a receding mass of fine curly hair. An untrimmed bushy beard hid a wide mouth. Above the long curved nose twinkled a pair of bright brown eyes "in which fun and humour lurked."

The toast that Russell made was fulsome and, in this context, worth quoting at length. The throng was by then in a good mood. According to the transcript, published two days after the event in *The Courant*, an Edinburgh newspaper, the speech was repeatedly interrupted by cheers. Drink had doubtless been taken.

"I claim the privilege of long acquaintance with Mr Currie, as a former parishioner, too," the minister began, "and well do I remember the future artist in his teens, sitting in the house of prayer almost side by side with the living bard, then past his prime. You will agree with me that ... having such a man, modest as he is talented, with the additional recommendation of being one of ourselves, Dr Rogers, the prime mover in this matter did well in entrusting to him the execution of the work which has just been inaugurated. (Cheers)

"As a work of art, it is admirable, even the uninitiated being judges ... . Our Forest ... can boast of its accomplished traveller, the pioneer of civilization [Mungo Park]; it can boast of its shepherd-poet; and now it can lay claim to its sculptor, too, who has stereotyped in stone the features and figure of them both." (Cheers)

"Reference might be made," the cleric continued, "to testimony of many from all quarters of the land, whose authority in such matters is unquestionable. I have

---

[3] One shepherd, though impressed with the pose of the dog at Hogg's feet and by the way that the fringes of the poet's plaid had been carved to look like real wool, was nonetheless critical of a couple of details. "Did ye e'er see a herd carrying a stick wi' nobs like they?" he demanded. "An' how could ony herd speel [climb] the hillsides w' sic bits [boots] as thon?"

heard Mr John Steell, who himself stands so high in the profession, speak in most laudatory terms of Mr Currie, for some small casts and carvings he had seen at Abbotsford.[4] Nothing but the imperative duties of his own studio would have prevented his being present here. Mr Robert Chambers has expressed his unhesitating opinion that no man he ever met possessed more original genius as a sculptor, or has succeeded better in the delineation of Scottish character.[5] Mr John Rochead - and this is perhaps the highest eulogy of all, because that of a distinguished, generous, and successful rival in the Wallace Monument competition - regards Mr Currie's spirited model of Sir William Wallace as conveying the best possible idea of a hero, and has proposed to the committee that a statue in accordance with that model should be placed in the interior of the monument."[6] (Cheers)

But what was most remarkable about Andrew Currie was not so much his skill, which was self-evident to all present. Rather, it was the fact that he had been trained not as sculptor, but as a millwright, a species of humble mechanic. Indeed, Andrew had only begun his career as a professional carver a few years previously, when he was over forty years old. He was completely self-taught.

"We may say of the sculptor, as of the poet, 'nascitur non fit,'" [born not made] the minister went on, confident that his audience could comprehend the Latin. "He is the child and nursing of nature herself, for the inborn tendencies are sure, sooner or later, to develop themselves, and rise above the force of circumstances. It has been so with Currie and with Hogg — [and] I might add, with Scott. All of them had come to years before breaking through the tame routine of their original vocation, and following out what each felt to be his mission."

---

[4] John Steell (1804~1891), preeminent Scottish sculptor of the period, whose works most notable works include the white marble statue of Sir Walter Scott in the Scott Monument in Edinburgh.

[5] Robert Chambers (1802~1871), Scottish publisher, geologist, proto-evolutionary thinker, author and journal editor whom Andrew met in Selkirk when Chambers was collecting materials for his book, The Picture of Scotland (1827).

[6] John Rochead (1814~1878), Scottish architect, designer of the Wallace Monument, the foundation stone for which was laid in 1861.

Poet and sculptor also had something else in common: insolvent fathers. Lack of funds had deprived both of proper educations, forcing them into occupations that would under normal circumstances have been beneath them.

"I believe that our friend had many wincings under the yoke ere he ventured to play the truant," the pastor added, "that, solitary and unseen, he spent much of the midnight oil, after laborious days, in poring over works of art; and that he employed hours stolen from his rest in moulding the plastic clay, or the more lasting wood, into forms of life and fancy and beauty. (Cheers)

"It was a bold step for a family man to take, to forsake the mechanical trade to which he was trained, and carve out for himself a different course of life. It looked as if he were casting aside the useful and remunerative wheel and axle to try the proverbial fickle wheel of fortune. And one cannot but admire the manly courage, the spirit of self-reliance, the confidence in a gracious Providence that had blessed him with such faculties and aspirations ... with which he appealed to a discriminating public. His brief career has vindicated the change and the choice. It is truly marvellous how, in so short a time, with no outward advantages whatever, no school of design, no friendly patron at home, but simply by means of his own chisel and mallet, he has proved himself every inch an artist." (Great cheers)

Marvellous indeed. The statue of the Ettrick Shepherd is Andrew Currie's masterpiece in stone. For the sculptor, the ceremonial unveiling on this wet afternoon at St Mary's Loch must have come as resounding confirmation that he had, at long last, found his vocation.

* * *

Two

Wrong Choice (1812~1829)

Andrew Currie was born on 6th November 1812 at Howford, a farm in the parish of Yarrow, Selkirkshire, "the least populous county in Scotland," into a family that was downwardly mobile and a world wracked by turmoil and conflict. Across the Border in England, aggrieved Luddites were smashing the new, automated looms and burning down the textile mills that housed them. Across the Channel in Europe, the Napoleonic Wars were raging. That Spring, at the bloody siege of Badajoz in Spain, Andrew's uncle John Sibbald Lang, an ensign in the Scots Brigade, had been shot through the head and killed, aged 25. That September, Napoleon began his disastrous retreat from Moscow, having failed to destroy the Imperial Russian Army at the decisive battle of Borodino. This Pyrrhic victory would be commemorated by Tchaikovsky in his *1812 Overture*, with its famous cannons-booming, chimes-ringing, kitchen-sink finale. First performed in 1882 it was, in the composer's own opinion, "very loud and noisy, but ... lacking in artistic merit."

Andrew was the first male child in his family to be christened Currie. His father had been baptised William Curror, then subsequently for reasons best known to himself changed his surname to the more common Currie. In those days no-one cared much about orthography: the spelling of the family name on parish birth records fluctuates wildly, from Curror to Currer to Curier. Curror was the default though, an ancient Scottish surname that supposedly derives from the Old French "coreor," meaning messenger, from which we get our modern word courier. There had been Currors in the Ettrick Forest since the thirteenth century, back when the forest still had trees and functioned as a royal hunting ground. In the early sixteenth century King James V drove out the deer, felled the timber (which he donated to rebuild the town of Selkirk after the English burned it down) and turned the land into sheep pasture. In Sir Walter Scott's words:

> The scenes are desert now, and bare,
> Where flourished once a forest fair,
> When these waste glens with copse were lined
> And peopled with the hart and hind.

There had also been Curries in this part of the world. But theirs is a different lineage whose name probably comes from the Gaelic "curraigh," meaning bog.

The Currors were a respectable family. In the mid seventeenth century they acquired Hartwoodburn and Brownmuir, adjoining farms located a mile or so south of Selkirk. In 1713 the estate was divided between two sons, the elder brother George receiving Hartwoodburn; his younger brother Thomas, Brownmuir. Though Hartwoodburn was soon sold, Currors continued farming at Brownmuir throughout the eighteenth century. But for families with multiple sons, there was never enough land to go around, nor money to acquire more.

In 1790 the sculptor's grandfather Andrew Curror (b 1732) took out a lease on Howford, a picturesque farm on a bend of Ettrick Water southwest of Selkirk. It was located just across the river from the village of Ettrickbridge-End, known to its hundred-odd inhabitants as "the Brig-End." Howford belonged to the Duke of Buccleuch, meaning that Andrew Curror had become a tenant farmer, a step down in the world from landed gentry. At least by then leases had been lengthened to encourage tenants to improve land that was not their own. The contract Andrew signed was for twenty-two years.

As the eighteenth century gave way to the nineteenth, Scotland was casting off the archaic and putting on the modern. Wave after wave of agricultural innovation swept through the Lowlands. Andrew Curror's father (b 1699), confusingly also named Andrew, had believed in the old superstitions:

"Mr. Andrew Curror had family worship every night before retiring to rest, when all his servants who fed in the house were present. During ripening and intaking of the crops he, like many other farmers, was afraid that the Devil might take it into his head to allow rain or wind to destroy his crops; therefore in his family prayers he besought earnestly that the Devil might be chained for a season to prevent such a misfortune happening. Some of the young and thoughtless members of his household conceived the idea of having some fun at the expense of the good old man. They quietly got up into the loft above the kitchen where the people assembled for prayers and took with them a chain. When the chaining of Satan was prayed for they rattled the chain with all their might, much to the astonishment and alarm of old Mr. Curror and the amusement of the audience, many of whom were in on the secret."

Andrew Curror the younger was by contrast a man who embraced the new ways. Witness the following letter written from Howford to his son William, the sculptor's father, dated 16 April 1796. As may be imagined from the symptoms Andrew describes, he was by then on his last legs:

"I have been in such a poor state of Health the last month that I could do nothing and was not able to ride the lenth of Selkirk, I am much worz than my ordinarie Asmatick ways, being troubled with a stopage of water, which keeps me from sleeping in the night, so that it is often ten eleven and some times twelve o'clock

before I get out of bed and when up am not able to look after the
people, therefore I wish you to come home as soon as possible ..."

William, then aged 24, had evidently been sent away to learn the ropes on
another farm, run by professional managers, which employed the new technology.
He was to report back on what he found there:

"As to the Mouldie Boarded plough you may take a good look of
one of them, so that the wright here may make one after your
directions ... ."

This refers to the revolutionary plough invented by James Small, a
Berwickshire blacksmith, in 1763. Small improved the mould-board - the wedge-
shaped part of the iron blade that turns the furrow - to such an extent that it could
be pulled by just two horses instead of the eight oxen required to drag the old
wooden ploughs it replaced.

A contemporary writer on the state of Scottish husbandry singled out Andrew
Curror's cousin Thomas as "a leader in the art of farming." At Brownmuir in 1796,
Thomas was experimenting with irrigation to encourage grass to grow earlier in
the season (thus benefiting ewes that were pregnant or suckling their lambs).
Having grown up in a culture that encouraged experimentation and an
entrepreneurial attitude, emigrant Scottish pastoralists like John Lang Currie, the
sculptor's younger brother, would deploy skills learned at home to prodigious
effect in Australia and elsewhere.

*

Andrew Curror died in 1797, aged 65, when William was just 25 years old. It seems
he left his son a significant sum of money, but the naive young man was cheated
out of his inheritance via legal action taken by a "polished" cousin — possibly a
minister. Certainly William sank into insolvency, unable to pay his debts. Among

them the most pressing would have been rent owing on the farm. He was ultimately rescued by the Langs, one of Selkirk's leading families. They mustered several "writers to the signet", that is, solicitors.[7] Starting in 1782, four successive generations of Langs would hold the influential post of sheriff-clerk of the shire. As local magistrates they dealt with minor procedures like estate disputes, fine payments, civil actions and bankruptcies.

Andrew Lang (1783~1842) was sheriff-clerk for twenty-seven of the thirty-three years that Sir Walter Scott was Sheriff of Selkirk. Scott thought highly of Lang, judging by a letter he wrote describing a surprise visit paid by Prince Leopold of Saxe-Coburg to Selkirk in 1819. In the marketplace, before an unruly crowd, the magistrate presented Leopold with the freedom of the burgh:

> "Lang made an excellent speech, sensible, and feeling, and well delivered. The Prince seemed much surprised at this great propriety of expression and behaviour in a magistrate, whose people seemed such a rabble, and whose whole band of music consisted in a drum and fife."

The Shirra was also on more than one occasion beholden to his clerk for "assistance in emergencies of impecuniosity." In other words, tapping him for a few quid when skint.

Andrew Lang had three older sisters, Margaret, Henrietta and Charlotte. Margaret married a farmer, Archibald Park, brother of the African explorer Mungo. Henrietta fell in love with another Park brother, Adam, who like Mungo was a doctor. But he jilted her and bolted down south, leaving poor Henrietta in the lurch. It was said that she was never the same again.

---

[7] Writers were licensed to draw up legal documents such as writs that required to be "signeted," ie, stamped with the private seal of the King of Scotland.

Eventually, in 1810, the family elders arranged a marriage for her with William Currie. By that time both were well into their thirties: William was 38; Henrietta, 32. Some thought it a mismatch. Nonetheless, the union produced six children — Jean, Andrew, Henrietta, John Lang, William and George, the last-named born in 1823, when Henrietta was 45 years old. It seems that under the terms of the nuptial settlement, William Currie's brothers-in-law agreed to take over the lease of the farm at Howford. It was renewed in 1812, the year of Andrew's birth, two years after the marriage, nominally in William's name. The annual rent was £222 which, given his debts, William would otherwise have been unable to pay.[8]

Judging by what their eldest son wrote about them, his parents were temperamentally incompatible. William was a kind-hearted, easy-going man who, like his son in later years, loved spinning yarns and telling funny stories. When not preoccupied with the business of farming sheep - lambing, sheering, selling at market - William would go out grouse shooting or trout fishing. On his way home, he would drop in on his cronies at neighbouring farms for a blether over "the indispensable tumbler" (or two) about the price of neeps, scurrilous goings-on in politics, and the latest exploits of the Ettrick Shepherd in *Blackwood's Magazine*.

Witty and well-read, William was a sceptic who scoffed at superstitions as old wives' tales. Like his fellow farmers he was conservative in his politics, but liberal in his opinions. He hated cant, especially the sanctimonious airs put on by

---

[8] The scale of Howford farm may be judged from the public roup (auction) that was held in Selkirk in May 1848 following Henrietta Currie's death. The farm's stock consisted of Cheviot sheep: 400 ewes with their lambs, 120 ewe hoggs (young female sheep), 20 wedder hoggs (castrated male sheep), 9 rams; Cattle: 6 milch cows, 2 queys (heifers) in calf, 3 two-year-old heifers, 9 one-year-old steers and heifers, 6 calves; and Horses: 3 excellent work horses, and one four-year-old filly, fit for saddle or harness. The implements of husbandry included three carts, one iron plough, two wooden ploughs, a scraper, two pairs of harrows, a roller, an improved turnip drill, an excellent pair of fanners, stable and barn furniture, horse harness, etc. The household furniture consisted of mahogany dining and tea tables, chest of drawers and wardrobe, mahogany chairs, four-posted and tent beds, carpets, feather beds, mattresses, sheets, blankets, dressing glasses [ie, mirrors], dinner and tea sets, a large variety of crystal, kitchen furniture, and dairy utensils. "There will also be sold a quantity of excellent rye grass hay."

Calvinists on Sundays. As he grew older he wearied of sitting in the kirk listening to dull sermons, preferring to go for a walk in order to study for himself "the work of the great Creator." Of William's appearance we know only that he was well-built and had grey eyes. These were so sharp his son believed that his father could see twice as far as most people, day or night. Though not musical, William had a melodious voice. His children regarded it a special treat when he read aloud to them before suppertime. Despite William's failings, Andrew adored his father "above any other being on earth."

About his mother Henrietta, on the other hand, her son had mixed feelings. The word Andrew typically uses to describe her is "pious." Though like her husband Henrietta had had a good education and was well-read with a taste for poetry, unlike him she was devout in her religion and strict in its observance. On Sundays, when the weather was too bad for the family to make the five-mile trek to the kirk, she would insist that her children read only "gude books." And when aged seventeen her eldest son returned from Edinburgh with a headful of what she believed were heresies his mother, concerned about the fate of his immortal soul, sent at once for the local dominie to set young Andrew back on the straight and narrow.

Andrew Currie sculpted a bust of Henrietta in her old age. He sent a plaster cast mounted on a circular wooden medallion to his brother John Lang Currie in Australia (who pronounced it "a perfect likeness"). The bust depicts a world-weary-looking matron whose regular, almost masculine features have a decidedly determined cast. But if there is such a thing as an artistic gene, Andrew inherited it from his mother. Two examples of her talent were displayed on the walls of the cosy little parlour at Howford. Above the mantlepiece with the peat fire glowing below hung a small, exquisitely-crafted picture in a gilt frame. Cut from white paper and mounted on a grey background, its subject was Melrose Abbey. In the foreground was a tree in whose foliage could be discerned a small bird singing. Facing the front window above a folding tea-table hung a larger work, also skillfully wrought, in another medium. An embroidered map of the world in two hemispheres sewn in threads of many colours, it showed lines of latitude and longitude on a base of fawn-coloured silk. From a distance the map resembled an engraving whose text, even down to the smallest print, was neatly and clearly delineated.

Though not well-off, like many Lowland Scottish families, the Curries were formidably literate. They were members of the Selkirk subscription library, founded in 1772. Every week or so a batch of new books from the library would arrive in a green bag. Its appearance was always a source of excitement for everyone. The family shelves boasted a collection consisting of perhaps a hundred and fifty volumes.[9] Many of these were on religious topics: histories of early Christianity, commentaries on the Bible, collections of sermons and allegorical texts like *The Pilgrim's Progress*. There were also a few children's books, their fly-leaves inscribed with the names of their owners. These included three that Andrew particularly loved: a pictorial book of Bible stories, an illustrated volume of national costumes of the world, and Oliver Goldsmith's history of the Earth with pictures of animals, birds and fish.

As a youngster, Andrew read widely. In addition to Shakespeare and his favourites, the poetry and novels of Sir Walter Scott, he also devoured books by such authors as Izaac Walton (*The Compleat Angler*), James Fenimore Cooper (*The Last of the Mohicans*) and the French romantic, Francois-Rene de Chateaubriand, as well as literary magazines like *Blackwood's* and *The Edinburgh Review*.

In his boyhood Andrew developed an intense love for "all the nooks and glens and picturesque spots" of the countryside between Selkirk and Howford. He and his chums would stroll along the riverside and climb the rolling hills "tak[ing] note of every old root, fern and flower on our way." Though "not remarkable for shining lights at school … usually unready with our tasks in Caesar and Virgil, we were ever ready for a ramble anywhere, and for being well posted up in the knowledge of hawks and owlets, howdie craws, game of all sorts, and fishing trout in the Ettrick."

---

[9] Andrew's brother John Lang Currie would accumulate a library consisting of some eight hundred books.

*

One metric for gauging the social standing of a family is the number of servants it could afford to employ. At Howford in 1825 the Curries had two serving women, a buxom lass and an old crone named Peggy Lovat. Their duties included cooking and cleaning, and spinning and carding the wool that Henrietta used to knit stockings for her children. As an infant Andrew also had a nurse named Betty Glen. Outside on the farm there was his boyhood pal the cow-herd laddie, plus at least one shepherd.

As always with hired hands, there were problems. William's father Andrew Curror had had a servant named Janet Grey. In 1789 she was tried by jury at the Court of Justiciary in Jedburgh and found guilty of the crime of child-murder. (Presumably the child was her own.) Two of William's servants drowned in the mill pond at Howford. On hearing of this tragedy, Francis Napier, the Lord Lieutenant of Selkirkshire, sent the Curries a Newfoundland puppy, whose mother he had brought back from his martial adventures in Canada. A practical explanation lay behind this noble gesture: Newfoundlands - relatives of St Bernards - were originally bred by fishermen as working dogs. They are known for their gentle nature, enormous size, and tremendous strength, which enables them to dive into the water and rescue a drowning person.

This extraordinary black-and-white shaggy dog - named Watch - had other unusual habits. He would dart at salmon in the mill pond, instinctively catching the fish behind the gills in order to render them paralyzed. His favorite pastime was leaping onto the parapet of the Ettrick Bridge to look for trout. On one occasion, Watch got overexcited, lost his balance and, much to Andrew's amusement, "down he flew, spreading all his legs out like a flying squirrel." The children had great fun making the poor dog dive for stones, much to the detriment of his teeth. As we shall shortly see, the famous Watch was to have an unfortunate influence on the direction of young Andrew's career path.

*

30 Carving History

By his own admission a timid boy and thought sickly by his mother, Andrew Currie was nonetheless a precocious child. Alas for the youngster, as things turned out, his aptitude for the mechanical manifested itself before his talent for the artistic. When Andrew was about seven years old, a threshing mill - another manifestation of the surging agrarian revolution - was erected at the neighbouring farm of Helmburn. This caused a sensation among "the simple denizens of the Forest." No-one had ever seen anything like it before. Andrew and his companion the cow-herd laddie went over to have a look. They were captivated by the sight. "This was the first time that I had ever seen a piece of machinery in motion," he recalled. "There was something so grand and bewildering in the water dashing over the bucket wheel, and the array of strange little wheels and revolving rakes tossing the straw from them." On their way home Andrew's playmate suggested that they should make their own water wheel. "The upshot was that, in a very few days, this part of the burn was studded with water wheels of all shapes and sizes and all in motion ... ."

Such invention and accompanying enthusiasm did not go unnoticed by the family elders. In particular, by Henrietta's brother William Lang, a successful Edinburgh-based advocate who used to return to the Borders for his holidays to shoot and fish. Despite the big gap in their ages - William was thirteen years younger than his sister - his opinion carried great weight with Andrew's mother. He pronounced that the youngster should capitalize on his obvious aptitude and train as a mechanic. Henrietta was not so sure. A mechanic had to be strong and little Andrew was far from robust. She had imagined that her brother the solicitor might take on the boy in his office, where the work would not be physically demanding. This was wishful thinking: there would only ever be room for one writer to the signet in the family. For this generation that would be Andrew Currie's cousin, chum, and exact contemporary, Andrew Lang's son John.

In the normal course of events, as eldest son Andrew would have succeeded his old man as tenant of Howford. A bright boy, he might even have gone up to the university in Edinburgh to study law. But his father was struggling financially, the farm's future was uncertain, and in any case there was no money to pay for further education. William thought it more prudent to apprentice his son to a trade. Though there was no shame in being a tradesman, it did mean getting your hands dirty: another step down in the world. The dogmatic uncle William having made up his mind, the matter was settled. From then on there was a tacit understanding in the family that the boy would become some sort of craftsman. That was how things stood until one autumn day some years later, when Andrew was about thirteen.

Uncle William took his nephew wild-duck shooting out on Howford loch. With them went the famous dog Watch, whose role was to dive into the water and retrieve the fallen birds. Following a successful morning's sport, while waiting for the young ducks to regroup from their hiding places among the reeds, the pair sat down to lunch out of sight of the loch. Afterwards, Andrew began whittling a piece of bog oak, carving the shape of a wild duck with the dog in pursuit in the water. "The softness of the material soon enabled me to bring out a rather spirited thing." His uncle was impressed. Perhaps his nephew was destined to be an artist rather than a mechanic. In fact, the carving was so good that William asked if he could take it home with him to put on his mantlepiece. Andrew willingly agreed. Unfortunately, however, the lad had carelessly laid down his handiwork on the heather. There Watch found it and "likely enough in bad humour for want of his dinner" the giant dog had chewed the piece to bits.

Back at Howford that evening, William had a long talk with his sister. He suggested that Andrew should come and stay with him in Edinburgh. William would engage an artist to teach the boy freehand and perspective drawing. Andrew was grateful for his uncle's suggestion. He meant to take him up on the offer. But as is often the way with such things, other arrangements were made for his schooling and Andrew never took art lessons. He would ever afterwards regret his failure to do so.

*

Andrew learned his ABC from old dominie Morton at the Brig-End parish primary school. In 1820, aged eight, he began six years at Selkirk Grammar School, traveling the seven miles back and forth to Howford every day. Then in 1825, disaster struck. An "awful fever" - probably typhoid - "prostrated our house, and took from us that dark-haired pensive boy William," the third of the Currie brothers, aged five, "myself escaping only by a hairbreadth." During those dreadful days, Andrew's aunt Margaret Lang, the writer's wife, came to their aid. "A ministering angel," he called her. In addition to tending the sick, she brought gifts to amuse the bedridden youngsters. They included pencils and a box of colours for her oldest nephew. Andrew began to draw. This was, he confessed, the first time in his life that he had had "a feeling for art." As he got older the feeling would grow stronger. It would manifest itself in the sketches of people, places, animals and birds that Andrew made in his notebooks wherever he went.

Among his relatives, after his father, Andrew loved his aunt most, even more than his mother. Margaret was nearly ten years younger than Henrietta and, despite having twelve children of her own to look after, somehow still had enough capacity left over to care for her sister-in-law's offspring as well. Though Margaret's maiden name was Suter - an old Selkirk family name meaning shoemaker - she was actually from Inverness, where her father was sheriff-clerk of Ross-shire. A portrait of her reveals a pleasant face with soft, rounded features and a calm, composed, sympathetic expression.

That autumn, Andrew fell ill again. This time it was thought that he would not survive. He clearly remembered the old wives exchanging significant glances and shaking their heads. His ailment was quite beyond the curative powers of the old Brig-End dominie, who practiced medicine on the side. Morton would examine the boy's tongue and take his pulse then, having prescribed such remedies as he had, let some blood. At length, it was decided to remove young Andrew to Viewfield, the house in Selkirk that belonged to his uncle and aunt Lang. There he would be near enough to receive treatment from Dr Anderson, a proper practitioner. It transpired that what ailed Andrew was goitre, a swelling of the thyroid gland caused (we now know) by iodine deficiency. Long and severe was his illness, but at last the growth was successfully excised.[10] Though Andrew would always bear the scar beneath his chin, he made a full recovery under the motherly care of his aunt, who never wearied in her attention.

For the rest of his schooldays Andrew would remain at the Langs' house, only visiting Howford for vacations. Viewfield was (and, though no longer a private residence, still is) a handsome, unostentatious grey stone Georgian building. The front of the house looks onto a magnificent view across the valley, hence the name. It may not have been here, but it was certainly around this time, that Andrew Currie first encountered the man who would be the single greatest influence on his life, Sir Walter Scott.

*

As a twelve-year-old attending Selkirk Grammar School under the tutelage of "Wishy-Washy o' the Back Raw," the nickname the boys gave to the rector, James Oliver (Back Row being an old Selkirk street), Andrew already knew that the Shirra was a great man. At that age, however, not yet having read any of his works, he could not make out why Scott was so famous. He and his pals, Robbie Park and John Lang, "being enterprising boys, in pursuit of knowledge of everything going on around us," used to sneak into the Court House - much to the annoyance of John's father Andrew - to watch Sir Walter trying cases.

Though Selkirk was "very litigious," most of the cases that came before the Sheriff were "astoundingly petty — affiliation (ie, determining parenthood of disputed babies), 'wrongous' dismissal, trespass, sabbath-breaking, toll disputes, disputed boundary lines." But though trivial, they nonetheless provided

---

[10] Back in those days attempts to remove goitre surgically often killed the patient, either through loss of blood or post-operative gangrene. Samuel Gross, an American doctor, wrote in 1846, "Can the thyroid in the state of enlargement be removed? Emphatically experience answers no. Should the surgeon be so foolhardy to undertake it ... every stroke of the knife will be followed by a torrent of blood and lucky it would be for him if his victim lived long enough for him to finish his horrid butchery. No honest and sensible surgeon would ever engage in it." Andrew was fortunate to have had a skillful doctor.

considerable amusement, both to the Shirra and his young audience "snugly ensconced behind the railings."

One of the first cases they witnessed was against Walter Paterson, who was summoned for an assault on a woman called Nan —. "In the main, as canny and inoffensive a tailor as ever drew stitch," Paterson on the occasion in question had had one dram too many at Gulen Robison's tavern on the Green (another old Selkirk street). He had been complaining about Nan, how he could not show his nose outside his own door without her abusing him. The origin of the bad feeling was that Paterson had fathered an illegitimate child on Nan, and had subsequently ill-used the unfortunate woman. Now, as he returned home up the Kirk Wynd, the mother of his baby accosted him, brandishing a besom in his face. She proceeded to give him a piece of her mind. Andrew describes what happened next:

> "Her words seem to have made him lose his usual prudence for, in a passion, he suddenly struck her with his hand on the side of the head. Next minute, another virago seized the besom, and floored the tailor on his own doorstep. A general melee ensued among the wives, to which [his blow] was but a flea-bite; however, his was the only one that came to court. As soon as the case was called, there looked very like a renewal of the wordy war, till Jamie Inglis, the town officer, was ordered to clear the court of the batch. But what was said in this short time, by some half-dozen women, so tickled Sir Walter that I well recollect him laughing while, with spectacles on, he seemed to be noting something down with a pencil."

For years after Andrew and his friends seldom missed a chance of attending court and enjoying the rich, free-of-charge entertainment it provided. Watching the Shirra, Andrew was, he recalled decades later, "riveted to the remarkable play of expression in that rugged face — I say rugged, for Sir Walter had more strongly-marked lines on his face than almost any man I ever saw: add to this his bushy overhanging eyebrows, which, when drawn down, gave him a severe, sombre expression which you feel, but cannot describe. The clock strikes, and Sir Walter gives a hasty glance upwards; the sombre face is lighted up, as he turns with some difficulty, for he had an unsightly club-foot; and you would swear, from that genial expression, that that could not be the same man you saw two minutes ago, so sudden and varied was his power of expression."

In later life Andrew told an acquaintance that he had met Sir Walter on more than one occasion, no doubt through his uncle the sheriff-clerk. It is unlikely that there was much substance to these encounters. Scott was an affable man with an approachable manner, but in the mid 1820s he was at the height of his celebrity, the most famous person not just in the Borders, but in the whole country. As a shy adolescent, Andrew would probably have been too star-struck to mumble much more than monosyllables.

Like thousands of other avid readers, Andrew devoured Scott's poems and novels, committing large chunks to memory. The Great Minstrel inspired in him a deep love of local lore. Like the Shirra Andrew would later become a keen antiquarian. Ultimately he was, in the words of his acquaintance, "saturated in the genius and personality of Sir Walter Scott." When Andrew became a sculptor, he would set up his workshop at Darnick, just down the road from Abbotsford, Scott's gothic mansion, for which he would carve some of his first pieces. Perhaps his proudest moment came when he was asked to sculpt for the Scott Monument in Princes Street Gardens two statues of characters from Scott's novels, a commission into which, as we shall see, he poured his heart and soul.

Even on holiday, Andrew would tie his travels to locations that Scott had mentioned in poems like *Marmion*. The sculptor's writings are peppered with references to Scott's life and work. His stories are crafted in emulation of the master's style, complete with passages in broad Lowlands dialect. The best - and most revealing - of them tells of an encounter between himself as a teenager and the gypsy Madge Gordon, whom Scott knew well and had used as the model for Meg Merrilies in his novel *Guy Mannering*.

When Andrew visited Edinburgh in the winter of 1828~'29, staying with his uncle William the advocate at the latter's lodgings at 118 Princes Street, he witnessed the Shirra "sitting listless in the Court of Session" at Parliament House in the Old Town, just off the High Street. (Since 1806 Scott had been a clerk of the court, a sinecure requiring him to do little more than to park himself at a table for several hours a day during the six months the court sat, signing his name to the occasional document.)

Andrew loved the time he spent in Edinburgh. During those precious happy days in the big city he was intellectually stimulated as never before, by the books he borrowed from the advocate's library, by the people he met at the jolly bachelor parties his uncle took him to, and by the lectures his friends smuggled him into at the university. His favorite lecturer, whom he never tired of seeing and hearing, was the famous professor of moral philosophy John Wilson. Contributing articles to *Blackwood's* under the pseudonym Christopher North, Wilson was also the preeminent magazine writer of his day. He was a handsome man of imposing physical presence and an eloquent orator. Behind his square desk Wilson seemed, one student who attended his large class in 1830 recalled, "like some great bust set on a square plinth." Andrew sketched the great man and, many years later, sculpted a medallion of him from memory.

At the university Andrew was amused by the unmistakable figure of John Leslie, a popular professor of mathematics. "Edinburgh's Falstaff" was a short fat man with a florid face and buck teeth. He dyed the white patches of his piebald hair purple. Another academic whose lectures Andrew attended was Robert Jameson, professor of mineralogy and natural history. Jameson's style of pedagogy was to spew forth "a blizzard of facts" in the hope that a few might stick. Charles Darwin, who had taken his classes a few years earlier, found them "incredible dull. The sole effect they produced on me was the determination never as long as I lived to read a book on geology." Andrew enjoyed listening to Jameson on meteorology. He was also impressed by the professor's superb collection, ranged in boxes all around the lecture room, of stuffed animals and birds, some of which he recognized from his nature rambles back home.

Edinburgh also had other, less high-minded attractions to offer. In the Lawnmarket on 28 January 1829, Andrew attended the public hanging of the body-snatcher William Burke. Also, the gory public dissection of the corpse the next day by the university's professor of anatomy, Alexander Monro.

All too soon it was time for the youngster to bid farewell to the high life of the capital and to return, heavy-hearted to the Borders. Andrew Currie's childhood had ended. Now he was about to embark on the first phase of his adult life, in a vocation that was not of his choice.

* * *

Three

Wheels & Spindles (1830~1847)

What a comedown it was, from the refined society of Edinburgh with its intellectual giants to the little village of Denholm, northeast of Hawick, where most of the inhabitants earned their living as humble stocking makers. In May 1830 the 18-year-old Andrew Currie arrived in Denholm to begin an apprenticeship under his new master, the millwright Robert Moodie. For a sensitive young man with a lively mind, the yoke would be hard to bear.

There was no escaping his fate. The articles of indenture had been drawn up, in a cruel twist of fate, by his cousin John Lang, himself just embarking on a career as a solicitor. They specified that the apprentice "during the full and complete span and period of five years ... shall faithfully, honestly and diligently, by night and by day attend to, serve and obey his said master in his art and vocation aforesaid, and he shall not during the said period of the apprenticeship absent nor divert himself from his master's work as a Millwright holyday or weekday on any pretense whatsoever ... ." Failure to comply would incur a heavy financial penalty, which Andrew well knew the "cautioner" [ie, guarantor] on his contract - his father and co-signer William Currie - was in no position to pay.

During the week ten hours a day would be devoted to "business among wheels and spindles." Even "holydays" would not provide much respite. In Denholm the villagers' social life, such as it was, revolved around the chapel and its associated meeting house. Moodie and his family were Cameronians, a strict Calvinist sect that would not tolerate talk of worldly matters on the sabbath. "Sunday is likely with me to be the most uncomfortable day of the week," Andrew predicted gloomily.

In the garret of his master's house where he boarded, he shared a room with his fellow apprentices. They were a coarse lot: Andrew would have no privacy among them. Early on he was mortified when his diary, which he had thought safely locked away, was discovered and read out aloud in the workshop, much to everyone else's amusement. He was cut off from family and friends. It was fifteen miles - a long day's walk - to his home at Howford. The following year fate would deal Andrew another crushing blow, with the death of his beloved father, aged just 59. Meantime, in order to survive, the young man quickly realized he would have to look for "a quiet nook for study" and cultivate "some congenial acquaintances." That would not be easy in such a small, out-of-the-way place as Denholm.

*

The trade that Andrew Currie learned was an ancient one. Millwrights were specialized mechanics who dealt with mills of all types — for grinding flour, sawing logs, making paper, and "fulling," that is, cleansing woolen cloth. They designed the wheel systems, carved the gear mechanisms, and built the machines. In the Borders, mills had generally been powered by water rather than wind. By the 1830s, however, the textile mills that were springing up in Galashiels and elsewhere were driven by steam engines that demanded a new and more complex set of skills. Ultimately, the pre-industrial trade of the millwright would give way to the modern profession of the civil engineer.

In addition to the carpenter's bench, a millwright had to know his way around the lathe and the blacksmith's anvil. "He could handle the axe, the hammer and the plane with equal skill and precision. He could turn, bore or forge with the ease and ability of one brought up in those trades." A knowledge of arithmetic and geometry was also required to "calculate the velocities, strength and power of machines." It was hard work: a millwright had to be physically tough and resilient.

Robert Moodie's specialty was threshing mills, water-driven contraptions like the one that had so bewitched Andrew as a boy. An ancestor of the combine harvester, the threshing mill used a series of corrugated rollers to hull grain from husks. It was invented in 1786 by Andrew Meikle, a millwright based at Phantassie, an estate in East Lothian about fifty miles north of Denholm. Meikle's threshing mill was, according to Sir John Sinclair, the distinguished Scottish economist and writer on agriculture, "unquestionably the most valuable implement that has been introduced into the practice of husbandry in the course of the last century."

For millennia wheat had been winnowed - separated from chaff - by hand, using flails, a laborious and time-consuming chore. Mechanization took the drudgery out of farm work. It also greatly reduced the need for farm workers. In 1830, just as Andrew Currie was beginning his apprenticeship, unrest among unemployed labourers boiled over in the form of the Swing Riots, so-called because landowners would receive written death threats signed "Captain Swing." Starting in the south of England, the riots quickly spread north. Sir Walter Scott worried that a general rebellion was about to erupt and that rule by "mobocracy" would ensue. Stationed with hussars in Sheffield the Shirra's son Walter was charged with keeping agitated workers in order. By February 1831, infected by her father's fears, his daughter Anne was terrified that "Captain Swing and all the radicals" would descend on their home at Abbotsford and put it to the torch.

*

Though unaffected by the Swing Riots, Denholm was not immune to turmoil caused by technological change. A wave of support for the Reform Act was sweeping the country. Introduced to parliament in 1831 and passed into law in 1832, the act widened the electorate by extending the franchise to the new cities that had sprung up during the industrial revolution.

Industry, so far as Denholm was concerned, meant stocking making. Since its introduction at the end of the eighteenth century, the manufacture of hosiery from wool and cotton had prospered to the point where, by the eighteen thirties, it had become the village's principle activity. Over eighty knitting machines - "frames" as they were known - could be heard clacking away. That was small by comparison with the nearby town of Hawick, where the Scottish stocking industry had originated and was still concentrated, but large for a place whose population numbered just a few hundred. Though the village boasted a few bigger stocking-making mills that employed multiple workers, most of Denholm's concerns were minuscule, many of them one-man outfits. It was literally a cottage industry, the hand-worked frames installed next to the windows of the thatched-roof cottages that lined the periphery of the Green, the large pasture that constitutes the centre of the village.

As in other industries, tensions arose between owners and workers over the adoption of advanced equipment. Employers charged operators weekly rent on their stocking frames, typically a shilling a week, which was deducted from their wages of around 14 shillings. This was a practice which the workers had long resented, arguing that in other trades employers provided machinery free of charge. The new machines were broader than the old narrow frames hence more productive, capable of knitting six pieces at a time. But they were also also more costly, so owners claimed a reduction in the price of the stockings they produced. As a result the workers strenuously opposed their introduction.

In general, unlike conservative members of his family such as his uncle Andrew Lang, Andrew sympathized with the working classes and their push for reform. "Why should the mass of workers in the kingdom, the sinews of the nation, not be elevated in the social scale and have a voice in the squandering of their hard-earned money?" he wondered. In his opinion the workers were asking for "no more than what is just and reasonable." But he did not support the radical element among Denholm's stocking makers: "Give them rope and we would have a repetition of the horrors of the French Revolution." Happily, such extremists seemed only a small section of the community; they did not represent, he thought, "the good sense of the working classes."

*

Denholm did have one claim to literary fame, as the birthplace of John Leyden (1775~1811). The son of a shepherd, Leyden grew up a brilliant, largely self-taught boy. After receiving coaching in Latin and Greek from the local minister, Leyden set off on foot, aged fifteen, for Edinburgh University. There, he would be mercilessly teased for his rustic appearance and uncouth lallans accent. Leyden would subsequently do much of the legwork for *Minstrelsy of the Scottish Border*, Sir Walter Scott's first major work, published in 1802. He doggedly pursued old songs and folklore, once according to Scott walking forty miles to bag the last two verses of a ballad. The young man had, the Shirra wrote admiringly, "an ardent and unutterable longing for information of every description."

In addition to Border ballads, Leyden's other great passion was for the travels of Mungo Park. These he longed to emulate. After completing work on the *Minstrelsy*, Leyden set off for India, where he soon established himself as an expert on indigenous languages. But on an expedition to Java led by the first Earl of Minto, another Roxburghshire man, in search of rare manuscripts Leyden caught a fever and died, aged just 36.

Andrew was cheered by the fact that he would do his millwright's training in the house where Leyden had been born, on the north side of the Green. Nearby, in a cottage in a cul-de-sac off the west side, was a subscription library that the Barrie family had established back in 1805. Andrew was delighted to discover its shelves contained many of the books on the list he had drawn up for his challenging course of self-edification. They included John Locke's *Essay Concerning Human Understanding* (1690); works by Francis Bacon, the originator of the scientific method, William Paley, author of *Natural Theology* and proponent of the argument from design, and Thomas Reid (1710~1796), the moral philosopher who founded the Scottish school of Common Sense. For general inquiries Andrew could look up

David Brewster's *Edinburgh Encyclopedia*, published in 18 volumes between 1802 and 1830. And for light relief after such "severe reading" he could dip into *The Pleasures of Hope*, didactic verses published in 1799 by the Scottish poet Thomas Campbell. Enormously popular in its day, the poem dealt with such contemporary topics as the French Revolution and the abolition of slavery. He carried his mother's copy of this slim volume with him in his coat pocket.

Andrew would keep himself up to date via a pair of weekly magazines, both of which began publication in 1832. Topics covered by *Chambers's Edinburgh Journal* included history, religion, science and language. *The Penny Magazine* was a high-minded illustrated weekly aimed at working class people who had no access to formal education. Intended as a counterbalance to more radical texts, it was published by the Society for the Diffusion of Useful Knowledge. Andrew liked *The Penny Magazine* "with its short articles on every sort of useful knowledge, and the woodcuts so cleverly done."

As well as the library, at the west end of its main street Denholm also had a reading room where people could sit and peruse the latest periodicals. A club had been formed there by locals with literary leanings. They included Thomas Murray, a tailor and linen-draper whose shop was located just down the street. Many years later Andrew would befriend Murray's son James, born 1837, another autodidact from unsophisticated origins. In his writings on historical texts the younger man would draw on the sculptor's prodigious knowledge of Border lore. An ardent antiquarian and philologist, James Augustus Henry Murray would win fame (and a knighthood) as the first editor of the Oxford English Dictionary.

In addition to Barrie the librarian and Murray the reading room clubman, another promising candidate for congenial companionship and edification was Jamieson (first name unknown) the naturalist. Described by locals as "a genius" this Jamieson seemed to Andrew a modest, unassuming fellow who did not join in the "athletic jumpings" and ball games that the apprentices played on the Green. "I often meet him on a literary walk like myself, poking among the bushes," he noted in his diary. "Can't make out what he is after, but shall make his acquaintance and learn something."

But the most important person Andrew would encounter during his five years in Denholm was Isabella "Belle" Hardie, whom he would court and eventually marry. Born in 1816, four years after Andrew, Belle was the daughter of George Hardie, a leading local stocking manufacturer.

*

The expected thing for Andrew Currie to do on completing his apprenticeship would have been to become a journeyman, hiring out his newly-qualified skills to a master millwright like Robert Moodie. But that was not the course the young man took. Instead, he used his initiative, leveraging local connections to make a bold and unexpected move. In 1835, just after the period of his indenture ended, it happened that a local grandee, Gilbert Elliot-Murray-Kynynmound, the second Earl of Minto, who had his seat at Minto House just north of Denholm, was appointed First Lord of the Admiralty. Fate had presented Andrew with a wonderful opportunity to gain experience of life in the wider world. The youngster grabbed it with both hands.

One of the duties of a First Lord was to oversee the dockyards in which the Royal Navy built and refitted its warships. It was thus in his purview to make appointments at these establishments. Among Her Majesty's dockyards was Chatham, on the Medway estuary in Kent. Chatham employed several thousand workmen, making it not only the biggest dockyard but one of the largest industrial enterprises in the country. Through the Earl's good graces, the 23-year-old was able to obtain a position there.

But first, before boarding the boat from Leith to London to begin his new job, the young man had an itch he needed to scratch. For recreation during his precious leisure hours at Denholm Andrew had always enjoyed making sketches, especially of animals. With his knife he had carved lifelike representations of birds. Now he wanted to know whether his work was any good, whether he had any chance of making a living as an artist. For an evaluation of his skills he approached a painter named Willie Allan (1782~1850), who three years later would become Sir William Allan, president of the Royal Scottish Academy.

It was a good choice. Allan had learned the hard way how tough it was to craft a successful career in the fine arts. The son of a humble officer at the court of session in Edinburgh, Allan from an early age had demonstrated a talent for drawing. He begged his father to let him train as an artist. Aged fourteen he was duly apprenticed, to a coach builder on Leith Walk who set him to painting coats of arms on carriage door panels. Happily his employer was so impressed with the boy's aptitude that he paid for a place for him at the Trustees' Academy, the precursor to Edinburgh College of Art. From there Allan went on to study at the Royal Academy School in London. On graduation, however, he "soon experienced the difficulties with which the fine arts, as a profession, have to contend in the great metropolis of merchandise: his superiority was not appreciated with that readiness which his youthful enthusiasm had anticipated, and the demands on his pencil were so few, as would soon have been insufficient to furnish him with the means of a mere subsistence." So, like many a Scottish youngster who cannot find work at home, he set out to look for it abroad.

In 1805 Allan sailed for Russia, a brave leap into the unknown. From St Petersburg, he travelled widely in the Ukraine among Cossacks, Circassians and Tartars, collecting costumes and weapons, and accumulating images in his sketchbooks. On his return to Edinburgh in 1814 he transformed these exotic source materials into large-scale tableaux. Again, it proved hard to establish a reputation for himself and a market for his work. "His countrymen, with their proverbial caution, were slow to perceive the excellencies that addressed them in such an unwonted form." However, he did eventually manage to find some appreciative supporters in the shape of Sir Walter Scott and his circle. A grateful Allan responded by painting scenes from Scottish history suggested by Scott's Waverley novels. These sold well.

Painter and novelist became good friends. Willie Allan painted the Shirra several times, notably in an intimate group portrait of 1819 that shows Scott at the home of James Hogg, on the occasion of the host's birthday. The writer-philosopher John Wilson is depicted making a toast to the Shepherd, who is seen swaying back in his chair, no doubt the worse for wear. Allan was a frequent guest at Abbotsford. There, he executed a melancholy drawing of "the Author of Waverley" at work in his study just a few days before Scott's death in September 1832.

Somehow, no doubt via one of his uncles, Andrew Currie secured an introduction to call on Allan when he was passing through Edinburgh on his way south. After scrutinizing the young man's work, the artist gave his opinion that the sketches were very creditable, for a beginner, but advised him to concentrate on sculpture. Thus was planted a seed, one that would take more than a decade to come to fruition.

*

Andrew Currie arrived at Chatham just as the Dockyard was undergoing the biggest upheaval in its history. The era of sail was ending, the transition to the age of steam had begun. J.M.W. Turner captured this momentous change in his elegiac masterpiece, *The Fighting Temeraire*, which he painted in 1839 while Andrew was still at HM Dockyard. It depicts the old warship, which had been built at Chatham in 1789 and seen distinguished service at the Battle of Trafalgar, being towed up the Thames by a soot-blackened steam-tug to her last berth, to be broken up for scrap. Beginning in 1832 with *HMS Phoenix*, an 800-ton paddle sloop, Chatham Dockyard would build many of the Royal Navy's early steamships.

Exactly what work Andrew did during his four years at Chatham is not known. The dockyard was equipping its machine shops with steam engines. These drove shafts from which overhead belts running the length of the workrooms would power lathes and cutters. A millwright would likely have been employed to help with the design, construction and operation of such shaft-and-belt systems. He might also have been involved in fashioning the wooden patterns used to make moulds for casting gears and other metal parts. One job we know that the young man did not do: carving the crude but colourful figureheads that warships, even in the age of steam, still mounted on their prows. That was the preserve of families of specialist artisans.

Though Chatham was only thirty miles southeast of London, traveling to the metropolis in those pre-railway days involved a non-trivial journey up the Thames by boat. It meant catching tides, the return trip taking much of the day. Not that Andrew had a lot of time to spend on leisure. He and his colleagues worked long hours: dawn to dusk in winter, six in the morning to six in the evening the rest of the year. However the young man almost certainly did manage to get to the British Museum. Given that sculpture and antiquity would become his twin passions, it was the obvious place for him to go. He saw - and doubtless, following his habit, sketched - some of the extensive collection of classical statues on display there. In addition to the Egyptian, Greek and Roman antiquities, this included the Parthenon marbles, brought back from Athens by Thomas Bruce, Earl of Elgin, and acquired by the museum in 1816.

During this period Andrew returned to Scotland once, in 1837, to see his family (and presumably also his fiancée, Belle Hardie). His mother and sister Henrietta walked from Granton, where they were enjoying a sea-bathing holiday, to Leith to see him on board for the return journey to London. He departed on the ill-fated paddle steamer SS *Pegasus*.[11] This ship boasted a magnificent winged-horse figurehead, which greatly amused the womenfolk. Thereafter it became a standing joke between them, Andrew sailing off in such a daft-looking ship, which had a horse with wings and webbed feet.

On his way south, as the *Pegasus* passed Lindisfarne, he made a sketch of the ruined monastery on the island. It was an eventful trip. At Hull, where they docked to break their voyage, a pickpocket tried to rob the young man. He was rescued by "an honest hospitable Jew" who "acted the good Samaritan" and invited Andrew to stay overnight with his family. This act of kindness greatly impressed him: "the hospitable treatment I got from these excellent people, without fee or reward, I have never forgot."

---

[11] In 1843 the *Pegasus* was wrecked off the Farne Islands with the loss of 51 lives.

Something else the young man never forgot happened just before he left Chatham. In September 1839, Andrew witnessed the departure from the dockyards, following a refit, of *HMS Erebus* and *HMS Terror* on an (ultimately unsuccessful) expedition to the Antarctic to locate the south magnetic pole. *Erebus* and *Terror* were bomb vessels, so called because they were constructed with specially reinforced hulls to withstand the enormous recoil from the three-ton mortars they carried. Such strengthening meant they were well suited to withstand thick ice. But as it turned out, not well enough.

After their return from the Antarctic, the ships were equipped with steam engines. In May 1845 they set off on a new voyage whose objective was to seek the Northwest Passage. Following a final sighting in Baffin Bay that July, the *Erebus* and *Terror* and their crew of 133 seamen disappeared, never to be seen again. Over the next ten years, the hunt for the missing expedition was seldom out of the news, as some forty search parties set out to look for the lost ships. Small wonder then that Andrew used to tell people he had seen the vessels leaving Chatham.

*

On 22 September 1839, newly arrived back from England, Andrew Currie, 27, married Isabella Hardie, 23, in Cavers, the parish that includes Denholm. Symbolically it was a nice match: boy from shoe-town weds girl from stockings-ville. Actually it would be a happy marriage that would last nigh-on fifty years. Belle became Andrew's "dear practical wife," "an excellent helpmeet" and "a ministering angel" to her somewhat unworldly husband. The couple set up house, and Andrew his millwright's workshop, in Earlston, a small Berwickshire market town "beautifully situated in a pleasant valley engirt by hills of moderate elevation" about four miles north of Melrose. It would be their home for almost twenty years.

Andrew and Belle's children were all born at Earlston, emerging at regular biannual intervals. Their first child, William, born in 1841, died in his fifth year. The rest all survived to adulthood. Margaret King, named after Andrew's beloved aunt and Belle's mother (whose maiden name was King), was born in 1843; Henrietta Lang, after Andrew's mother, in 1845; George Hardie, after Belle's father, in 1847; Helen, after Belle's mother (who was known as Nelly), in 1849; William John, after Andrew's father and younger brother, in 1851; and the baby of the family, Andrew Lang, in 1854.

Ironically, just as Andrew was putting down his roots in the Borders, his siblings and cousins were ripping theirs up and heading overseas. In general, people emigrate because they cannot have what they want at home and hope to find it elsewhere. What the Scots - especially the younger sons of tenant farmers - wanted most was land. Historians have dubbed the exodus from the Borders that occurred during the mid nineteenth century "the Lowland clearances." Unlike Highlanders, who mostly opted for for Canada, Lowlanders tended to prefer Australia, in particular the Western District of the brand-new colony that would later be dubbed Victoria.

In 1835 a boatload of pioneers from Van Diemen's Land established an illegal settlement on the banks of the Yarra river. This was the origin of the city of Melbourne (named for Queen Victoria's prime minister and mentor). In defiance of the faraway authorities, the squatters began ousting the aboriginal inhabitants and grazing their sheep and cattle on the pastures thus vacated. The following year, recognizing a fait accompli, the government in London threw up its hands and declared the country open for settlement. A land rush ensued.

In 1839 two of Andrew's cousins - 23-year-old Thomas Lang, who had trained as a doctor, and his 16-year-old brother William - arrived at Port Phillip (gateway to Melbourne) then headed west to stake out a sheep farm. In 1841 they were joined by their brother Gideon Scott Lang and Andrew's younger brother, John Lang Currie (b 1818). No sooner had John arrived than he contracted typhoid fever and nearly died. But he recovered and together with Tom Anderson, an old Selkirk Grammar school friend of Andrew's, managed to scrape together £750. With this money they bought a 32,000-acre station and stocked it with 1,500 sheep.

In November 1848 Andrew's two remaining younger siblings, George (b 1823) and Henrietta (known in the family as "Hen," b 1815), arrived at Port Phillip after a journey lasting 144 days. There had been no reason for them to stay following the death earlier that year of their mother. She had been living with their eldest sister Jean whose husband, William Scott, had managed Howford since William Currie's death. The livestock were sold off and the family left the farm for good.

"Melbourne is an astonishing place considering that twelve years ago there was not a single house," a wide-eyed George wrote in his journal. "Now it is more than twice the size of Hawick." At his brother John's sheep station, where he would spend the next three years before striking out on his own, the scale was even more impressive. "I must say I never had a proper idea of it from the letters we used to get," George wrote to his sister Jean. "Instead of two shepherds or three as I always thought would be their utmost, there are including themselves nearly thirty people on the station ... [it] contains 50 square miles ... about 40 times the size of Howford farm.

"Over every part the pasture is of the richest kind, infinitely superior to any you will find in Selkirkshire and capable of holding 20,000 sheep when fully booked; at present they have between ten and twelve. ... The stations ... are not leased like farms; the squatters being virtually proprietors of the land, as securely as the Duke of Buccleuch is; it can never be taken away from them as long as they pay the squatting license, some fifty pounds a year. ...

"To tell any of the Ettrick farmers of the immense quantities of sheep here and the sums of money turned over by the settlers, they will only shake their heads, but one might as well try to raise the dead as make them believe it." There was of course also "the wonderful climate" which, as one of the Langs wrote to yet another relative contemplating emigration, "would reconcile anyone to the abandonment of Selkirk, Scotland."

*

For Andrew Currie, Earlston proved more than just an attractive place to live. It was also a town that boasted a colourful history stretching back more than five hundred years. The most famous denizen of Earlston, or Erceldoune as it was formerly known, was Lord Thomas Learmont aka Thomas the Rhymer. Sir Walter Scott had been fascinated with the Rhymer, whom he saw as the progenitor of Scottish poetry. In the *Minstrelsy* Scott wrote one of his best ballads about this most fabulous of Border bards. A bafflingly elusive figure, half man, half myth, Thomas lived in Earlston during the thirteenth century. On a wall of the local parish church is an inscription in stone: "Auld Rymr['s] Race Lyes In This Place." Today, all that remains of his keep is a single, dilapidated stone wall known as Rhymer's Tower.

The legend went that one day, tired from chasing after a deer, Thomas was resting at Huntley Bank, when the Fairy Queen - a lady dressed in green silk, riding a milk-white palfrey - appeared to him. The couple kissed, Thomas was bewitched, then the Queen whisked him off to her enchanted kingdom beneath the Eildon Hills, where he remained for seven years. Having initially been forbidden to speak, Thomas was ultimately granted the power of prophecy. On his return to the land of mortal men he predicted, in rhyming couplets, many events that subsequently took place, including the death of King Alexander III in 1286, and the battle of Bannockburn in 1314. For this ability to accurately foretell the future, he was dubbed True Thomas. After a further seven years, he was summoned back to Fairyland and disappeared, never to be seen again.

Scott was so taken with the legend of Thomas that he extended his estate to incorporate Rhymer's Glen, Huntley Burn, and the Eildon Tree, under which the fateful kiss had supposedly occurred.[12] He took J.M.W. Turner to see the glen on a visit the artist made to Abbotsford in 1831, the year before the author's death.[13] But

---

[12] "The Eildon Tree," according to James Murray, "stood on the declivity of the eastern side of the three Eildon Hills, looking across the Tweed to Leader Water, Bemerside, Earlstoun, and other places connected with Thomas. Its site is believed to be indicated by the Eildon Stone, 'a rugged boulder of whinstone' standing on the edge of the road from Melrose to St Boswells." In a footnote, Murray adds, "Mr Currie has a verbal tradition that the tree stood not by the stone, but a quarter of a mile higher up the base of the hill, where he says, 'the site of it was pointed out to me thirty years ago [ie, c 1845] by the late James Williamson of Newstead, and I believe I could still plant my stick on the spot.'"

[13] Some confusion here, too. "Na, na! Huntley Bank is not by the Huntley Burn," Andrew told a visitor circa 1880. "It is up the hillside as you go to St Boswell's shortly after you pass Melrose." And then, "with a shake of the head, he added, as if my inquiries recalled old associations, 'Aye, but the Rhymer's Glen is no' kept as it was in Sir Walter's days.'"

though a romantic, Scott was no fool. The natives were too credulous, he complained: "in no part of Scotland ... has the belief in fairies maintained its ground with more pertinacity than in Selkirkshire."

In December 1839, not long after Andrew Currie and his bride had moved to their new home, a cottage near Rhymer's Tower, the ancient past dramatically came to life. "The rumour spread in Earlston that one of the Rhymer's most celebrated prophesies had been fulfilled." The prediction concerned the fate of the poet's own family:

> The hare sail kittle [shall litter] on my hearth stane
> And there will never be a laird Learmont again.

"I well remember running with all the rest of the town, to see the hare's nest; and sure enough there it was — two young hares in a nettle bush in the fireplace!" Andrew wrote excitedly, adding, "I saw it, with my own eyes."

This event seems to have kindled in him what would become a lifelong passion for antiquity. Antiquarianism, the search for a long-lost past, suited Andrew's curious mind and romantic nature. In this, as in so much else, Scott had shown the way. A keen antiquarian himself, the Shirra had even penned a book entitled *The Antiquary* (1816), which he subsequently claimed was his personal favourite among the Waverley novels. In it, the author parodies himself in the shape of the eponymous main character, Jonathan Oldbuck aka Monkbarns. At a time of unprecedented change, Scott felt that it vital was to preserve as much as possible of the past before it vanished for ever. The Borders, he felt, were positively saturated with folklore:

> Nor hill nor brook we passed along
> But had its legend or its song.

In addition to verbal legacies, there were also tangible artifacts to be dug up from the numerous archaeological sites on either side of Hadrian's Wall. Ancient invaders like the Romans had left behind a treasure-trove of buried antiquities such as armour, coins and pottery.

Andrew set himself to learn everything he could about Earlston in general and Thomas the Rhymer in particular. He began by taking down oral histories. Local people he quizzed included the last of the Learmonts, an old bachelor called Robert, a weaver by trade, from whom he learned many of the town's traditions.[14] James Williamson of Newstead (site of the ancient Roman garrison of Trimontium) showed him the location of the Eildon Tree. And from an 85-year-old named Rob Messer, "a very intelligent matter-of-fact man, well-versed in all traditionary lore about Earlston, and possessing a wonderful memory," he recorded a rather more prosaic account of the disappearance of True Thomas:

> "D'ye see thae auld waa's i' the front of yer ain shop? Weel man, ah mind o' that bein' a gey an' substantial hoose i' ma young days, and Tammas the Rymer was last seen gaan' oot o' that hoose ane nicht afore the derknin', and he set off up the Leader [Water, the river that runs past Earlston] for Lauder Cas'le, but he ne'er gat there, he never was sene againe ... he was carryan' money wi' him to some Lord or great man up there, that he was intimate wi'. But my granfaither uist to say, an' nae doot he had it handit doon, that the Leader was i' great fluid at the time, an' that Tammas the Rymer had been robbit an' murdert an' his body thrawn into the water, whulk micht take it to Berwick. An' that's likker-like than the Fairy story. Sae ye hae'd, as ah had it, frae thaim that was afore us."

---

[14] Last, that is, of the local Learmonts. It turns out that the fates of the Curries and the Learmonts are intertwined in another, unexpected way. Thomas Livingstone-Learmonth (1783-1869), having made a fortune as a merchant in Calcutta, moved on to settle in Hobart. In 1838 he sent his teenaged sons Thomas junior and Somerville from Tasmania up to Victoria to find suitable sheep farming land. They bought 20,000 acres and named the property Ercildoune. During the latter part of the nineteenth century the Learmonth brothers and Andrew's brother John Lang Currie competed against each other to win prizes for their merino rams. Eventually, in 1920, John Lang's son Alan bought Ercildoune for £100,000. A stone from Rhymer's Tower was shipped from Scotland and placed in its antipodean counterpart.

Sometimes his work provided opportunities to learn about the past. Nearby the ruins of Rhymer's Tower was an ancient water-mill. "Rhymer's Mill was renewed by me in 1843," Andrew wrote. "The old one had a stone in the gable with the words **Rhymer Mill** in antique letters." .

When James Murray published his *Full Text of the Romance and Prophecies of Thomas of Erceldoune* in 1875, he acknowledged his debt to "my friend, Andrew Currie Esq." The author had been "zealously assisted by the local researches of Mr Currie ... the well-known Sculptor and Border Antiquary ... to whom I am indebted for much local information as to the Rhymer." In fact, so learned in local lore was Andrew that Murray believed him a native of Earlston.

"Love of the Border country was one of his strongest characteristics," wrote Andrew's pupil Lillias Cotesworth. "He knew almost every foot of ground for many miles around his first home at Earlston, and there was no legend or tradition with which he was not acquainted. No matter where he lived, he said that his heart remained in Earlston, the village where he began his married life so humbly, and in his last years he still spoke of it with romantic affection as a far-off haven of happiness surrounded with all the glamour of love and youth and early friendships, as vague and beautiful as the land of Fairy, to which the Laird of Learmont so mysteriously departed."

It was in Earlston, while still working as a millwright, that Andrew's talent as a sculptor was first recognized. But as we shall see in the following chapters, it would blossom elsewhere.

* * *

Four

High Road & Low Road
(Sculpture in C19 Scotland)

Sculpture is expensive. Historically, this meant that only wealthy individuals and opulent organizations like the church could afford to own it. In the first decades of the nineteenth century a Scottish nob wishing to have himself immortalized in marble or bronze had to commission an Englishman, like Sir Francis Chantrey of London, or (ideally) an Italian, like Antonio Canova of Rome, the preeminent sculptor of his day.

In 1822 the English essayist William Hazlitt sneered that "Scotland is of all other countries in the world perhaps the one in which the question, 'What is the use of that?' is asked oftenest. But where this is the case, the Fine Arts cannot flourish." Then, just a few years later, everything changed.

In Victorian Scotland a great wave of nationalistic enthusiasm arose for erecting monuments, paid for by public subscription and carved by native-born sculptors. The country had lately nurtured literary celebrities like Robert Burns and Walter Scott. Proud citizens clamoured to celebrate their compatriots in stone. World-famous writers and poets joined heroes from history like William Wallace and Robert the Bruce as favourites in the petrified pantheon. It would be a rare

Scottish sculptor who did not carve at least one of these figures. Some, like Andrew Currie, would produce versions of all four.

Most of the local artists began their careers as stone masons, practitioners of an ancient trade that had long thrived in Scotland. Formerly, monumental masons had walked the line between craft and art, carving figures and foliage on headstones and suchlike. Now, they found new, more lively outlets for their skills.

Prior to 1850 indigenous sculptor-masons could take either of two distinct career paths, one high, the other low. The high road was taken by likely lads who, having demonstrated outstanding talent, would be dispatched to the Trustees' Academy in Edinburgh (or, occasionally, the Royal Academy School in London). In the classroom they would learn the basics of draughtsmanship, working first "from the flatt" - copying pictures - then "from the round" - copying plaster casts. Thence the tyros, if lucky enough to find a patron to pay their way, would go on to Rome. In the Eternal City they would study the techniques of marble carving and bronze casting, working as assistants to masters like Bertel Thorvaldsen, the Dane who inherited the mantle of greatest living sculptor on the death of Canova in 1822. Thorvaldsen insisted that only through rigorous imitation of classical models could a stone mason metamorphose into a fine artist.

Preeminent among the high-roaders were Thomas Campbell (1790~1858), a humbly-born marble-cutter from Edinburgh, and Laurence Macdonald (1799~1878), an ornamental mason from the tiny Perthshire village of Findo Gask. Having made the leap from rough-hewn artisan to polished society sculptor, neither wasted much time back in their native land. Campbell set up his studio in London, where his clients were predominantly English. Macdonald - dubbed "our Canova" by *The Edinburgh Literary Journal* - having failed to establish a business in the Athens of the North returned in 1832 to Rome, where he took over Thorvaldsen's studio in the stables of the Palazzo Barberini. A visit to Macdonald's became de rigueur for upper-class Brits doing the grand tour. Dukes and duchesses would pay dearly have themselves captured in polished white marble in the guise of a Grecian warrior or a Roman empress, complete with toga. The ability to achieve a good likeness was key to success.

The sculptor-masons who took the low road were, by contrast, mostly self-taught. Unlike the high-roaders, whose stock in trade was portrait busts, the low-roaders specialized in what art historians call "genre" figures, meaning rustic characters taken mostly from the poems of Burns and the novels of Scott. They worked, not in pricey marble and bronze, but in the much cheaper (and less durable) freestone and plaster. The best-known practitioners in this group were John Greenshields (1792~1835), Robert Forrest (1798~1852), and James Thom (1802~1850). All three had their studios in the west of the country: Thom in Ayr, Forrest in a quarry near Lanark, Greenshields just down the road "in a beautiful loop of the Clyde." At the height of Forrest's fame the coach service between Lanark and Glasgow advertised short stops to enable curious passengers to alight and view his work.

Thom was discovered chiseling funerary monuments in a churchyard by David Auld, the custodian of the Burns Museum in Alloway. Encouraged by Auld, in 1829 Thom carved life-sized seated figures of Tam O'Shanter and his drunken companion Souter Johnny out of blocks of rough-grained red sandstone. These works were subsequently exhibited, first in Edinburgh - where punters were charged a shilling for single admission, half-a-crown for a season ticket - then in London. In the Scottish capital alone some eighteen thousand people paid to gawk at Thom's work. In twenty-two months the show grossed the extraordinary sum of £8,900 in entrance money. Orders poured in for sixteen five-foot replicas, plus several for one-third-scale reproductions in stone. Moulds were also struck of a bust of Burns that Thom had made. The stucco casts sold for a guinea apiece. "Mr Thom's figures of Tam and Souter have been exhibited with applause in almost every part of the united kingdom," enthused a contemporary anthology of eminent persons. "[F]rom the highest to the lowest, there is scarcely a house which does not contain a cast of them."

Such success was bound to attract imitations. Greenshields, whose preoccupation had hitherto been carving busts of the royal family, immediately began work on the Jolly Beggars, a group of eight figures from the Burns cantata of that name. Visiting him at his humble thatched-cottage studio around this time, Sir

Walter Scott thought the young man showed great promise. Greenshields was a "heaven-born genius" who needed to study the best models under the tutelage of an eminent practitioner like his friend Chantrey. The Shirra urged him not to fritter away his talent on mere caricature:

> " ... the perdurable character of sculpture, the grim and stern severity
> of its productions, their size too, and their consequence, confine the
> art to what is either dignified and noble, or beautiful and graceful: it
> is, I think, inapplicable to situations of broad humour."

Undeterred, Greenshields finished his figures and in 1831 exhibited them in Edinburgh and London. After seeing the Jolly Beggars, the ever-generous Scott changed his mind. "Tell John that he has taught me to read Burns in my old age," he informed the sculptor's brother, "say to him that the group is faultless.'"

Not to be outdone, Forrest exhibited his own versions of Tam O'Shanter and Souter Johnny, begun more than ten years earlier, at the Calton Convening Rooms in Edinburgh in 1834. Then Thom returned with a new show, featuring Burns's Landlord and Landlady and Scott's Old Mortality and his Pony. But the rash of similar exhibitions had sated the public's appetite for genre figures and this second exhibition flopped. In 1836 Thom left for America in pursuit of an agent who, after showing some of his works in that country, had pocketed the proceeds. Thom settled in the US, where he died of tuberculosis in a New York lodging house in 1850, "a sadly disappointed man." His Old Mortality ended up, appropriately enough, in a cemetery at Laurel Hill, outside Philadelphia. Unable to sustain the market for his work, Forrest also faded from view. He is said to have supported himself through the lean years by carving anonymous funerary monuments.

*

Just as popular interest in exhibitions of crude genre figures was waning, however, a new market for sculpture opened up. The impetus was the death of Sir Walter

Scott, which occurred in 1832. The Shirra was already "the most pictured and busted [sic] man of the age" apart from the Iron Duke (of Wellington). Now, cities all over the country hastily organized design competitions for monuments to commemorate "Scotland's darling son." First out of the blocks was Glasgow.

Both Forrest and Greenshields entered the competition. Having already completed a statue of Scott, Greenshields had the jump on his rival. On the pedestal of this accomplished work (now in Parliament House, Edinburgh) Greenshields carved the words "Sic Sedebat," meaning "He Sat Thus," his proud point being that he had taken his statue directly from the life, not from some second-hand source like a print. Since the competition called for an erect figure, the organizing committee urged Greenshields to replicate the head of his previous work on the model he submitted. This he reluctantly agreed to do. His design was adopted, but the sculptor did not live to see the realization of his work. It was completed in 1837 and installed on an eighty-foot column in Glasgow's George Square by a high-roader, Alexander Handyside Ritchie. Two years later Ritchie would produce his own, original statue of Sir Walter Scott. It stands outside the Shirra's Court House in the Market Place, Selkirk. More on him shortly.

Not to be outdone by Glasgow's upstart effort, Edinburgh launched an international competition for a grand monument to Sir Walter Scott, who had after all been born in the city's Old Town. To be built on a prime location (originally Charlotte Square, ultimately Princes Street Gardens), its focal point would be a twice-life-size statue of the Great Minstrel. The artist chosen out of thirty contenders to carve it was not some Englishman or Italian, but an untried 34-year-old local named John Steell. Steell's magnificent seated figure of the Shirra in white Carrara marble is thought to be the first such statue commissioned in Scotland from a native sculptor.

Born in 1804, the son of an Aberdeen carver and gilder who subsequently moved to Edinburgh to teach woodworking at the Trustees' Academy, Steell served the conventional high-roader apprenticeship, putting in four years at the Trustees' followed by several months in Rome. Back in Edinburgh, he joined the newly-founded Royal Scottish Academy. Steell was a driven, ambitious character blessed with the kind of personal charm that made him a natural salesman. Commissions poured into his studio, mostly for portrait busts in the approved neoclassical mode. Unlike his predecessors, he had no need to relocate to London.

In 1840 Steell won the competition for an equestrian statue of the Duke of Wellington in bronze for a site outside Register House in Edinburgh. In order to cast the statue, he built Scotland's first bronze foundry. This enabled Steell to crank out copies of his work to meet the demand. His bronze statue of Robert Burns was purchased by New York (Central Park, 1880), Dundee (1880), London (Embankment Gardens, 1884) and Dunedin (New Zealand, 1887). In 1838 Steell was appointed Sculptor to Her Majesty the Queen. In 1844 he carved the statue of Queen Victoria that sits atop the Royal Scottish Academy building in Princes Street, Edinburgh. In 1876, following the unveiling of his memorial to Prince Albert in Charlotte Square, he was knighted, becoming the first sculptor to be thus honoured since Chantrey.

*

Occasional commissions for public monuments conferred great prestige on a sculptor. As a result the competitions were keenly contested. Other than Greeenshields none of the genre sculptors ever managed to win a public monument commission. Even well-credentialed practitioners were sometimes disappointed in their expectations. Andrew Currie entered four such competitions - Mungo Park (Selkirk, 1859), James Hogg (St Mary's Loch, 1860), William Wallace (Stirling, 1860), and Robert the Bruce (Stirling, 1872) - and won three of them, in at least one case beating a high-roader. Not bad going for a late starter.

The statue of Mungo Park, his first major commission, pitted Andrew against Handyside Ritchie. Born in Musselburgh in 1804, the son of an ornamental plasterer, Ritchie had like his contemporary Steell studied at the Trustees' Academy then gone on to Rome, where he worked under Thorvaldsen. After his return to Scotland, in 1838 he set up a studio in Princes Street. Ritchie specialized in public monuments and busts for aristocratic customers. The former include the statues of Scott in Glasgow and Selkirk, a figure of William Wallace in Stirling (1859), and one of John Leyden in Denholm (1860).[15]

That Andrew was able to beat such an accomplished fine artist is testament to his ability. Also, to the fact that he was the only proficient sculptor located in the Borders, which no doubt influenced the partisan selection committee's decision.[16]

One of Handyside Ritchie's first big commissions had been a monument to Sir Charles Marjoribanks sculpted in 1832 in the Border village of Coldstream. Perched for some reason on top of a seventy-foot column, this statue was destroyed by lighting in 1873. Ritchie having died several years previously, Andrew was asked to do the restoration, based on Ritchie's model.

*

Never having had drawing lessons or been to Rome, Andrew was obviously not a high-roader. To be sure he did many genre figures, but also some works that can be categorized as fine art. As relatives and friends of his subjects attested, he was able to capture a good likeness. He is thus not easy to pigeon-hole.

---

[15] Known locally as "Wee Wallace," to distinguish it from the much larger statue by D.W. Stevenson on the Wallace Monument, Ritchie's version depicts the great patriot clad in a toga, demonstrating about as much regard for historical accuracy as Mel Gibson. The eccentric Glasgow-born sculptor Patrick Park (1811~1855), also a pupil of Thorvaldsen, came up with a more daring solution to the fraught question of how to garb ancient heroes. Around 1851 Park produced, on spec, a model for a statue of William Wallace that would be eighteen feet high — and utterly nude. Park had hoped to win public support to fund the translation of his model into bronze, for installation on the Calton Hill. But the prospect of a naked giant in their midst proved altogether too much for the prudish citizens of Edinburgh. It was suggested that the sculptor might like to add a fig-leaf; but, having unsuccessfully argued that Wallace was a mythical figure and as such did not require to be clad, in a fit of pique Park dashed his model to pieces.

[16] Andrew's only potential rival in the Borders was his namesake, the journeyman mason and genre sculptor John Currie of Dumfries, with whom he is often confused. The confusion is exacerbated by the fact that John Currie also carved versions of Edie Ochiltree and Old Mortality, coincidentally the same two characters that Andrew would later execute for the Scott Monument. However, John Currie's fleeting success occurred during the the late 1830s and early 1840s, when he exhibited his genre pieces in Edinburgh and Liverpool. By the time Andrew began his work as a sculptor more than a decade later, John Currie had long since faded into obscurity.

Andrew was self-taught, but this in itself is by no means unprecedented. The great Chantrey himself liked to boast that he had never had even "an hour's instruction" in sculpture in his life. Andrew was trained as a millwright, not a stone mason. His first commissions, the ones that established his reputation, were wooden pieces. Again, this is not unheard-of. Chantrey initially worked as a wood carver and gilder. Steell and Thorvaldsen both came from wood-carving backgrounds.

What makes Andrew unique is that he did not begin his career as a professional sculptor until he was well into his forties. As Andrew's friend, the Border writer William Shillinglaw Crockett, put it in a letter to *The Scotsman*, "he did extraordinarily well for one who, late in life, changed his occupation to carve a livelihood in the service of art." His peers seem to have held him in high regard. Steell was reportedly impressed by some small wooden carvings by Andrew he had seen at Abbotsford. John Rochead, the architect who designed the Wallace Monument, was also a supporter.

Perhaps the best way to gauge Andrew's status is by comparing him with the group of sculptors who were commissioned to carve character statues for the Scott Monument in commemoration of the centenary of Sir Walter's birth in 1871. Many were members of the Royal Scottish Academy. They included two of the most eminent fine artists of the day, Andrew's contemporary, William Brodie (1815~1881) and D.W. Stevenson (1842~1904). Along with Steell, they dominated monumental figure sculpture in Scotland during the second half of the nineteenth century. Both were high roaders. Brodie had studied under Laurence Macdonald in Rome. Though his specialty was portrait busts and architectural sculpture, he is best-known for his bronze monument to Greyfriars Bobby, the faithful grave-guarding terrier (1872). Stevenson began his artistic career in Brodie's studio in Edinburgh, where he worked for eight years. On returning from Rome, he assisted Steell on the Prince Albert Memorial. His best-known piece is the massive - three-ton, fourteen-foot-high - bronze statue of William Wallace on the outside wall of the Wallace Monument in Stirling (1887).

Of the 24 statuettes commissioned for the Scott Monument in 1871, Brodie accounted for five, Stevenson three. Evidently they did not consider genre sculpture beneath them. Being chosen to contribute pieces for such a prominent landmark was seen as a high honour. Andrew Currie was immensely proud of having been selected to do his two characters, Edie Ochiltree and Old Mortality.

Even with the new opportunities available to sculptors, earning a living was always hard. Andrew never made much money from his work, and in this he was not alone. Clark Stanton RSA, another member of the Scott Monument group, was "continuously in debt" throughout his life. Handyside Ritchie died virtually penniless, leaving an estate valued at just £6 10s 6d. Even John Steell, the greatest of them all, is buried in an unmarked grave.

* * *

Five

Late Developer (1848~1860)

The census of 1851 listed Andrew Currie as a "millwright employing 3 men" in Earlston. By the time the next census rolled around a decade later, Andrew had changed his vocation, his location — and not long afterwards would change his religion, too.

The change of occupation came first. Ever since he was a boy Andrew had enjoyed woodcarving. "[H]e was always busy with his knife," wrote Lillias Cotesworth, who as a girl in the 1870s used to take twice-weekly clay modeling lessons from Andrew at his studio. She came to know him well, and left by far the most intimate account we have of his life:

> "[D]uring leisure hours, [he] shaped many skillful Gibbons-like
> bits of foliage and lifelike representations of birds, every delicate
> feather showing ... ."[17] He also "moulded clever original groups
> in the red clay, some of which is still found near the Black Hill."[18]
> These might include "an 'auld wife' on the lookout, her hand

---

[17] Grinling Gibbons (1648~1721), an English sculptor and woodcarver known for his exquisite decorative work at Hampton Court and elsewhere.
[18] "[A] picturesque conical eminence, crowned with the remains of a Roman camp" outside Earlston.
NB "clever" here means skillful, as in "clever with his hands."

over her eyes, her garments windswept; a shepherd and his dog;
or a classical head copied from some picture."

It was just a hobby, but Andrew was proud of his handiwork. He showed off his best pieces in the window of his millwright's workshop. One day Lillias's father, William Cotesworth, a young English gentleman, happened to be passing and was taken by what he saw. Cotesworth, then 21 years old, was the owner of Cowdenknowes, a beautifully-situated mansion that overlooks Leader Water about a mile south of Earlston. He had inherited the house from a Liverpool merchant called James Gilfillan, a friend of his father's, who bought it in 1841 from the bankrupt Home family.

The library needed some furniture. The gentleman inquired within: would Andrew be interested in making him a bookshelf with carved embellishments? Indeed he would. Especially since it was for Cowdenknowes, a house in whose keep, as Andrew well knew, Thomas the Rhymer had been wrongfully imprisoned and on which as a consequence he had laid a curse, that it would never pass from father to son.

This first commission was destined not to be a quick job. Begun in 1848, according to dates the sculptor carved into its base, the bookcase and its extension would not be completed until 1883, thirty-five years later. How to account for this extraordinary delay? According to Lillias Cotesworth, the problem was partly one of Andrew's dilatory nature:

> "He was no mechanical worker, but possessed the true soul of an artist; to him a delicate vine tendril, the dainty curves of a leaf, or a slender foxglove were 'a joy forever,' and he would produce them with little effort. But when inspiration was not there, when he did not discover a model to suit his fancy, he found it difficult to 'buckle to,' and finish what he had begun. This proved to be so with the bookcase he carved for the library at Cowdenknowes ... ."

Nonetheless it was, ultimately, a fine piece. "Almost every leaf is different, and nothing upon it is without meaning, from several quaint and graceful heads to clusters of bulrushes and dock leaves. But how often have I heard tell that, if questioned as to when he intended to proceed with the task, and how near it was to completion, he would smile, consciously shake his head, and make some evasive answer, his eyes twinkling, for he was well aware of his own inability for steady plodding labour."[19]

Despite this apparent dilatoriness, a friendship grew between Andrew and his first benefactors, which deepened after Lillias became his pupil. Much later, when "[a]s a result of some grave misfortune" the Cotesworths sold Cowdenknowes and returned to England (thus fulfilling the Rhymer's curse), they asked Andrew to extend the bookcase, so that it would fit into a room in their new house in Berkshire. "[H]e thought it all out with the greatest care, putting his best work into the clever addition."

The new section featured at one end a figure of King David I of Scotland holding a model and the charter of Melrose Abbey (an edifice that was, as we shall see, of great significance to Andrew). It was carved out of a piece of wood "as old as the abbey itself, True Thomas with the doe that led him astray, and, woven among delicate leaves, a ribbon with the words, 'Farewell to Leader's river, Farewell to Ercildoun.'" The hooded head of Thomas, with its beard, long curved nose and downward-sloping eyes, is almost certainly a self-portrait of the artist.

*

The bookcase was the beginning. But it was with his next large carved wooden piece that Andrew Currie made his name as a sculptor. Known as the "fairy flower stand," this featured graceful blossoms mingling with fairy figures, including (inevitably) Thomas the Rhymer. It was shown along with two smaller works, a goat's head and a dead partridge, at the Royal Scottish Academy's annual

---

[19] Another possible explanation: perhaps Andrew hadn't been paid for his work, and was being evasive to spare the young girl's feelings. William Cotesworth had no money of his own; the life-rent on the Cowdenknowes estate had been left to his father.

exhibition in Edinburgh in 1855, held that year for the first time in the Academy's new galleries at the foot of the Mound. The function of this exhibition was (and is) to show the best new art - paintings, prints and sculptures - from around the country. The works are not only on display, they are also on sale. At the grand old age of 43 Andrew had become a professional sculptor.

Why had he abandoned what was apparently "a prosperous concern" to devote himself to the precarious life of an artist? It was, as the Reverend James Russell, who had known Andrew since he was a youngster attending Yarrow Kirk, would subsequently assert, "a bold step for a family man to take, to forsake the mechanical trade to which he was trained, and carve out for himself a different course of life."

In fact, Andrew seems to have had little choice but to dispose of his millwright's business: his health had "given way." What exactly this means we do not know, but it seems likely that, after twenty five years of punishing dawn-to-dusk physical labour, his body could not take any more. Or perhaps he had simply grown tired of a job that gave him no outlet for his creative abilities. At any rate, "it was then that he devoted his mind to art."

The fairy flower stand won much praise in Edinburgh, but did not find a buyer. Andrew did however manage to make his first sale: the delicate carving of the partridge was bought by James Hope-Scott. Through his marriage to Sir Walter Scott's granddaughter Charlotte Lockhart, Hope-Scott had become the proprietor of Abbotsford, the baronial-style castle that the Shirra built for himself near the ruins of Melrose Abbey. Hope-Scott would be an important and influential figure in the sculptor's professional and personal life. He would become Andrew's patron, commissioning many pieces, both for Abbotsford and the church that he would build in Galashiels. More of him anon.

Hope-Scott was sufficiently impressed with Andrew's fairy flower stand to allow it to be exhibited at Abbotsford after the RSA show ended. In November 1855, flattered by the many congratulations he had received but frustrated at its failure to sell, Andrew resolved to dispose of his signature piece by raffle. This was unusual, but by no means unprecedented. In 1815, when Willie Allan's painting

Circassian Captives did not find a purchaser, Sir Walter Scott, John Wilson and their cronies clubbed together and held a raffle for it, selling tickets at ten guineas each to a hundred subscribers. In Dumfries during the early 1840s, Andrew's namesake the genre sculptor John Currie had raised funds by raffling his group, *Old Mortality and his Pony*.

Andrew's raffle was more modest than Allan's: he sold ninety shares at a pound apiece. The winner was Lady Polwarth, wife of Lord Polwarth, Henry Francis Hepburne-Scott, a cousin of Sir Walter's, and his executor. His lordship's seat was Mertoun House, near St Boswells. Andrew was delighted: "it is very gratifying to me," he wrote to Lord Polwarth, "that my workmanship will be honoured with a place in Mertoun House as my preference was that it might remain by Tweedside."[20]

*

Having turned professional, Andrew now needed a studio with enough space to allow him to sculpt on a more ambitious scale. His workshop at Earlston was too small. It was also too out of the way: access to potential customers was essential. Andrew found the solution in Darnick, a "picturesque and thriving hamlet" on the banks of the Tweed in Roxburghshire. In the mid nineteenth century Darnick had a population of around four hundred. He moved there with his family in 1857.

Darnick - the name means "village on the moor" - is located west of Melrose, about a mile from the Abbey, just down the road that leads to Abbotsford. "The village of Darnick," according to one mid nineteenth century guide, "... attracts the attention of tourists in consequence, chiefly, of its possessing the finest specimen of

---

[20] Lord P was evidently a man of parts. In the same letter Andrew thanks him for a technical tip: "I flatter myself that I have now succeeded in your Lordship's very valuable suggestion about hardening the clay, viz, by boiling it with a proper mixture of lime, which makes an extremely hard and fine substance."

Alas, the fairy flower stand is no longer at Mertoun House. It may have disappeared when the Polwarths cleared the house at the time of its sale in 1912 (though it is not mentioned in the auction catalogue). Its current whereabouts are unknown.

the ancient Border keeps." In fact, Darnick boasted a cluster of three fifteenth-century peel towers, aka fortified "bastel" houses. In olden days, these were places of refuge that could be defended against bands of marauding reivers or invading armies. Two were more or less ruins. Sir Walter Scott had coveted the third, intending to turn it into a repository for his collection of antique armour. His intention being known, his friends took to mocking him as "the Duke of Darnick."

However, Scott's interest awakened a determination in the hereditary owner, an Edinburgh merchant named John Heiton, to restore the tower as a retirement home for himself. This he eventually did in 1859, "assisted by the antiquarian and artistic judgment of Mr Currie." (Another account claims that Andrew actually superintended the restoration work.) The tower was thoroughly done over "from base to bartizan [overhanging wall-mounted turret], the whole of the apartments and everything connected with them" suitably remade "in primitive style." A happy bonus derived from this work. Andrew would subsequently use some leftover oak beams, well-seasoned timber that had originally been adzed in the fifteenth century, as raw material for his carvings. Notably, for the addition to the Cotesworth bookcase and a second, much larger, bookcase that he would later make for his older sister Jean and her farmer husband, William Scott of Ladhope.

Oil painting of Darnick Tower, believed to be by AC. Fisher's Tower is at left
(private collection)

Andrew established his studio in a wooden shack behind one of the ruined peels. This was known, after the family who formerly owned it, as "Fisher's Tower." A visitor to the tower in 1864 noted that "its doorway on the north side still shows the groove cut in the stonework to receive the outer strong door of wood or iron, and the large strong hooks on which it hung still remain. On the lintel is cut the IHS and the initials apparently of JF."[21] How Andrew the antiquary must have loved living in a house on which history was quite literally engraved!

Oddly enough, he was not the first sculptor to have been based in Darnick. That was John Smith, a member of a family of mason-builders who were responsible for constructing a number of houses, churches and bridges in the area. Smith is best-known for the enormous 31-foot red sandstone statue of William Wallace, erected in 1814, that stands facing the Ettrick Forest at Dryburgh.[22] But by far the most important point of contact for Andrew with sculptors from bygone days was to be found nearby, at Melrose Abbey.

*

Founded as a Cistercian monastery by King David I in 1136, rebuilt by Robert the Bruce after its destruction in 1322 by the English, then devastated by Calvinist zealots in 1569, Melrose Abbey was, as Robert Chambers wrote in 1827, "the most beautiful of all the ecclesiastical ruins scattered through this reformed land. To say that it is beautiful, is to say nothing. It is exquisitely — splendidly lovely ... an object possessed of infinite grace and unmeasurable charm." Running out of superlatives, Chambers passed the baton to Sir Walter Scott and his description of "St David's ruin'd pile" in *The Lay of the Last Minstrel* (1805):

---

[21] IHS is "a common Christogram, based on the first three letters of Jesus in Greek." JF may be the initials of a member of the Fisher family.
[22] Sir Walter Scott loathed this crudely-carved colossus, calling it a "horrible monster." So much so that, according to James Hogg, he once confessed that he would like to "blow up the statue of Wallace with gunpowder ... in such a style that there will not be one fragment of it left."

Was never a scene so sad and fair ...

... slender shafts of shapely stone,
By foliaged tracery combined;
Thou would'st have thought some fairy's hand
'Twixt poplars straight the osier [willow] wand
In many a freakish knot had twined;
Then framed a spell, when the work was done,
And changed the willow-wreaths to stone.

This sounds not unlike the effect that Andrew had striven for, in wood, with his fairy flower stand.

Like other great medieval monasteries and cathedrals, Melrose Abbey had been ruthlessly destroyed by mobs of fanatical iconoclasts. They were whipped into a frenzy by protestant demagogues like John Knox, who railed in his sermons against idolatry, the worship of graven (sculpted) images. Much like the Taliban blowing up the Buddhas of Bamiyan in modern times, these vandals targeted statues of figures. Melrose Abbey had been home to some of Scotland's finest religious sculptures. In particular, its eastern window mounted thirteen statues representing Jesus and his apostles. The dissolution of the monasteries left such treasures vulnerable. Most egregiously, to the wrath of an over-zealous weaver from Gattonside who one night, armed with a hammer and chisel, climbed a ladder and knocked off the statues' heads and arms. Next day this monster boasted to everyone he met that he had "fairly stumped thae vile paipist dirt nou!" He was thereafter known locally as "Old Stumpie."

As at Earlston, Andrew threw himself into learning all he could about the history of the Abbey. He quizzed the local old folk, soon discovering that few knew much about its antiquities. Andrew also undertook hands-on rescue work, "exhuming and otherwise collecting numerous fragmentary remains of the sculptured stones belonging to the Abbey." He arranged them in order within the ruins to "form a special object of attraction for the pilgrims who visit St David's pile." His efforts seem to have been successful. "[I]n consequence of some excavations made by by Mr Currie, the sculptor at Darnick, there is good reason to suppose that among the debris about Melrose there may be many of the statues which occupied niches of the old idolatrous pile, and which fortunately escaped the hammer of Old Stumpie," wrote John Heiton (owner of the peel tower and probably Andrew's landlord) in a letter to *The Scotsman* in 1865.

In addition, Andrew applied himself to acquiring expertise on the stones that he found in the Abbey's graveyard. "[He] is as learned in tombstones as Old Mortality himself," wrote George Huntley Gordon, a former amanuensis to Sir Walter Scott, in a letter to *The Athenaeum* in 1864.[23] "[He] has done much more than clean or restore them, as he has *made* many in a style which reminds one of the monuments of bygone ages. He is also the sculptor of some busts of much merit." According to the anonymous author of a letter to the *Freemason's Magazine* in 1868, Andrew gave the historian James Wade "all the information necessary to compile his book," *History of St Mary's Abbey, Melrose*, published in 1861. (In which case, it is odd that Wade did not credit him.)

The Abbey was not the only object of his study. During the late 1850s and early 1860s Andrew was actively involved in archaeological discoveries in other parts of the Borders. For example, he participated in an attempt to clear up the mystery surrounding some large flat stones that had been dug up by a ploughman near Yarrow Kirk in 1804. One of them bore a Latin inscription. Bones and ashes were discovered underneath, indicating a burial chamber of some sort. "[The stone] was examined by Sir Walter Scott, Dr John Leyden, Mungo Park, and others of antiquarian lore." But was it, as Leyden thought, a Roman relic or was the inscription Christian, as Professor James Pillans of Edinburgh University suggested?

In 1857 Andrew obtained the Duke of Buccleuch's permission to take a plaster cast of the inscribed stone. He donated the cast he made to the Museum of the

---

[23] Old Mortality is a character from Sir Walter Scott's eponymous 1816 novel. He is based on Robert Paterson, a zealous Cameronian who devoted his latter years to tending and mending the graves of otherwise forgotten Covenanters (seventeenth century presbyterian die-hards), traveling around graveyards all over the Borders. See Chapter Eight.

Society of Antiquaries in Edinburgh where it was subsequently photographed. During his research, Andrew also made discoveries that helped establish the age of the remains. In particular, some items that were found in the garden attached to a nearby shepherd's cottage. "At that time," he wrote many years later, "when I took the cast from the inscribed upright stone, the shepherd ... had previously turned up in his garden ground a bronze battle-axe and a polished black ring, like an optician's eye-glass. This I got from him and it is now in the Antiquarian Museum. I failed to get the bronze axe, which was used as a useful chopper in the shepherd's house, but I made a sketch of it at the time."

On 13 February 1860, at a meeting in the library of the Royal Institution on the Mound in Edinburgh, Andrew Currie was admitted as a Fellow of the Society of Antiquaries of Scotland. This allowed him to add the initials FSA after his name. He would henceforth often be referred to as "the Border sculptor and antiquary." Unfortunately, active fellows of the society are required to pay annual dues; after four years Andrew either neglected, or was unable, to renew his membership.

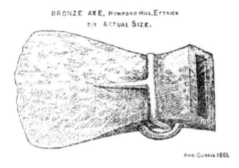

BRONZE AXE. Howford Hill, Ettrick
⅔ Actual Size.

And. Currie 1865.

*

For all its rich history, Darnick's most attractive feature from a professional sculptor's point of view was its proximity to the home of Sir Walter Scott. Following the author's death in 1832, Abbotsford became a mecca for literary pilgrims. From all over the world devotees descended in droves to pay homage at the Shirra's shrine. All tourists want souvenirs to take home with them. Andrew catered to this passing trade. Indeed, according to Lillias Cotesworth, he "lived chiefly by selling to tourists busts and bas-reliefs of Sir Walter Scott, Hogg, Burns, etc, and copies in wood or plaster of ornaments from Melrose Abbey."

One American visitor, a reporter from the *New York Times*, arrived in the area in 1882 to gather material for an article commemorating the fiftieth anniversary of the Great Minstrel's death. He noted that it was "a neighborhood where [Scott's] memory is still held in the highest regard; where every hilltop, every ruin, almost every house and tree, brings to the minds of the people some recollection of him; where portraits of him appear in the homes alike of noblemen and peasants; where plaster casts of the characters in his books are on all sides for sale at little more than a song ... ." He interviewed an old woman, the keeper of a wayside inn on the Abbotsford road, who remembered Sir Walter well. Among other things, she told him that the Shirra had been always "on the lookout for a bit of talk with odd characters; some of them out of his books are made most beautiful by Mr Currie, in Darnick."

"This latter statement," the reporter explained, "was made in reference to a self-educated sculptor, who lives in an adjoining village, and who, though a man of scant reading, has succeeded in molding statues of 'Old Mortality' and other like characters in such fashion as to display truly remarkable talent and win a reputation, not only on the border, but in other parts of Scotland." The American evidently imagined that "self-educated" meant that Andrew was barely literate. Actually, as we have seen, he had received a robust Scottish grammar-school education, and was very well read; it was sculpture that he had taught himself. In journalism, it is always better to check your facts than jump to conclusions.

*

For sculptors, anniversaries represent a unique sales opportunity. The first one to crop up after Andrew's move to Darnick was the Burns centenary, 25 January 1859.

On 8 January that year, a classified advertisement appeared on the front page of *The Scotsman*:

BUST OF BURNS

A. CURRIE, SCULPTOR, DARNICK, by Melrose, having, in anticipation of the Centenary of the Birth of Burns, been ordered to execute for The Royal Caledonian Society of London a life-sized Bust of the Poet, for the Original Painting by NAYSMITH, begs to intimate that the work will be completed in a few days, and that he will be ready to supply CASTS from the same, to be forwarded to any part of the country in time for the Celebration.

How many casts Andrew supplied is not known. However, we do know what happened to two of them. One, "fresh from the studio of Mr Currie of Darnick," was displayed "encircled with a chaplet of holly and berries under a canopy of chastely arranged evergreens" next to the chairman's seat during a public dinner held in the bard's name on 25 January at the Abbotsford Hotel. Fifty guests attended.

A more elaborate commemoration took place in Andrew's former home town of Earlston. "The popularity of the celebration of this event caused an excitement in this village quite unprecedented." The shops shut at noon and all business was suspended for the day. At exactly three o'clock a procession led by a band started from the public reading room. "Hundreds joined arm in arm and proudly followed the beating drum and numerous flags that were wafted to the breeze." At around half past six, after much haggis had been consumed, a crowd of almost seven hundred people gathered in the store room at Wilson's mill. The audience sang *Auld Lang Syne*, then the chairman of the meeting got up to introduce "a very unexpected guest ... none other than the immortal Burns."

Well, not exactly the poet himself - he had been dead for over sixty years - but a bust of him, done by Andrew Currie. "I believe that this bust may be confidently relied upon as a correct likeness of the original," the chairman continued, "and in saying this no higher compliment can be paid to any artist. I have great pleasure in informing you that we are wholly indebted for this valuable present to Mr Currie of Darnick, who has also honoured us with his presence here tonight. I therefore request that this meeting tender to Mr Currie their warmest thanks for this handsome gift." (Loud and continued applause)

Earlston had mustered seven hundred. At London's Crystal Palace, *fourteen thousand* people turned up for a gathering at which another bust of Burns was unveiled. This was not by Andrew Currie, as some mistakenly thought, but by his contemporary, the high roader William Calder Marshall. Given that Marshall and Andrew (and every other sculptor of Burns) were working from the same source - Naysmith's portrait of the bard - the confusion is understandable.

Though a handy source of income, plaster casts of authors and their characters were small stuff. Andrew would shortly begin work on a much more ambitious scale, and in stone, a new material for him, as we shall see in the next chapter.

* * *

Six

Native Sons (1858~1860)

In 1858 a small item from Selkirk appeared in *The Builder*, an architectural journal:

"The committee for the erection of a monument to the distinguished African discoverer, Mungo Park, have selected the design of Mr Andrew Currie, of Darnick, sculptor. There were various competitors, but only two who sent in models, Mr Currie and Mr Ritchie of Edinburgh."

How did he do it? How did a neophyte sculptor with little or no previous experience of working in stone, let alone on such a grand scale, manage to win the competition to carve a prestigious public monument? Especially when pitted against Alexander Handyside Ritchie, a distinguished rival who had trained in Rome under the great Dane Thorvaldsen; and who moreover had local track record, namely, his imposing statue of Sir Walter Scott which stands outside the Court House in Selkirk's Market Place?

Two possible explanations: First, as the old saw goes, it's not what you know, it's who. Andrew was well-connected locally. And second, he may have underbid his better-qualified opponent. Certainly not much money was available for the Mungo Park memorial. The original meeting on how to commemorate the town's most famous son had been held at Selkirk Town Hall back in December 1841, just two years after the erection of Richie's monument to Scott, thirty-six years after Park's death. The members took their time making up their minds: the raising of subscriptions in the Border counties for a monument to Park did not commence until sixteen years later. Even then enthusiasm was muted: "the committee failed to collect an amount sufficient to defray the expense."

Enter the Reverend Charles Rogers, who would become one of Andrew Currie's biggest boosters. Chaplain to the garrison at Stirling Castle, Rogers was a prime mover in the mid nineteenth century mania for nationalist monument building. Notably the Wallace Monument outside Stirling and, as we shall see, the statue of Robert the Bruce that Andrew would subsequently undertake for the castle esplanade. Rogers had an unhappy knack for getting himself entangled in disputes, often over how the funds he had collected were spent. For the Mungo Park memorial the reverend managed to raise an additional £30 - "from persons friendly to the movement in India" - thus "the balance was procured." At last, plans for the monument could go ahead.

*

Though now almost forgotten, Mungo Park won considerable fame in his day as an intrepid "traveller," as explorers were then known. He was born in 1771, the same year as Walter Scott, the seventh child in a family of thirteen (five died young), at Foulshiels, a farm which his father rented from the Duke of Buccleuch on Yarrow Water about four miles from Selkirk. Park was brought up strictly in the Calvinist tradition. From this, it was said, he derived his grim determination.

Like the Curries, the Parks were tenant farmers, but sufficiently well-off to pay for a good education for young Mungo. Like Andrew, he attended Selkirk Grammar School. At age fourteen he was apprenticed to Thomas Anderson, the local doctor, whose patients included the Currie family. Park went on to Edinburgh University, where he studied medicine, subsequently qualifying as a surgeon.

On his first expedition, to Sumatra in 1792-3, Park discovered in himself an extraordinary self-sufficiency and a compulsive wanderlust. In 1794, with the backing of Sir Joseph Banks, president of the Royal Society and founder of the African Association, he was chosen to lead an expedition to chart the course of the

River Niger. After many hair-raising adventures in West Africa, Park returned to Scotland in 1797. He spent the next year writing an account of his journey. Published in 1799 *Travels in the Interior of Africa* became an instant best-seller.[24]

Park married his childhood sweetheart Alison Anderson, the daughter of his old master. Attempting to settle down in the Borders, he became friends with the young Walter Scott, who was then working on *The Lay of the Last Minstrel*. But the dark continent continued to haunt Park: he told Scott that he would "rather brave Africa and all its horrors," than wear out his days riding the gloomy hills as an underpaid country doctor.

In 1805 Park mounted a second expedition to find the source of the Niger, this time under the sponsorship of the Colonial Office. Its official objectives were "the extension of British commerce and the enlargement of geographical knowledge," in that order. But Park underestimated the enormity of the task he had set himself: heading for Timbuktu he and his entire expedition (which included his brother-in-law Alexander Anderson and George Scott, another Selkirk man) disappeared, never to be seen again. It seems that Park was killed during a skirmish with hostile locals at Boussa, a village in what is now Benin.

Having been born seven years after his death, Andrew never knew Mungo Park. But the two families were intimately linked. His aunt Margaret Lang married one of Mungo's brothers, Archibald, a sheriff's officer (who had introduced the traveller to Walter Scott). His mother Henrietta Lang had been in love with (and jilted by) another brother, Adam, also a surgeon. She also knew Mungo well. "My pious mother was schooled with [Mungo]," Andrew recalled, "and in her house [Viewfield] he prepared much of his first account of Africa. Her opinion was that she never had experience of a better Christian man, so unselfish, so charitable and benevolent even to his enemies."

---

[24] It also introduced a new expression into the English language. "Mumbo Jumbo" - derived from the Mandinka word *maama-jomboo* - was a character Park encountered on his travels. Donning a mask and costume made of bark this individual would perform a dance the purpose of which was to intimidate women. The term came to mean an obscure ritual, hence obfuscatory language or gibberish.

Andrew would draw on family connections to help him achieve a good likeness for his statue of Mungo Park, using "paintings, engravings and information supplied by the niece of the traveller." Familial ties were obviously an advantage. So was being "a native of the Forest." However, most significant in Andrew's winning the commission to sculpt the monument to Mungo Park was undoubtedly the fact that John Lang, his cousin, exact contemporary, and best friend from childhood, was on the selection committee.

John had taken over from his father Andrew Lang as sheriff-clerk of Selkirkshire in 1841. On 2 April 1858, he wrote a letter to his cousin in Darnick:

Dear Andrew:

A Meeting of the Park committee was held last night, to consider the various Designs etcetera, but in consequence of various Members labouring under the disadvantage of not having seen anything by you, as by two others who give Designs, in the shape of a Bust or Statue and being unable, therefore, to judge of the comparative eligibility of the artists, the Meeting was adjourned for ten days or so, with the view of enabling such members of the committee as might feel disposed to call upon you and other parties referred to and to inspect such specimens of the art as you and they could show them.

I inform you of this as a friend, desirous that you should be prepared for the work and I trust that you will be able to show something good to those who may visit you (as I intend to do) and satisfy the committee, through them that the job belongs to your department of art.

I shall call on you someday next week.

Dear Andrew, I am yours sincerely,

John Lang

The committee reached its decision shortly afterwards: Andrew's design got the nod.

*

According to *The Scotsman*, "The sculptor, Mr Currie, has been successful in getting a stone from Denholme [sic] quarry of sufficient size for the full-length figure (eight feet) of Mungo Park. The stone is being rough-dressed at Mr Laing's quarry, and is capable of receiving an almost marble-like polish." The monument was erected opposite the house formerly occupied by Dr Anderson at the junction of High Street and Back Row. The statue represents Park standing in an easy attitude, a sextant in his right hand. In his left hand he holds a scroll on which is inscribed a paraphrase of the last sentence from his final letter to Lord Camden, the secretary of the Colonial Office: "Though I succeed not I would at last die on the Niger."[25]

"He is habited in a loose travelling cloak, with under-belt," Charles Rogers wrote. " The head, which is uncovered, presents an open massive brow, the features being in perfect repose. The likeness is admirable." The statue stands on a tapered pedestal at the base of which are four ornate carved lion's heads. The pedestal surmounts a massive plinth, the total height including the statue being twenty-eight feet.[26] On the front panel of the plinth, under decorative foliage at the centre of which sits a medallion bearing a Hippocratic serpent-and-staff, the symbol of medicine, the inscription reads:

---

[25] The original reads: "Though all the Europeans who are with me should die, and though I were myself half dead, I would still persevere, and if I could not succeed in the object of my journey, I would at last die on the Niger."

[26] On the side panels of the plinth two bronze bas reliefs were added in 1905, the centenary of Park's death. Sculpted by the Galashiels-born latter-day high roader Thomas Clapperton (1879~1962), they depict Park being tended to, and guided by, solicitous natives. In a further attempt to guild the lily, four somewhat overwrought, not to say irrelevant, life-size bronze figures of Africans (two musicians, a mother and child, and a slave girl), also by Clapperton, were added at the corners of the plinth in 1913.

MUNGO PARK

BORN AT FOULSHIELS

SELKIRKSHIRE

10TH SEPTEMBER 1771

KILLED AT BOUSSA ON THE

NIGER, AFRICA 1805

The monument was inaugurated on 2 March 1859, "amid enthusiastic demonstrations. The hiring market for hinds [herdsmen] being held upon the same day, the influx of strangers from the surrounding country, particularly from the vales of Ettrick and Yarrow, was very considerable." At two o'clock a procession formed at the monument to Sir Walter Scott in the Market Place then moved off along High Street towards the monument. It was led by the Burgh Flute Band, the Incorporated Trades, the Merchant Company, the Hawick Brass Band, St John's Lodge (Melrose) of Freemasons and the Provost, Magistrates and Town Council of Selkirk.

"The picturesque costume of the Masons, bearing the paraphernalia of 'the mystic craft,' attracted general admiration, while the manly, muscular forms of the numerous body of Hammersmen commanded special attention. The reminiscences of former days were on this occasion recalled by the sight of the original banner brought from the field of Flodden by the men of Selkirk, which has not been displayed in our streets since the visit of Prince Leopold to our ancient burgh in 1891."

The procession arrived at the monument. "The scene at this point was imposing in the extreme. On all sides ... were assembled thousands of the sons and daughters of 'the Forest,' the former apparently emulating each other in the depth and fervour of their enthusiasm. The adjoining buildings, too, were crowded with spectators — in fact not an available nook or corner whence a view of the proceedings could be obtained was without its due quota of occupants."

After a prayer to open the proceedings, "the statue was uncovered by Mr Currie, the sculptor, amid deafening cheers, the band playing, in exquisite style,

Auld Lang Syne." The inaugural address was delivered "in a loud and distinctive voice" by James Johnstone of Alva, the largest landlord in that one third of the parish of Yarrow not owned by the Duke of Buccleuch.

"Mungo Park was physically a good type or sample of our Forest men, well-trained and pliant, with a handsome intelligent countenance," Johnstone declared, laying it on thick for the locals. "I have said a good type, for as our 'Flowers of the Forest' are amongst the fairest and comeliest of the daughters of Europe, so are our men of the finest and manliest moulds — above the average height of men, and generally intelligent and prepossessing of countenance."[27] Such shameless flattery drew predictable roars of approval from the crowd. "Mr Johnstone concluded by paying a well-deserved compliment to the sculptor, Mr Currie. At four o'clock, about sixty gentlemen dined together in the County Hotel in honour of the inauguration."

Heady stuff, but even better was to come the following year, as we have seen, with the celebrations that attended the inauguration of Andrew's masterpiece in stone, the statue of the Ettrick Shepherd at St Mary's Loch.

*

The massive block out of which Andrew carved his statue of Mungo Park had been hewn from Walter Laing's quarry at Denholm Hill. It was transported to the sculptor's studio in Darnick by rail, to Melrose Station on the Waverley Line (which terminates at Edinburgh's Waverley Station), from nearby Hassendean. The six-ton slab of freestone that the Duke of Buccleuch donated for the statue of the Ettrick Shepherd came from the Whita Hill quarry at Langholm, over thirty miles distant from Melrose. Unfortunately the railway line would not reach Langholm until 1864. This meant that the ponderous block had to be transported to the nearest station, Hawick, some twenty miles away by road, via horse-drawn wagon. It

---

[27] Just like in Garrison Keillor's (fictional) town of Lake Wobegon, Minnesota, "where all the women are strong, all the men are good-looking, and all the children are above average."

would be an epic journey, like something out of ancient Egypt, filled with drama and incident.[28]

The problems began at the quarry. Whita, which supplied the hardwearing grey sandstone from which the majority of Langholm is built, is situated on the other side of the hill above and to the north of the self-styled "Muckle Toon." In a letter of 30 November 1859 to *The Border Advertiser*, demonstrating considerable literary flair, Andrew himself describes what happened:

> My Dear Editor, — I am now safely arrived at home, after a very eventful excursion with men and horses from Langholm, where we went on Tuesday last, to convey the colossal figure of the Ettrick Shepherd (rough hewn into shape) to Darnick. As the varied incidents of his procession from the high precipitous hill above Langholm to Darnick have been both disastrous and - now that I am sitting safe at my ain fireside sound in life and limb, I will add - somewhat ludicrous, I make no apology in giving you a brief description of an event which I shall remember to the end of my days.
>
> You are, no doubt, aware that this stone is the magnificent gift of the Duke of Buccleuch, being of great dimensions, and, on that account, difficult to find in a solid and pure state. I had to suggest to the committee that, probably, to save expense, and from the difficulty of getting a stone, I would be obliged to adopt a smaller model. Before doing so, however, the case was laid before the Duke, who is the largest subscriber to this memorial. With a generosity and public spirit which mark all his acts, he replied that if it was to be found in any quarry of his, he should have pleasure

---

[28] Shipping huge chunks of stone is intrinsically fraught. In Italy the 30-ton block of white Carrara marble from which John Steell carved his magnificent statue of Sir Walter Scott crashed through the bottom of the boat onto which it was being loaded. To drag it from Leith docks to Steell's studio on Princes Street required 25 horses.

in furnishing it. Langholm responded to the call, that the bard of Ettrick was in her sandstone rock on Langholm, and within sight of Ettrick Pen [highest of the Ettrick Hills], his native ground. Long and arduous has been the extraction of this fine block, but at last it was accomplished under the able superintendence of Mr Burnet, his Grace's clerk of works. The next stage being to shape the block, I sent two men with moulders, who, in the course of a fortnight, hewed it into a rude representation of a sitting figure, or Egyptian mummy.

All this was plain sailing compared to the "engineering difficulties" required in the next stage — viz, the translation of this mass weighing six tons along a narrow and bad road winding on the face of a steep hill, and thence straight down to Langholm town, in some places at an angle of 30 degrees, and making here and there sundry strange turns and convolutions like the figure 8. This was a task in the success of which I had frequently grave doubts, and so had the canny folks of Langholm. For when Mr Burnet and I had mustered our forces at the foot of the Kirkwynd on Tuesday morning last, great was the shaking of heads among the wise ones, and the sage advices, as such a mass of rock conveyed down that road was unexampled in the annals of Langholm.[29] I must say, however, that many of these gratuitous advices and remarks were very judicious, and were given with the best intention, though the general opinion gathered from the long faces was, "Poor man, he little kens what he's about: come down! it'll never come down!" But I had long before made up my mind, that it should come down — if not by wheel carriage, it should come by sliding on a sledge.

---

[29] The Kirk Wynd is the street up which riders gallop in pursuit of their leader, the Cornet, during the chase which is the highlight of the annual Langholm Common Riding.

I need not now detail the process of raising the block out of the bed of quarry on to a strong waggon. All this was satisfactorily managed on Friday morning by 10 AM, and on a signal from Mr Burnet, the mass emerged slowly out of the interior and onto the flank of the mountain. From this spot the eye ranged over a wide expanse of the Solway blazing in the morning sun; beyond were Criffel [prominent hill in southern Galloway], and far to the east rose the blue top of Ettrick Pen. The morning was bright, and so were my spirits, for I felt a confidence in the success of the operation, resulting from skilful men and well-directed labour. The road was planked for a short distance, and the planks over which the waggon wheels had passed were lifted to the front. In front and rear were two sets of ropes for men to pull by, and uphill a guy rope to be used by six spare men should occasion require. In this manner, and without a single casualty, was the whole extent of Langholm hill traversed, a distance, I should say, of fully half-a-mile. One o'clock found us at the top of that steepest and worst of all roads, terminated by the Kirkwynd of Langholm, which forms part of it. The difficulty now was to prevent the mass acquiring a momentum and running away. I need not say that had such a misfortune taken place no power could have stopt it, and there would have been in all probability a new street formed through Langholm, not to speak of the loss of life. All the men were now moved to the rear (except a few on each side with ropes to prevent the waggon from lurching) and by half-past two o'clock the huge stone was safely landed in the Market Place of Langholm, amid the cheers of some hundreds of men, and the congratulations of all parties interested in the work.

After a careful inspection of the waggon wheels before starting on the following morning, we found everything to all appearance correct. After spending a pleasant evening with Mr Burnet —

looking over his interesting fossils of the coal formation, and some ancient cannon found about Hermitage Castle [semi-ruin near Newcastleton, Roxburghshire], I started homeward on Saturday morning on the outside of the Hawick coach. The waggon with six horses had preceded me three hours. The route intended was by Mosspaul, Branxholm, Hawick, and Selkirk, to Darnick. The morning was calm and pleasant, and the day promised to be fine. After the exciting work of the last two days, I anticipated some pleasure and recreation in my homeward journey, especially in this romantic vale of Ewes Water. It will be presently seen how my pleasant anticipations were demolished like a house of cards.

I had just made the acquaintance of my fellow-passengers, one of them a well-to-do looking English gentleman, of portly dimensions, who was vastly excited all the way up by the sight of so many pheasants and other game, and who was just in the midst of [explaining] an interesting method of taking pheasants in Lancashire ... when within a mile or so of Mosspaul Inn the waggon hove in sight, drawn up on one side of the road, the drivers seemingly resting on the bank. On nearing them, however, I was hailed with, "There is a wheel broke." This was extremely awkward. I dismounted in hopes that it might be trivial, but a slight inspection convinced me that my coaching was over for that day. I found one of the waggon wheel felloes [metal segments that make up the rim] was broken quite through.

Two courses were now open to me, either to go back to Langholm, some ten miles, and have the wheel repaired, or repair it on the spot, and proceed to Hawick that night. I adopted the latter course, in the hope of saving a day. I found there was a blacksmith about three miles off, and as the iron plates I required could only be got by my own directions, I set out at once for the smithy. I found the blacksmith a very decent, obliging old man, who, on stating my case, set to work at once, and in a very short time made me two strong circular plates with bolts. He gave me a lecture before beginning, however, on his view of monuments. He was not sure about them. "They savour too much of Popery, and incline folk to worship the creature more than the creator; but we are commanded to help one another, and as ye need help, therefore, whatever ye want command my services." There was no self-interest here, for the good old man would scarcely receive payment for his work when finished.

In course of two hours we had the waggon again in motion, and the repair was now the strongest part of the wheel. As we drew up shortly after at Mosspaul Inn I commenced, while the men were getting refreshments, a further strengthening of the wheels, and making every provision for our journey. This was the more necessary, as night was closing in, and we were approaching the worst part of the road, where, should the waggon break down, all passages would be stopped. Moreover, the lives of men and horses would be risked, and in this outlandish place (Mosspaul) no possibility, without great expense, of again raising such a mass of stone. All these considerations crowded into my mind, and determined me to make every effort in my power to reach at least the smithy of Teviothead, three miles, where assistance could be had if need was. I therefore directed each of the drivers to be constant by his horse's head (there were six horses and three drivers). I myself with a lantern undertook to manage the drags behind, to show the light on the road, and to keep a sharp look-out on every side lest anything give way. It was now "between the gloamin' and the mirk."[30]

---

[30] "'Tween the gloaming and the mirk, when the kye comes hame," is a line from a song, appropriately enough, by James Hogg.

The night was wet and lowering, with the mist careering along the sides of these high green hills, when our pondrous freight again moved on with a grinding, ominous sound. Onward we swung through the darkness till we neared Linhope, when I thought it advisable to make a survey. We accordingly halted, and I found our prospects anything but cheering. Another of the waggon wheels showed symptoms of dissolution, but I did not deem it expedient, before the men, to appear as if there was anything wrong. The night was now very wet, and I was drenched to the skin, but I felt it not. We were now only half-a-mile from the village of Teviothead, yet I felt some anxiety lest we might break down before we even reached the place. Fortune, however, favoured us.

We drew up and halted in front of a cottage a little below the level of the road. On entering the smithy I was informed that the vulcan of the place had decamped, no-one knew where. Of that, however, I made light. I felt thankful that I had tools, iron, and a forge. In that department I felt perfectly at home. I now doffed my upper clothes (very wet they were) and girded myself with vulcan's apron, which I found carefully laid by on the bellows, and, amid the tittering of the smiddy loungers, I set to work to make some wingalls [sic] to bind the iron and wooden rings of the wheels together. The ridicule of the rustics was soon changed into a better feeling, and for the next hour I kept all hands busily at work, and, to their credit be it said, each seemed more anxious than another to assist. On moving again, with a considerable accompaniment of men, women and bairns, I felt so much confidence in the machine that I now for the first time dropt leisurely behind, and deputed my lantern to an active mason lad.

Everything now went on satisfactorily for some miles. We had at length reached the level road at Branxholm, when I heard a peculiar cracking sound, like the splitting of wood, given out by one of the wheels. I listened attentively, and soon found out the cause. It was wood and iron, no longer able to stand the tear and wear caused by seven tons in motion. It was now giving way to the pressure in all directions and breaking up before my eyes. Another wheel was also on fire at the same time. The case was now hopeless and desperate. I immediately had the horses removed and sent on to Hawick, distant three miles, leaving the waggon opposite Branxholm till I should make proper repairs on the following week.[31]

Accordingly on the Monday morning following, I set tradesmen to work, and about dusk we were again in a position to resume our journey. I was just looking round the waggon to see that all was right, when some person laid a hand on my shoulder with the words, "Are ye weel? I heard of ye on Saturday night as ye passed my cottage at Teviothead in much tribulation." It was the bard of

---

[31] In a letter to another newspaper, *The Caledonian Mercury and Daily Express*, Andrew wrote a lyrical account of what confronted him when he went back:

"Just at daybreak on Monday morning, I returned to the scene of the catastrophe. The first rays of the sun were tipping the neighbouring hills and the tower of Branxholm, when I caught a view of the figure. Having been rough hewn at the quarry into the shape of a sitting figure, there was presented the appearance of one of those Egyptian figures in the British Museum; the hands resting on the knees, and the eyes, in the rays of the bright morning sun, gazing fiercely into the windows of Branxholm Hall."

The statue in the British Museum that most closely corresponds to Andrew's description is the red granite statue of Sobekemsaf, an Egyptian king of the 17th dynasty (c 1590 BCE). Unfortunately, this figure was not acquired until 1907 thus cannot have been the one that he recalled from his visit(s) to the museum.

As so often with Andrew, the spot had a specific literary resonance. The first canto of Sir Walter Scott's *Lay of the Last Minstrel*, the romance which had made the poet's name, begins with the lines:

> The feast was over in Branksome tower
> And the Ladye had gone to her secret bower
> Her bower that was guarded by word and spell,
> Deadly to hear, and deadly to tell ...

Teviot.[32] I answered him, "I hail your appearance at this particular time, Mr Riddell, as a good omen, for the Ettrick Shepherd, like St Cuthbert, has refused to move from this spot till the spell is broke, and who so appropriate as his brother bard; therefore give the signal, and wish his memorial God speed!"[33]

This was responded to heartily by the bard, and onward amid the uproar of sounds made by the grumbling waggon, and the shouts of the onlookers, rolled the pondrous mass, and in a short time we arrived at Hawick Station. I had no wish to run further risks, and, therefore, I saw my freight safely deposited in a truck, which came safe to hand, to Darnick Station and in a short time after, the mass of sandstone rock safely deposited in my yard. Thus has Hogg's memorial been in its passage along the Borders, somewhat like his own fitful life — though moving along scenery romantic and beautiful in itself, and associated with Border story and ballad — it was yet accomplished with care, and sorrow, and anxiety arising from the fear of *breaking down*!

*

Though the years 1858 to 1860 represent Andrew's coming of age as a sculptor, there were setbacks as well as triumphs. In 1859, he submitted to the competition for the Wallace Monument at Stirling a model of the great thirteenth-century Scottish patriot. Why he did this is not clear, the competition having called for architectural rather than sculptural submissions. Perhaps, as with the Scott Monument, there was also a subsidiary competition for a statue.[34] However, John

---

[32] Henry Scott Riddell (1798~1870), a minor poet, was, like James Hogg, the son of shepherd.
[33] When marauding Vikings forced the monks of Lindisfarne to flee, they took with them the coffin of their former bishop, St Cuthbert. When the cart carrying the coffin reached Durham, it stopped, and refused to move any further, no matter how hard the monks pushed.
[34] The statue of Wallace by D.W. Stevenson outside the monument was not erected until 1887.

Rochead, the Edinburgh-born, Glasgow-based architect whose design won the competition, was sufficiently impressed with Andrew's submission he recommended to the committee that a statue based on the sculptor's model of William Wallace should be made and placed in the interior of the monument.[35]

A more dramatic blow came in October 1860 with the sudden death of one of Andrew's assistants, John Henderson. According to *The Scotsman*, Henderson was "an intelligent and clever workman. It was by him that the greater part of the fine figure of Mungo Park's statue in Selkirk was chiselled, as well as the drapery on the Hogg Monument at St Mary's Loch, lately inaugurated."

It was a Monday morning and Henderson, "who was suffering from an affection of the lungs" (probably tuberculosis, the leading cause of death in nineteenth-century Scotland), had returned that morning from a visit to friends in his native Denholm. He started work on a monument to be erected in Melrose Abbey to the poet Robert Bower.[36]

---

[35] It seems that no such statue was ever made.

[36] Robert Bower was procurator-fiscal of Melrose and a promising poet who published a volume of ballads and lyrics in 1853. The monument (gravestone) to him stands in the cemetery at Melrose Abbey. Under an ogee arch the inscription reads:

Robert Bower ... was a lover of all that is true and good a steady and patriotic defender of public rights and a man who in his literary genius and aspirations lacked only the health and length of life to distinguish him great which Nature sometimes denied to her most gifted sons. He died 18.4.1859 aged 33 years.

On each side of the stone, at the base of the arch are two carved heads. The one on the right is King David, under whose aegis the abbey was founded in 1136. The one on the left is damaged: who it represents is not known.

The inscription on the stone also includes Robert's father, John "Johnnie" Bower (1785~1843), who was the custodian and cicerone of Melrose Abbey, "employed to keep it in order and show it to strangers." A devotee of the *Lay of the Last Minstrel*, he took pains to identify every aspect of the ruins mentioned in the poem, much to the amusement of its author. "The fictions of Scott had become facts with honest Johnnie Bower," wrote the American author Washington Irving on a visit to Abbotsford in 1817. "From constantly living among the ruins of Melrose Abbey, and pointing out the scenes of the poem, the *Lay of the Last Minstrel*, had, in a manner, become interwoven with his whole existence ... ."

"One of the ingenious devices on which the worthy little man prided himself," Irving continued, "was to place a visitor opposite the Abbey, with his back to it, and bid him bend down and look at it between his legs. This, he said, gave an entirely different aspect to the ruin. Folks admired the plan amazingly, but as to the 'leddies,' they were dainty on the matter, and contented themselves with looking from under their arms."

"Mr Currie, after giving him some directions about the carving, went into his private room, but shortly afterwards heard a noise as if of someone staggering in the passage leading through the house. On going out he found Henderson with his hand on his breast, vomiting blood. Before he could be assisted to a chair, the poor man fell down dead, having only had time to ejaculate the word 'Gone!'"

Henderson's untimely death did not leave Andrew working on his own. In the census of 1861 for the parish of Melrose, village of Darnick, he is listed as a "sculptor employing 2 men." During the next decade there would be no further commissions for public monuments. But a new market would shortly open up in the shape of religious works, for two very different patrons.

* * *

Seven

Tracts & Tractarians (1861~1870)

In December 1863 Andrew Currie placed a classified advertisement in the *Border Magazine Advertiser*. It listed the range of wares his studio could supply:

MONUMENTAL SCULPTURE

MONUMENTS, GRAVESTONES, TABLETS, CHIMNEY-PIECES

PEDESTAL PILLARS, CRESTS OF ARMS, VASES

In Marble and Sandstones, by

ANDREW CURRIE,

SCULPTOR

DARNICK BY MELROSE

How many of these items did Andrew actually make? According to his obituary in *The Scotsman*, "he did many small commissions both in wood and marble and other mediums." The catalog of his work is made up mostly of large pieces, like monuments; the anonymous small ones would not have merited a mention, hence most have long since slipped between the cracks. But even some of the larger works are missing. For example, in a photograph taken in 1867 of the artist working at his studio a large bust of a bearded subject can be seen. Who is it of, and where is it now? We do not know.[37]

One large piece we do know about - photographs exist - that has disappeared was carved by Andrew in 1863. A group consisting of two winged angels, it was installed above the doorway on the second floor of the Drummond Tract Building at the corner of King Street and Murray Place in Stirling. It was his first commission outside the Borders.

William Drummond (1793~1868) and his half-brother Peter Drummond (1799~1877) were prosperous nurserymen and seed merchants who found different ways to express their fervent evangelist faith. William suffered from what was described as "statue mania." This he combined with a morbid fascination for Scottish martyrs. In what was formerly "a wilderness famed for bad behaviour" between the esplanade of Stirling Castle (the future site of Andrew's statue of Robert the Bruce) and the Valley Cemetery, he established what became known as the Drummond Pleasure Ground. Dotted around it are statues of the protestant reformers John Knox, Andrew Melville and Alexander Henderson; plus James Renwick, the last of the Covenanter martyrs. Also, a marble group consisting of Margaret Wilson and her like-minded younger sister Agnes, collectively known as the Wigtown martyrs, who reputedly were drowned in the Solway in 1685 for refusing to abjure the Covenant. A guardian angel hovers behind them and a lamb rests at their feet.[38] These statues were all the work of Handyside Ritchie. Nearby, bizarrely, is a massive stone pyramid that William erected. It is dedicated to all those who suffered martyrdom in the cause of religious freedom.

In 1859 William Drummond contributed £100 to match a similar amount raised by Charles Rogers to pay for Ritchie's neoclassical statue of William Wallace, which ended up above the porch of the Athenaeum at the head of King Street. It was probably Rogers who introduced Andrew to Peter Drummond. Peter had a bee in his bonnet about observance of the Sabbath. He was upset by the tendency

---

[37] For a list of works by Andrew Currie known to be missing, see Appendix One.
[38] The lamb subsequently had to be removed when the group was enclosed by a cast-iron cupola designed by John Rochead, of Wallace Monument fame.

of Stirling's recalcitrant citizens to decamp to the neighbouring village of Cambuskenneth, spending the Lord's day there in idleness and drunken dissipation at public houses. It occurred to Drummond to publish his views in the form of an admonitory tract. His first effort having been successful, he next turned his attention to shutting down local theatre-going and horse-racing. Within a few years this energetic killjoy was cranking out religious pamphlets in prodigious quantities. His Stirling Tract Enterprise would ultimately print a cumulative total of over half a billion items, for distribution all over the world.

In 1861 Peter Drummond commissioned Andrew to carve the pair of angels for the new Italianate tract depot he built in King Street at a cost of £5,000. In addition to the angels, sculpted heads of heroes of the Reformation were positioned above the windows of the first floor.[39] Drummond's tract enterprise continued to expand rapidly, moving to new premises in 1887. The next owner of the King Street building was the British Linen Bank. It has since changed hands several times. According to one source, the angels were taken down in 1923. "They were made of plaster, and much decayed."

*

---

[39] One wonders whether the likes of Calvin and Zwingli, both of whom had encouraged the destruction of graven images, would have been pleased to see themselves thus represented.

Andrew's main patron during the eighteen sixties was James Hope-Scott. Though he and Hope-Scott were exact contemporaries, their backgrounds could hardly have been more different. Hope-Scott was born James Robert Hope in Buckinghamshire in 1812, the blue-blooded son of a baronet and grandson of an earl. He was educated at Eton and Christ Church College, Oxford, where he was befriended by John Henry Newman and William Ewart Gladstone. "An immensely serious, religious, philanthropical Englishman," Hope trained as a barrister. He made a fortune during "the railway mania," the speculative frenzy that swept Britain during the 1840s, representing the interests of rapidly expanding railway companies in front of parliamentary committees. Eventually he became a QC. In 1847 he married Charlotte Lockhart, grand-daughter of Sir Walter Scott. The couple moved to Abbotsford. Initially they rented the house then, on the death of her brother in 1853, ownership passed to Charlotte. Her husband changed his surname to Hope-Scott.

Hope-Scott was chief legal advisor to the Oxford Movement. Founded by his priest friend Newman, this was a group of high-church Anglicans who, following the passage of the Reform Act of 1832, became concerned about control of the Church of England. Newman and his circle at Oxford argued against what they saw as the vulnerability of the church to secular forces and for the reinstatement of its lost apostolic heritage. They voiced their concerns in a series of pamphlets called *Tracts for the Times*, hence became known as "Tractarians." The Tractarians were accused by evangelicals and others of being closet Catholics. In 1841 Newman published his ultimate tract, number 90, asserting in effect that the Anglican and Roman churches were not incompatible. Four years later he converted to Catholicism. In 1851 Hope, reacting to what he perceived to be intolerable interference by the state in ecclesiastical affairs, followed suit.

The Tractarians in general and Newman in particular adored the works of Sir Walter Scott. His Waverley novels brought vividly to life the pre-Reformation past, a romantic middle ages, complete with idealized medieval church. The Tractarians mourned the Great Minstrel's death and held a memorial service each year on his anniversary. Sir Walter, they liked to point out, had worshipped at the tiny Scottish

Episcopal Church, whose services were famously high-church. In fact Scott had shown little interest in the forms of religious devotion. He was certainly not, much as the Tractarians tried to claim otherwise, pro-Rome. "Popery," Scott wrote in his diary for 1829, was "a mean and depraving superstition," adding that "the Catholic superstition may sink into the dust, with all its absurd ritual and solemnities."

Over Christmas 1852~3 Newman visited his close friend Hope-Scott, staying at Abbotsford for six weeks. During that time the cleric celebrated mass in the basement of the house. Newman was not impressed by the quality of the accommodation. The bedrooms were cramped and there was little privacy. Abbotsford had been opened to tourists five months after Scott's death in order to raise money to pay off his remaining debts. Sightseers would arrive first thing in the morning and peer in through the windows, much to the annoyance of breakfasting guests like Newman. Overall, "Conundrum Castle" was not in good shape. The garden had gone to seed, the trees were left untrimmed, everything had been neglected. Hope-Scott set about improving his wife's inheritance. During the years 1855 to 1857, he added a chapel and a new wing for the family. He built a terrace and constructed an "ingenious arrangement of access by which the tourists might be admitted to satisfy their curiosity, while some sort of protection was afforded to the domestic privacy of the inmates."

*

As we have seen, Andrew Currie first encountered James Hope-Scott in 1855. Their initial meeting probably occurred at the RSA exhibition where the latter purchased his small carving of a partridge. Evidently Hope-Scott was sufficiently impressed with Andrew's work to allow his fairy flower stand to be exhibited at Abbotsford after the RSA show had ended. Hope-Scott hired the Darnick-based builder John Smith to make the improvements to Abbotsford. Following his move to Darnick in 1857, Andrew advised on the restoration of Darnick Tower. It is thus conceivable that he might also have assisted Hope-Scott with his renovations. Sir Walter Scott's nearly-deaf amanuensis George Huntley Gordon evidently thought he had, although Gordon was mistaken about Andrew being related to Smith:

> "His predecessor and uncle, Mr Smith, executed many of the medieval ornaments with which Scott took so much pleasure in embellishing his "romance in stone"; and Mr Currie is the sculptor of similar ornaments on the outside of the eighteen or twenty rooms which Mr Hope-Scott has added, in such excellent keeping with the rest. He is learned and skillful in the ecclesiastical and domestic architecture of the Middle Ages."

When he moved to Darnick Andrew was already knowledgeable about Abbotsford and its environs. The first thing he did on arrival was to visit the Turn-Again Stone. This was the Shirra's favourite spot, where he used to sit enjoying a splendid view of Melrose Abbey.[40] As was his wont, Andrew set about gleaning historical information from the local old folk. For example, Scott had planted with his own hands an oak tree to commemorate Wellington's victory at the Battle of Waterloo in 1815. Andrew learned the whereabouts of this tree that from an elderly man called Gordon Wayness, who had dug the hole for it. "Ye couldna hae waled [chosen] an uglier ane, Sir Walter," Andrew recorded Wayness telling the Shirra. "Ugly let him be; I'll not change him," Scott replied.

Around the same time that Hope-Scott bought the carving of the partridge, he also acquired two other small pieces from Andrew. All three feature the same dark

---

[40] Located at the bottom of a slope on the Abbotsford estate, this flat stone marked the spot where in 1526 a violent death had occurred. Scott of Buccleuch, aka Wicked Wat of Branxholm, sought to snatch the boy-king James V from the grip of the Earl of Angus. The attempt went awry, but in the subsequent pursuit one of Angus's men, Andrew Ker of Cessford, stumbled, fell and was slain by Elliot of Stobs, one of Buccleuch's retainers, who turned and skewered him with his spear. The outcome is mentioned in Scott's *Border Minstrelsy* and captured in a couplet from the first canto of his *Lay of the Last Minstrel*:

> Gallant Cessford's heart-blood dear
> Reek'd on dark Elliot's Border spear

staining that had been polished to reveal the amber-yellow wood. They are still at Abbotsford. At least one was likely commissioned by Hope-Scott. A delicate rendering of the Paschal Lamb - a symbolic prefiguration of Christ - it is based on a carved boss from the vaulted roof of the chapter house at Dryburgh Abbey, where the Shirra is buried. Having grown up on a sheep farm, Andrew excelled at carving ovines, witness the many lambs, ewes and rams that occur in his work.[41] The other piece, a seated old man, an (not the) Ettrick Shepherd, is based on a local character he remembered from his youth. Hence the inscription on its base: "He lived in Yarrow." At least two other versions of this figure are known to exist, meaning that it was one of Andrew's stock pieces.

Having his work on display in the house of Sir Walter Scott must have been enormously gratifying for Andrew. According to the writer Sir George Douglas "... a lady who knew him intimately [probably Lillias Cotesworth] has assured me of her belief that he would rather have executed work for Abbotsford than for Westminster Abbey itself." But in the autumn of 1860 when Hope-Scott requested Charles Rogers to undertake the completion of the monument to John Leyden in Denholm, he did not recommend Andrew for the job. In the event, the monument was designed by the Edinburgh architect Hector H. Orrock and sculpted by Handyside Ritchie.

*

Before 1853 Roman Catholics in the Melrose area had nowhere to worship. A priest came over from Hawick once a month to celebrate mass in a private house in Galashiels. On taking up residence at Abbotsford, Hope-Scott took steps to remedy the situation. He began by erecting a small chapel and a school. But as the manufacture of tweed in Galashiels grew, the population increased rapidly. A full-scale church was required. Hope-Scott bought some land at Darling's Haugh. He

---

[41] Most notably a magnificent figure of a ram, carved in 1874, which stood on top of a wall at the Buckholmsie Skin Works in Galashiels. Following the demolition of the works in 1983, this too has disappeared.

commissioned a design from William Wilkinson Wardell, a London-based architect and Tractarian sympathizer who had converted to Catholicism in 1843, aged 21. Wardell was the protege of Augustus Welby Pugin, a pioneer of the gothic revival movement and himself also a Catholic convert.

Wardell based his design for of Our Lady & St Andrew on a medieval Franciscan church in Bruges. The Tractarians insisted that gothic, a style that had hitherto been associated with ascetic gloom and vulgar superstition, was the only proper architecture for a Christian church. They argued that the prevailing neoclassical style was essentially pagan, its model being Greek temples. Moreover, the ancients had used slaves to build their places of worship, whereas medieval European gothic cathedrals and monasteries had been the work of free craftsmen and were thus products of a morally superior society. Construction by Smith of Darnick commenced in 1856. By the end of the following year the shell of the church was "fit for use in a rough way," Hope-Scott wrote to his friend Newman. "I shall not be hurried in the decorative part, which I cannot afford to do handsomely at present." Ultimately, he would spend £10,000 of his own money on the church. Donations from the congregation would take care of the rest. The whole thing would take almost twenty years to complete.

Decking out the interior of Our Lady & St Andrew was a job for ecclesiastical specialists. When Wardell's health broke down, forcing him to depart for the warmer climes of Australia, George Goldie, an architect and designer of Roman Catholic churches, took over the remainder of the work. The high altar and lady chapel were ordered from the workshop of Thomas Earp of Lambeth. Pugin's designs were used for the casts of religious figures. The only non-specialist, the only local artist to be commissioned was Andrew Currie. Could this conceivably have been a consequence of a pivotal event in Andrew's life, his conversion to Catholicism?

On 18 December 1864, according to Galashiels parish records, Andrew Currie, aged 52, was received into the Catholic Church. In "Rome's Recruits: a List of Protestants who have become Catholics since the Tractarian Movement," published in 1878, "Andrew Currie, sculptor," is one of almost two thousand names mentioned. Did Hope-Scott have anything to do with Andrew's conversion? We cannot be sure, but it seems plausible. After all, how many other Tractarians living near Darnick did he know?

It has been suggested that Andrew Currie might have converted merely in order to win the Galashiels church commission. But such a cynical ploy would have been completely out of character. As his writings make clear, he was utterly serious about his new faith.

*

Though the proximate cause will likely never be known, Andrew's writings provide some insights into the reasons for his conversion. From an early age he had disliked Calvinism. His father William Currie "hated cant, and the putting-on of that sanctimonious air on Sundays so common with Calvinists." Andrew took particular exception to the dogmatic Calvinist catechism. This is a set of a hundred and seven questions and answers that begins:

> What is the chief end of man?
> To know God by whom men were created.

In nineteenth-century Scotland, learning the catechism was a standard part of religious indoctrination. Children were expected to memorize it, and woe betide any boy or girl who failed to parrot the proper response. "I believe in Christianity, but not through the medium of Calvinism and its exponent, the single catechism, of which I have a mortal horror," Andrew wrote in his diary of 1830. "Not that it is connected with tears and tawse and bubbly noses, but from its revolting principles, at which my nature rebels ... ."

On his return from Edinburgh to the Brig-End as a precocious youngster in 1829, Andrew sparred with old dominie Morton about the "sophistry of Calvinism." As an instance of that sophistry he wanted to cite the core Calvinist notion of predestination, that "God fore-ordains everything that comes to pass." In which case, went the argument, since "sin comes to pass," it followed logically that "God is the author of sin." But out of regard for the old man's feelings, he held back.

The dislike between Andrew and Calvinists was mutual. "We seem instinctively to know and repel each other, I suppose by some unknown principle of sympathy and antipathy." He well recalled his first encounter with the fundamentalists, as a boy at a "sederunt," a camp meeting on Howford Croft: "a goodly collection of dour-looking carles [men] in faded tartan cloaks and plaids. ... How they scowled at a few of us youths who were profane enough to do a little bit of romping between the rows of sitters on the green brae side!"

Some coins were stolen from a collection dish, a misdeed for which Andrew was blamed. He protested his innocence, but in vain. His punishment was "first a sound thrashing from father and mother and lecture on the enormity of my crime; next, the dose repeated by dominie Morton with supplementary lecture and fearful tawse; then old wives in the Brig-End talking, with pursed-up mouth and contracted brow, a stern look at the sinner as he passed their door." No wonder young Andrew hated Calvinists! Just his luck that Robert Moodie, his millwright master at Denholm, turned out to be an "Auld Licht" Cameronian, a member of a sect so strict they would not speak of worldly matters on the Sabbath.

Much later, at Melrose Abbey, Andrew was confronted with the shattered remains of statues destroyed by Calvinist zealots like Old Stumpie. As a romantic by nature with a passionate interest in antiquity, is it any wonder that he would be drawn to the church that had commissioned such creations, a church moreover whose history stretched back unbroken into the mists of time? But being a Catholic convert cannot have been easy: anti-papist prejudice was still rampant in mid nineteenth century Scotland. According to one of the priests who was dispatched to Galashiels in 1852 to establish the church there, the mission was a difficult one:

"People of this place are becoming dreadfully bigoted and are inflamed by ministers and masters. Those who come to our services are turned out of their meetings. Even those who work here, painters and carpenters, are publicly denounced. Landlords have decided not to let any house to a Catholic or an Irishman."

*

Resulting from his researches at Melrose Abbey, Andrew had become as we have seen "learned and skillful in the ecclesiastical ... architecture of the Middle Ages." About a year after his conversion, he began work on an altar for a side chapel of the Church of Our Lady & St Andrew. Dedicated to St Patrick, it was first used in July 1866 in the presence of the Bishop of Northampton. The altar is not, it must be admitted, a particularly successful piece: the design is far too cluttered. Happily, Andrew was not responsible for the design. That was done by the architect Joseph Scoles, yet another specialist in Roman Catholic churches and their accoutrements. The altar's main features are two panels surmounted by ornate gothic arches. They depict St Patrick converting the Irish to Christianity. Between them is a figure of the saint standing on a plinth. There is a great deal of superfluous decoration. The best part is the relatively plain front panel, in the centre of which is a carving of a lamb in a hollowed-out four-leafed shamrock.

The massive hexagonal stone pulpit, which Andrew carved from light-coloured sandstone four years later, is a much stronger work. The design is simpler, the upper half featuring three panels under gothic arches with bas-reliefs of Biblical scenes. They depict St Paul in prison, St Peter being given the keys to the kingdom of heaven, and Jesus with the twelve apostles. The panels are supported by a solid lower half with garlanded pilasters.

In between carving the two religious pieces, Andrew also undertook a secular commission for Abbotsford. His first wife Charlotte having died in childbirth in 1858, three years later Hope-Scott married Lady Victoria Fitzalan Howard, eldest daughter of the Duke of Norfolk and god-daughter of Queen Victoria. It was announced that Her Majesty would visit her god-daughter in August 1867, calling into Abbotsford for tea on her way north to Balmoral. Seeking a suitable way to commemorate the royal visit, Hope-Scott came up with an idea. The Queen was a dog fancier. She had once owned a deerhound, supposedly the royal dog of Scotland. As it happened, Sir Walter Scott's favourite dog, Maida, immortalized by John Steell in white marble at the Scott Monument, was also a deerhound.[42] Hope-Scott commissioned two "couchant" deerhounds to be placed on either side of his front door. It was a rush job: Andrew got the dogs done and delivered just two hours before the Queen arrived. Whether Her Majesty noticed them is not recorded.

The Church of Our Lady & St Andrew officially opened for public worship in August 1873. Unfortunately Hope-Scott did not live to see it, having died three months previously. It was said that he never recovered from the grief of losing his second wife, who had died like his first, in child-birth, two years earlier. On a column at the back of the church, a small (unsigned) brown plaster bust of James Hope-Scott looks down from a framed medallion. Is this, perhaps, a final tribute from sculptor to patron?

Andrew Currie had lost his best customer. He would undertake one more work on a religious theme, a statue of the sacred heart for St John's Church in Portobello, a suburb of Edinburgh, but that would not be until 1877.[43] Meantime, as we will see in the next chapter, he had a new commission to execute, one that was very much to his liking.

* * *

---

[42] In 1827 Edwin Landseer painted Maida at Abbotsford. He subsequently recycled Maida's likeness in other portraits, including one of Queen Victoria in Windsor Park done in 1835.
[43] Whether this statue was ever executed is unclear. If it was, it no longer exists.

Eight

North of the Border (1871~1872)

Little more than a month after Sir Walter Scott's death in September 1832, a public meeting was convened at the Assembly Rooms in Edinburgh by the Lord Provost, John Learmonth, to discuss how to commemorate "Scotland's darling son" in the city of his birth. In Spring 1836 an open competition was launched, offering a prize of fifty guineas. Fifty-four entries were received, twenty-two of them for gothic structures. This was entirely appropriate, since gothic was known to be Scott's favourite style. (Though some fretted that it would clash with the prevailing neoclassical Georgian aesthetic of Edinburgh's New Town in Charlotte Square, the site originally proposed.)

The winning design duly incorporated pointed arches, ribbed vaults, flying buttresses and crocketed pinnacles. It reminded many of Melrose Abbey, especially since the proposal was signed "John Morvo," the name of the medieval master mason believed to have been responsible for the construction of St David's Pile. John Morvo turned out to be the pseudonym of George Meikle Kemp, a 45-year-old joiner, draftsman and self-taught architect. A painfully shy man with an extreme aversion to shaking hands, Kemp feared that if he had submitted the entry under his own name, his lack of track record would have counted against him.

Kemp was the son of a shepherd. He had served his apprenticeship as a carpenter, then worked in a millwright's workshop in Galashiels. Proximity to the

Border abbeys - Dryburgh, Jedburgh, Kelso and Melrose - enabled him to visit them often, making sketches and noting differences in style. Melrose was his favourite: in 1830 he drew three large, exquisitely detailed views of the ruins. They provided the inspiration for his winning entry.

Among the main features of Kemp's design for the monument were sixty-four niches intended to hold statues of characters from Scott's works. (Statues of actual historical figures mentioned in the novels would also be commissioned.) By the time the monument was inaugurated in August 1846 only eight of the niches, on the lower level, had been filled. In December 1870, with the Great Minstrel's centenary less than a year away, further funds were raised. Statues would be commissioned for the 24 niches at the base of the four great flying buttresses and elsewhere on the monument's second level. A new, high-powered subcommittee was convened to select suitable sculptors. Its members included such prominent artists as Sir George Harvey, president of the Royal Scottish Academy, James Drummond, curator of the National Gallery of Scotland, Robert Herdman, a specialist in historical paintings, James Ballantine, a maker of stained glass windows, and (Andrew's supporter) the architect John Rochead. Sketches from the candidates were examined and a preliminary selection made. However, when the list of names chosen was published, controversy ensued. Witness this indignant letter of 23 January 1872 from "A Subscriber" to *The Scotsman*:

"Is this the best representation of Scottish sculptors for such a work? I would have imagined that when the committee chose one of those from London, they would have endeavoured to secure the services of Mr Calder Marshall RA, and that they would not have omitted, in the western metropolis [ie, Glasgow] Mr Mossman or Mr Ewing, who are undoubtedly better qualified for the work than one or two of the comparative novices in the list; or, in the very vicinity of Abbotsford, Mr Currie, a clever [skillful] sculptor, and familiar with every stone of Melrose Abbey, which suggested to the architect of the Scott Monument so much of that fine design."

In response to the public outcry, it was announced that the sculptors would be requested to prepare half-size models of the figures and submit them for approval to the subcommittee. "It was also resolved to employ Mr Currie, sculptor, Darnick, to execute a statue of Old Mortality ... ." In addition Andrew would be employed to execute a statue of another character, Edie Ochiltree. "He delighted in the Waverley novels," wrote Lillias Cotesworth, "and immense was his satisfaction when asked to undertake two of the figures for Scott's monument in Edinburgh. Edie Ochiltree and Old Mortality were those chosen, and he threw his whole soul into the work."

*

Like many of Scott's characters Edie Ochiltree, the "light-hearted beggar" from his novel *The Antiquary* (1816), was based on a real person. Andrew Gemmels was well-known for many years throughout the Borders as a "gaberlunzie" or wandering mendicant. "He had been a soldier in his youth, and his entertaining stories of his campaigns, and the adventures he had encountered in foreign countries, united with his shrewdness, drollery, and other agreeable qualities rendered him a general favourite, and secured him a cordial welcome and free quarters at every shepherd's cot or farm-shading that lay in the range of his extensive wanderings ... ." Evidently the itinerant lifestyle suited him: Gemmels died in 1793, aged 106.

In *The Antiquary* Scott had provided a detailed description of Edie Ochiltree for the sculptor to work from:

> "A slouched hat of huge dimensions; a long white beard, which
> mingled with his grizzled hair; an aged but strongly marked and
> expressive countenance, hardened, by climate and exposure, to a
> right brick-dust complexion; a long blue gown, with a pewter badge
> on the right arm; two or three wallets, or bags, slung across his

shoulder, for holding the different kinds of meal, when he received his charity in kind from those who were but a degree richer than himself ... ."

All these items Andrew faithfully reproduced, adding a begging bowl in the figure's left hand and a stout staff in his right. Other touches included "knee-breeches, somewhat out at the knees, and much requiring repairs, and his waistcoat, which seems also to have suffered from the elements." But how to render the gaberlunzie's face? The Border writer Sir George Douglas reported that the sculptor "took great pains to make the acquaintance of a descendent of 'Edie Ochiltree,' for the express purpose of studying the family features." The happy result is a visage wearing an expression that is, as Lillias Cotesworth put it, "sly and waggish," or - to use a good Scots word - pawky. This is just so, for in the novel Edie repeatedly punctures to humorous effect the pseudo-scholarly interpretations that Monkbarns, the antiquary of the title, places on objects dug up on his land.

Behind his figure of Edie Andrew carved a stone on which is inscribed the letters "A.D.L.L." In the novel Monkbarns claims they stand for *Agricola Dicavit Libens Lubens* - "Agricola has dedicated this gladly and with pleasure" - thus proving the site was that of the battle between the first-century Roman general Gaius Julius Agricola and the Caledonians. But the beggar reveals that the initials actually stand for *Aiken Drum's Lang Ladle*, Aiken Drum being a character from a nonsense song.[44]

---

[44] There cam' a man doon frae the moon, doon frae the moon, doon frae the moon,
    And they ca'd him Aiken Drum
  And he played upon a ladle, a ladle, a ladle; he played upon a ladle,
    And they ca'd him Aiken Drum ...

This was the signature tune of Daft Jock Gray (1776~1837) aka Jock the Ladle, "a poor wandering simpleton," who served as the model for the character of the fool Davie Gellatley in Scott's first novel, *Waverley* (1814). Scott was no doubt attracted attracted to Daft Jock because, although "he had no capacity for the learning taught at the parish school ... he caught at a wonderfully early age, and with a rapidity almost incredible, many fragments of Border song, which he could repeat, with the music, in the precise manner of those who

In addition to the finished figure of Edie Ochiltree on the Scott Monument Andrew also carved another, somewhat cruder version in stone of the same subject that is now in the gardens at Abbotsford.

The sculptor had gone to great lengths to find a descendent of Andrew Gemmels. For his statue of Old Mortality, real name Robert Paterson, he did not have the same difficulty, having been personally acquainted in his youth with Paterson's grandson, Nathaniel. Robert Paterson was born circa 1713 at Haggis Ha, a farm near Hawick. A stonemason by trade, he spent much of the latter part of his life wandering around the Borders with his old white pony, from one cemetery to the next. He repaired the gravestones of Covenanter martyrs, "cleaning the moss from the grey stones, renewing with his chisel the half-defaced inscriptions, and repairing the emblems of death with which these simple monuments are usually adorned." Paterson's nickname derived from his age and habitual proximity to the deceased. He died in 1801.

In the eponymous novel *Old Mortality*, written in 1816, the same year as *The Antiquary*, Scott presents a vivid picture of Paterson's appearance:

"An old man was seated upon the monument of the slaughtered presbyterians, and busily employed in deepening, with his chisel, the letters of the inscription ... . A blue bonnet of unusual dimensions covered the grey hairs of the pious workman. His dress was a large old-fashioned coat of the coarse cloth called hoddingrey, usually worn by the elder peasants, with waistcoat and breeches of the same; and the whole suit, though still in decent repair, had obviously seen a train of of long service. Strong clouted shoes, studded with

---

instructed him ... . Jock was abandoned to the oral lore he loved so much, and of this he soon possessed himself of an immense stock." Jock Gray anecdotes are legion. Andrew Currie undoubtedly knew Daft Jock (he mentions him in passing in his Reminiscences). He produced a plaster cast of the mendicant dressed in his usual outfit, consisting of "a rather shabby suit of hodden grey," with knee-breeches and ridge-and-furrow stockings fastened by flashy red garters tied neatly in a rose-knot.

hobnails, and gramoches, or leggings, made of thick black cloth, completed his equipment."

To these details, Andrew added a plaid draped over the left shoulder, and a stooping posture, the figure leaning on his stick. The expression on his face is, as Lillias Cotesworth put it, "serious and serene." The features are surely derived from those of the Reverend Nathaniel Paterson, whom Andrew knew well as a teenager. A keen naturalist and outdoorsman, Paterson had been the minister at Galashiels Kirk from 1821 to 1934. His wife was the daughter of Robert Laidlaw, a good friend of Sir Walter Scott. Paterson also became a welcome guest at Abbotsford. In the autumn of 1828, when he was aged 16, after leaving school but before beginning his apprenticeship, Andrew met the minister, as he recounts at the outset of his reminiscences:

"[I made] the acquaintance of an excellent man, Dr Paterson, whose friendship in after years till he left Galashiels, I always look back upon as one of the pleasant passages of my young life, and from whom I learned much. I have yet in my eye those never-to-be-forgot pleasant Sunday evening walks, starting from the Manse at Galashiels and making the circuit of Galashiels hill, by the old Selkirk road, thence eastward till we returned."

Paterson achieved a measure of fame for his book, *The Manse Garden* (1836). It says much for Andrew's precocity that the reverend gentleman was prepared to tolerate the youngster's company on his rambles. As with his carving of Edie Ochiltree, the sculptor adds context behind the figure of Old Mortality. A mallet leans against a gravestone, over which is looped a rope with a stake for tethering the old man's pony. On the gravestone itself, which is inscribed in Paterson's distinctive style of lettering, can be seen the words:

[HERE] LYES [THE] BODY OF FERGUSSON SHOT ON THIS SPOT BY GRAEME
[OF] CLAVERHOUSE 1684

The reference is to John Graham of Claverhouse - "Bluidy Clavers" to his enemies - who hunted down and killed many Covenanters. They included Robert Ferguson and three of his companions, at the Water of Dee, in December 1683. Andrew also carved at least one lesser version of Old Mortality. A half life-size wooden figure of the old man was auctioned in Edinburgh in 1985.[45]

Some commentators rate Andrew's two statues on the Scott Monument as his best works. A problem for the contemporary viewer is that the statues, located on the upper tier of the north-east buttress, are hard to see both from within the monument (from the gallery on the first level only their profiles are visible) and from without, looking up from Princes Street. For one thing, to prevent fouling by pigeons, the statues are covered by chicken-wire. For another - a more serious issue - the figures, like the monument itself, are blackened by dirt.

They are made of sandstone from the Binny quarry in nearby Ecclesmachan. This was described as "a very nice material, less costly to work than others and of a better colour; for ornamental carving it is particularly good." The downside is that the stone exudes bitumen. Atmospheric particles, such as the soot expelled from the funnels of countless steam trains passing along the Waverley Line below, have stuck to the oily patches. At the time of the monument's construction, this ability to attract dirt might have been seen as a virtue, since it allowed the stone to rapidly acquire the patina of age. Today, however, it has made the structure a nightmare to clean.

* * *

---

[45] The sandstone figure of Old Mortality and his pony housed in the grounds of Dumfries Museum which is sometimes mistakenly attributed to Andrew Currie is in fact by his namesake, John Currie.

Nine

Last Order (1872~1877)

Along with the Scott Monument, the other great gothic memorial erected around this time was the Wallace Monument, just outside Stirling. When the foundation stone for this colossal edifice was laid in 1861, a crowd of some 70,000 is said to have gathered, making it one of the biggest public events to have occurred in nineteenth-century Scotland. As with most such undertakings, ambition outran resources, the project blew its budget, the contractor went bankrupt and the architect, John Rochead, never received his fee. The monument was not finished until 1869.

At this distance it is hard to understand why William Wallace should have been honoured with a monument before his exact contemporary, Robert the Bruce. After all, both were heroic leaders in the Wars of Scottish Independence. But whereas Wallace had some success fighting the English before being captured and cruelly executed, the Bruce actually won a decisive battle against the English at Bannockburn in 1314. Apparently, for romantics, the gory bed holds more appeal than victory.

In the autumn of 1869, aware that Robert the Bruce had been neglected by previous generations, a group of expatriate Scots gathered at the Grampian Club in London to discuss building a national monument to him. They settled on the idea of a statue that would catch the warrior king immediately after his triumph at

Bannockburn, having ipso facto achieved independence for Scotland, in the act of sheathing his sword. The main mover in these discussions, as with the Wallace Monument, the statue of the Ettrick Shepherd, and other nationalistic commemorations, was the Reverend Charles Rogers, formerly chaplain to the garrison at Stirling Castle and latterly translated to London. Though essentially well-intentioned, Rogers was an inveterate schemer who was forever embroiling himself in controversy. The Bruce monument project would be no exception.

In April 1870 Rogers brought along his friend, the elderly illustrator George Cruikshank (1792~1878), to a meeting of the newly-formed monument committee. The artist was invited to submit a design for the statue. Cruikshank is best-known for his early work, savage caricatures of the royal family and contemporary politicians in the great satirical tradition of Hogarth and Gillray. In later life Cruikshank turned to illustration, notably of books by his friend Charles Dickens. He also underwent, much to Dickens' annoyance, a pauline conversion from prodigious boozer to rabid teetotaler.

Though Cruikshank was born in London, his father Isaac - also a caricaturist (and a raging alcoholic) - came from Edinburgh. George identified himself as a Scot: he claimed that the Bruce had always been one of his heroes. Now, here was a last chance for him "to establish his reputation as an artist who had served the people of his ancestors." Certainly Cruikshank invested heavily in his design, taking considerable care over the details. From fourteenth-century manuscripts at the British Museum, he confirmed that the Bruce had worn chain-mail around his head in battle. As a consequence, the king would have been close-shaven (to prevent his facial hair getting caught in the links). He also ascertained the style of coronet the Bruce had worn atop his armour.

Cruikshank produced a sketch depicting the king "looking down with pity on the slain," of both sides, on the field of battle as he sheathes his sword. He proposed that the statue should be cast in bronze and set on a pedestal of granite, for a total height of twenty-two feet. He found an appropriate suit of armour, which he himself donned and posed in (Cruikshank was prone to identify with his subjects). His friend, the sculptor John Adams-Acton, carved a five-foot model.

Meanwhile, unbeknownst to Cruikshank, Rogers had been hedging his bets. In April 1872 the London committee asked Andrew Currie to submit a photo of a design of Robert the Bruce which he had made some years previously and which Rogers had evidently seen. (Why Andrew had made this design is not clear: doubtless the idea of erecting such a monument had been around for awhile.) Towards the end of May, Rogers sent Cruikshank the photo of Andrew's sketch. The news that he had a rival came as a nasty surprise to the old man. Explaining that in order to ensure originality, his policy was never to look at the designs of other artists until his own was finished, Cruikshank returned the envelope containing the photo unopened.

"Over the next fortnight George discussed the project with Rogers several times," Robert Patten wrote in his biography of Cruikshank. "By the middle of [June] the artist was convinced that he had been commissioned to execute the monument ... ." He proceeded accordingly.

*

Cruikshank's original estimate for the bronze statue was £2,000. But, much to his surprise and the committee's dismay, subscriptions dried up. For a while it seemed as if the project might collapse. "With the view of preventing such a deplorable catastrophe, it was finally resolved to appeal directly to the Scottish people in Scotland, and for the purpose of carrying on the movement with increased zest, the headquarters of the committee were changed from London to Stirling ... ."

Enter, as chairman of the new "local" committee, Stirling-born Major-General Sir James Edward Alexander, soldier, author, traveller, freemason, enthusiastic homeopathist and all-round man of action.[46] His first task was to locate an appropriate site for the monument. The field of Bannockburn had seemed the obvious choice, but Alexander rejected this option, arguing that "the statue would be exposed to injury and few people would see it." He then applied to the Secretary

---

[46] A few years later Alexander would be the main mover behind the relocation of Cleopatra's Needle from Egypt to the Embankment in London.

of State for War for a spot on the esplanade at Stirling Castle - an open space in front of the fortified gate - where "a great many strangers who come to view the ancient castle and town will see and admire it." This site was also historically apt, since it was the attempt to relieve the strategically vital castle, held by the English and under siege by the Scots, that had been the cause of the battle. In February 1872 Alexander's request was granted.

Next came the vexed issue of what material to use for the statue. Bronze was costly: the limited budget would not stretch that far. Undaunted, the resourceful Alexander came up with what he thought was a capital idea. Half-a-dozen condemned bronze cannon were lying around the castle taking up space: why not melt them down to cast the statue?[47] But despite his best efforts, this time the general could not win over the War Office bureaucrats. They told him there was no precedent for turning guns into statues; an act of parliament would be required.

Since bronze was out of the question, "nearly imperishable freestone" would have to do instead. But the carving would not be commissioned from Adams-Acton, who was English and, more to the point, expensive. In March 1872 Rogers approached Cruikshank with a compromise. Reluctantly, the illustrator agreed to allow his design to be carved, in stone, by a Scottish sculptor previously unknown to him, called Andrew Currie. "There were several competing artists," according to *The Scotsman*, "but Mr Currie's offer was found the most suitable." Nonetheless, Cruikshank felt that the original sculptor deserved some recognition. He proposed that the monument's pedestal should carry an inscription:

> Designed by George Cruikshank 1870
> Modelled by John Adams-Acton 1870
> Sculptured [sic] by Andrew Currie 187—

There was also another problem: the committee was unhappy with the proposed pose. Cruikshank had conceived the Bruce looking down with pity upon

---

[47] The British Army officially declared heavy calibre bronze pieces obsolete in 1816.

the slain. But with the new elevated site, a mile and a half away from Bannockburn, this attitude was no longer appropriate. In 1874, at Alexander's urging, the artist modified his design so that the head was raised, looking across the esplanade towards the battlefield. But Cruikshank was still asking for too much money. In addition to the funds already raised, he estimated that a further £1,000 would be required.

In August 1876 Rogers visited Andrew at Darnick. His mission was to persuade the sculptor to adopt Cruikshank's design. Andrew was indignant, refusing "to entertain for a moment the idea of looking to any design but my own." Following an exchange of letters, an impasse was reached. Recognizing that concluding an agreement with Rogers would be impossible, Andrew entered into negotiations with the local committee via its chairman, General Alexander. The outcome was satisfactory: "I was empowered by them to erect the monument *from my own design*, that being the only footing on which I would undertake the work." But confusion over whose design would be used persisted. The following month (September), *The British Architect and Northern Engineer* reported that "[t]he monument to King Robert the Bruce, promoted by General Sir J.E. Alexander and Dr Charles Rogers of London was, at a meeting held in Stirling ..., entrusted to Mr Andrew Currie ... . The monument will mainly consist of a colossal statue of the patriot king, sheathing his sword in the moment of victory. It was designed by Mr George Cruikshank ... ."

Andrew had evidently underbid his English rivals. "He undertook this labor patriotically," Alexander said in his speech at the monument's inauguration, "and much for the honour which he hopes to derive from its successful achievement than from any hope of pecuniary recompense."

"I am glad the honour of the designing the statue was conferred on me," Andrew replied in his speech, "because I consider it to have been an honourable privilege."

The seven-ton block of stone from which Andrew carved the statue came from the Fairloans quarry in Northumberland. This was, supposedly, the same freestone that had been used for the pillars of Melrose Abbey, "whose beautiful foliated capitals [are] as sharp now as if they had been recently carved." As the sculptor knew better than most, more than mere stone connected the Bruce with Melrose. In 1322, after the English army sacked the Abbey, it was rebuilt by order of (and with money from) King Robert. In 1329, as he lay dying, the monarch requested that his embalmed heart should be buried at Melrose Abbey, after it had been carried into battle "against God's foes." His last wishes were faithfully carried out.[48]

In 1818, when the king's body was exhumed from its resting place at Dunfermline Abbey, the ribs were found to be sawn through, indicating that the heart had indeed been removed. In 1921 a leaden casket containing a human heart was discovered beneath the floor of the chapter house at Melrose Abbey.

*

The statue of King Robert that Andrew carved is nine feet high. It was cut from a block of freestone weighing about five tons. The statue rests on a stepped pedestal ten feet high and six feet wide. On the front is carved in deep relief a Scottish shield with lion rampant. To one side, under the king's right foot, is a pointed inscription:

DESIGNED AND EXECUTED BY A. CURRIE, SCULPTOR.

To ensure accuracy, Andrew approached the statue of the Bruce with his usual thoroughness. "[T]he sculptor has taken the utmost care to reproduce the armour of the period," reported the *Stirling Observer & Midland Counties Advertiser* approvingly, "his success in every detail being really wonderful. The fine bordering of the tunic, the ornamentation of the baldric [belt worn across the chest], the edging of the robe, and the chain armour on the legs and body are particularly noticeable. The gauntlet on the right arm may be objected to by some

---

[48] Well, more or less: the Bruce's desire had been that his heart should be carried to the Holy Sepulchre on a crusade against the infidels. There being no crusade underway at the time of his death, a campaign against the Moors in Grenada had to suffice.

critics, as it is of steel plate instead of the chain order, but it is quite capable of proof that the former was in use during the reign of Edward II. Over the shoulder hangs the royal robe, and surmounting the open helmet, which is plumed, is a coronet representing the improvised gold crown which the historians say distinguished the Bruce from the ordinary knights in the decisive battle. The face has, as we understand, been modelled on the features of a descendent of the Bruce [possibly the Earl of Elgin], and it presents a noble countenance with an expression of devout thankfulness, skillfully blended with that of conscious dignity." It also sports a manly beard which, though full and curly, the neck being uncovered and the chin jutting, seems unlikely to get caught in the helmet's chain mail.

As with his figures on the Scott Monument, the sculptor added some context behind the statue. A Scottish shield rests on a rock surrounded by thistles, the national emblem. Above it, the crook of the quigrich (crosier) of St Fillan can be seen. This was held aloft by Maurice, Abbott of Inchaffray, to bless the Scottish army before the battle. The prelate also brought with him a silver reliquary known to contain the left arm-bone of the saint, as a reminder to the troops that God was on their side.[49]

Propped against the base of the shield is the head of a battle-axe. This is a reference to the Bruce's famous encounter, on the day before Bannockburn, with Henry de Bohun. Riding a powerful warhorse and rigged out in full armour, the English knight spotted the Scottish king inspecting his men and, lowering his lance, impulsively charged. The Bruce, mounted on a grey palfrey and wearing no protection, cantered towards to his opponent. Then, when the thunderous charge was almost upon him, he swerved aside, stood up in his stirrups, and brought his axe down so hard that it bifurcated de Bohun's helmeted bonce. The king had taken a huge risk, for which his generals afterwards rebuked him. However, showing the sang-froid that endeared him to his men, the Bruce regretted only that he had broken the shaft of his axe.

---

[49] Among its various miraculous properties, St Fillan's left arm was reputed to glow. This luminosity usefully enabled the saint to write his sermons and study scriptures after dark.

The axe head was modeled on an actual weapon Andrew found at the Antiquarian Museum in Edinburgh. It had been discovered on the field of Bannockburn, "another evidence of the extreme carefulness of the sculptor. The effect of the whole is highly impressive."

*

After its completion by Andrew in his studio at Darnick, the statue was sent up to Stirling by goods train. It was elevated into its position on the pedestal, under the sculptor's personal supervision, ready for the inauguration. This took place on Saturday 24 November 1877, accompanied by the usual pomp and circumstance. Fortunately the weather, though cold, was bright and cheerful; the sky was clear, the air hazy.

The day having been declared a general holiday, the citizens of the royal burgh turned out en masse to witness the pageant and proceedings on the esplanade. From an early hour visitors had flocked into town from outlying hamlets to take up positions that would give them a good view of events. The parapet walls of the castle were clustered with eager spectators, while venturesome others had perched on the red-tiled roofs of houses on Castle Hill. The esplanade itself was a swaying sea of faces.

At one o'clock the town bells began to ring out merrily. At half-past one the procession mustered in the Corn Exchange yard. At two o'clock the participants sallied forth, amid cheers from onlookers. The Bannockburn brass band struck up - what else? - *Auld Lang Syne*. Banners flying, the procession marched down King Street (passing beneath Andrew's angels on the Drummond Tract Depot). It was a stirring sight: "the crowds which lined the route appeared to be highly gratified by the spectacle."

A detachment of police led the way. Next came a contingent of Oddfellows and Foresters, friendly societies, "headed by their chiefs on horseback, and attired in orthodox green uniforms." The Good Templars, members of a temperance organization, formed an advance guard for the Sons of St Crispin, the boot and shoe guild (Crispin being the patron saint of shoemakers), "led by their king in white robes and bestriding a lusty steed."

"Guarded by worthies bearing ancient halberds" came the precious blue blanket of Stirling, the ancient banner of the seven incorporated trades, granted them by Mary Queen of Scots. The members of the Guildry, the municipal corporation, "were easily picked out, as each carried a staff with a green banneret fluttering from its point. Then came the Dean and his Council, succeeded by the town drummer and town sergeants with halberds, looking sufficiently quaint in their scarlet uniforms, knee-breeches, and three-cornered hats."

In front of the Town Clerk and Chamberlain marched a stalwart "son of the rock" - as natives of Stirling are known - carrying a velvet cushion, on which lay the silver keys of the Royal Burgh. Behind the officials walked the Provost and Magistrates, wearing their chains and seals of office. Next came representatives of the committee, including General Alexander and the Reverend Rogers. The latter had on his arm Mrs Simpson, sister of the late lamented Sheriff Henry Glassford Bell, who had chaired the inauguration of Andrew's monument to the Ettrick Shepherd seventeen years previously. The sculptor and the master of works, who was responsible for erecting the statue, brought up the rear.

It had been hoped that the Earl of Elgin, a lineal descendent of the Bruce, would honour the proceedings with his presence. But he declined, sending in his stead a yeoman who bore aloft the two-handed sword of King Robert the Bruce, "a weapon of very formidable dimensions."[50] Efforts had also been made to borrow the crosier of St Fillan but the Society of Antiquarians refused to let it out of their safe-keeping.

By half-past two the cavalcade had made its way with difficulty up the steep and narrow Baker Street, which was almost blocked by spectators. On arriving at the esplanade, the processionists filed along the outside of the hollow square which had formed in front of the statue. The speakers took up their positions on a

---

[50] The impact of this gesture would have been somewhat diminished by the fact that the same sword had also made an appearance in the Wallace Monument procession, just six years previously.

platform provided close to the monument. When all was ready, a prayer was said, then Lady Alexander withdrew the cord holding together the sheet enveloping the statue, formally uncovering it to the full view of the assembled multitude. Cheers arose. These were presently drowned by a thunderous royal salute of twenty-one guns from the castle ramparts. The band launched into *Scots Wha Hae*, "in a more solemn than inspiring manner."

After speeches from General Alexander, Provost Christie, Reverend Rogers and others, Baillie Anderson got up to propose a toast to the sculptor:

> " When I look upon the statue which has been unveiled, and consider the amount of thought and study it has cost Mr Currie to develop its various proportions, I say he is entitled to our thanks. While we think of the amount of care and attention that are required in executing a work such as this, the statue shows that Mr Currie is an artist of no mean order. Our ancient little burgh is visited yearly by thousands of tourists from all parts of the world. We have a number of sights which those parties enquire after to go and view, and I am sure not the least will be the Bruce statue, and by that means the reputation of Mr Currie as an artist will be carried to all ends of the earth. I trust that he will be long spared and that this is not the last order he will have, but that he will have many, and that he will execute them with the same taste and care as he has exhibited in this one."

A nice thought, but wishful thinking. The statue of the Bruce would not be the last order Andrew Currie executed, but it was his last large-scale public commission. In November 1877 he had just turned 65. His belatedly-begun career as a sculptor was drawing to a close.

Illustration of AC's statue of Robert the Bruce made at its unveiling

When George Cruikshank saw illustrations of the statue in the papers he realized that, contrary to his expectation, his design had not been employed, his contribution not even mentioned. Understandably, he felt "very much aggrieved." No-one had told him anything. In a letter to *The Times* of 6 December 1877, Cruikshank wrote bitterly:

> "Although Mr Andrew Currie, the sculptor, has carved the figure as sheathing his sword according to my original design, yet he has

unfortunately altered the chain armour that should surround the face, and has also given a beard, and the headgear is so altered that the coronet could not be seen from a distance. I therefore take this opportunity of informing the public, and particularly the people of Scotland, that the figure intended to represent their great military hero may do for someone else, but it is entirely and totally different about the head from what King Robert the Bruce appeared when on the battlefield of Bannockburn. So, after all this trouble and expense, here is an utter failure, and this in consequence of these alterations being made, and, I may add also, in consequence of the extraordinary way in which the Chairman of the Bruce Committee acted, in not having the statue sculptured in an exact manner from the design made by me."

Recriminations followed. Cruikshank accused Rogers of having substituted Andrew's design for his. Rogers retaliated, claiming (unjustly) that Cruikshank had only made a sketch, Adams-Acton had done most of the work. The great caricaturist died shortly afterwards.

In fact, to judge by contemporary illustrations, so far from being an utter failure Andrew's statue of the Bruce was, at the time of its unveiling, a stunning success. Some actually thought it his masterpiece. Alas, in the intervening hundred and thirty-plus years, the "near-imperishable freestone" from which the statue was carved has proved to be anything but. The plumes on the helmet are long gone, the pedestal is flaking, and overall the monument looks somewhat forlorn. The stone has eroded so badly that parts of the statue - the Bruce's sword, the border of his shield, the battle-axe head - have had to be replaced with a lighter-coloured material. Though necessary, the repairs look slightly peculiar.

What has gone wrong? After all, another statue of the Bruce, also done in freestone at the Bruce's putative birthplace of Lochmaben, near Lockerbie, has worn much better. Unveiled in 1879, just two years after Andrew's statue, this was sculpted by the high roader John Hutchison. Is the damage due to the fact that the elevated site at Stirling Castle is especially exposed to the elements? Certainly that doesn't help, but the real problem is that the statue was carved "on the cant." That is, in places the laid-down sediment of the stone faces vertically rather than horizontally, greatly accelerating decay. This seems odd, since getting the orientation right was a well-known principle of masonry. But as we have seen, Andrew was trained as a millwright, not a mason.[51]

Despite its decrepitude, when it catches the light, with the Wallace Monument on the Abbey Craig in the background, Andrew's statue of the Bruce is still an imposing sight. As such, it represents a fitting finale to his work as a sculptor of public monuments.

* * *

---

[51] Andrew's other large-scale works in stone - Mungo Park and the Ettrick Shepherd - have been painted, perhaps to avoid similar erosion.

Ten

Family Matters (1875~1881)

In early September 1875, before he began work on his statue of the Bruce, Andrew Currie took a short holiday. Ostensibly his purpose was to do antiquarian research and perform a pilgrimage. But he also had another, sentimental objective.

The trip seems to have begun on the spur of the moment. James Henderson, an old schoolmate from Selkirk Grammar days, back in the Borders after twenty-five years in Canada, dropped into Andrew's workshop in Darnick on his way to see Melrose Abbey. As it happened, Andrew had to be in Selkirk the next day. The old friends got together for a wander round the town, swapping stories about people and places they had known in their youth half a century ago. They climbed Peat Law, visiting local landmarks like the Three Brethren cairns and Tibby Tomson's grave along the way.

A few days later Andrew, James, and his brother John Henderson set off from Selkirk for Berwick-on-Tweed, a journey of less than thirty miles. There, they met a friend of Andrew's, a local schoolmaster called John Logan. From Berwick Bridge, the four of them sailed up the Tweed as far as the village of Horncliffe in Northumberland. They hiked over to Branxton, the site of the greatest catastrophe in Scottish history, Flodden's fatal field. The battle took place in 1513. Estimates vary, but at least 10,000 men - including King James IV and many of his nobles - are thought to have perished there. Andrew was keenly interested in Flodden, reading everything he could get on the subject. He had long wanted to see the battlefield with his own eyes, to test his book-derived knowledge against reality.

Andrew made a point of locating the knoll where the king had fallen and was buried. "I lingered on this spot, hallowed with so many memories ... ." He looked around for a souvenir. "Much to my surprise, while poking the soil with my walking stick on the knowe top, I turned up a stone ball about two inches in diameter and, a little further down, a human bone — a fragment of a thigh bone. At first I had some compunctions about removing the bone, but on being told that this field, at present in grass, would be ploughed next year, I decided to carry it home, and enshrine it among my sacred relics."

For a native of the Ettrick Forest like Andrew, who had grown up in Selkirk, Flodden was charged with special significance. The town had responded readily to the king's call to arms, sending as many as a hundred of its men under the command of William Brydon, the town clerk. They acquitted themselves bravely in battle, but only a few had returned. As proof of their valour, the remnants brought with them a pennant taken from an English company. It was carried back to Selkirk by a weaver named Fletcher, the only survivor from a family of five brothers. This flag was subsequently displayed on festival occasions, such as the riding of the marches. Andrew remembered having seen it in his youth.[52] After three hundred years, the pennant had become so tattered and faded that it was known derisively as "the weaver's dishclout."

A mournful song, *The Flowers o' the Forest*, tells of local women grieving over the loss of their loved ones at Flodden:

I've heard them lilting at the ewe-milking,

Lasses a-lilting before the dawn of the day;

But now there is moaning in ilka green loaning [every green pasture]

The flowers o' the forest are a' wede away [all carried off] ...

---

[52] As we have seen, the flag was carried in the procession for the inauguration of the monument to Mungo Park in 1859, but perhaps Andrew missed it.

The prime of our land, are cauld in the clay ...

According to *Border Counties' Magazine*, Andrew had "set himself to tell 'red Flodden's dismal tale' in a series of carved wooden figures, to bear the suggestive name of 'The Flowers of the Forest.'" As of 1880 only one figure had seen the light, *The Ewe Milker*, in both wood and plaster versions. It was "a beautiful conception, representative of the Arcadian time when as yet there was only heard 'The liltin' at our ewe-milkin,' but which, further on in the series, is designed to re-appear, not in the upright buoyant position, but recumbent and mournful, emblematic of 'The moanin' in ilka green loanin.' Every figure will thus be symbolical, and record at a glance a scene or incident of the 'order, sent our lads to the Border,' [such] as that of Brydon the Town Clerk parting with his family, [and] will tell the whole story of the Flodden flag. The vision of such a group has long haunted Mr Currie, but other engagements have always intervened and kept it in the background; but now it is to be be hoped he will find leisure to complete what he has so successfully begun." If he ever did find the leisure, the other figures in the series have long since disappeared.

Flodden, like so many aspects of Andrew's life, had a connection to the works of Sir Walter Scott. The original title of *Marmion*, the Great Minstrel's 1808 epic, was *Flodden Field*. Andrew and his friends visited the well of Sybil Gray, which is mentioned in the poem:

> A little fountain cell,
> Where water, clear as diamond-spark,
> In a stone basin fell.
> Above some half-worn letters say,
> 'Drink weary pilgrim drink and pray
> For the kind soul of Sybil Gray
> Who built this cross and well.'

He noted critically that the ancient well had been supplanted by "a modern piece of sham gothic fountain and basin." The inscription had also been altered to read:

> Rest weary pilgrim rest and stay
> By the well of Sybil Gray.

The alteration had apparently been been the work of the proprietor, the Marchioness of Waterford, who, as a good Calvinist, did not believe in saying prayers for the dead. Andrew disapproved of the change: "surely it is unfeeling to hamper and desecrate the ancient stone and inscription of its pious Catholic founder," he wrote in his reminiscences.

Such was Andrew's interest in Flodden that he revisited the scene the following year. He made sketches of Twizel Bridge, which English troops crossed on their way to the battle, and details of Twizel Castle.

*

The Henderson brothers having left to return to Canada, Andrew continued on the second leg of his holiday with John Logan as his sole companion. On the morning of 3 September 1875, in misty, drizzling rain, the two men made the three-mile crossing on foot, over the sand at low tide, to Holy Island. Conditions were so miserable Logan suggested going home. Andrew would have none of it: "We don't go back till we accomplish the praiseworthy object of our pilgrimage," he told his friend. That was, to visit "the holy spot whence emanated the light of Christianity to the pagan tribes around."

The monastery at Lindisfarne was founded in the seventh century by St Aidan, an Irish monk who came across to Northumbria from Iona. One of his followers later established the monastery at Melrose, which would be the training ground for future bishops of Lindisfarne. Notably St Cuthbert, "that truly great man," Andrew called him, the missionary monk-bishop who ultimately became a hermit.

Though Andrew had never visited Holy Island before, he had seen it several times, as a passenger on a passing ship. The first time had been on his initial voyage to England, from Leith to London, in 1835. Two years later, he had amused himself by making sketches of Lindisfarne and other islands in the Farne group aboard the ill-fated steamer *Pegasus*, which was wrecked on rocks off the Farnes in July 1843 with the loss of fifty-one lives. Now, in the churchyard at Holy Island, he found the graves of some of the drowned.

The two friends pottered around the venerable ruins, Andrew taking notes and making drawings of various stones and historical detritus he found there. Then, with the tide coming in, it was time to retrace their steps. On the way home, they read relevant passages from *Marmion* and discussed what to do the following day. Logan suggested visiting local sites, but Andrew had other ideas. His plan for the next morning was to walk along the Magdalen Fields, between the old city wall of Berwick and the sea cliffs, "in the footsteps of my noble daughter."

Andrew's second daughter, Henrietta Lang Currie, had worked for several years as a schoolmistress at Catholic primary schools in Berwick-upon-Tweed and later Barnard Castle. In 1871 she had returned to the Borders to marry Francis Xavier Greiner, a Galashiels watchmaker. The following summer Henrietta died in childbirth, aged just 27. Father and daughter had been particularly close: Andrew felt her loss deeply. There would, he reflected sadly, "[n]ever be another who will accomplish the work of a long life in such a short one, as she did. No, spring will succeed the storms of winter, and the flowers will blossom on the Magdalen Fields where she loved to walk and gather them for the altar, but centuries may run their course ere they see another Henrietta L. Currie."[53]

Andrew felt guilty that he had never come to visit his devout daughter in Berwick, as he had promised he would. In letters to her father Henrietta had often talked of them going to Lindisfarne together. Eventually she had arranged a school

---

[53] The Magdalen Fields are now a golf course.

outing to Holy Island, paying for the hire of two carts out of her own pocket. In Berwick, Henrietta had lodged at Logan's home. After his walk Andrew sketched the house, focusing on the window, with its little box of marigolds, of the room on the first floor which had been hers.

As well as Henrietta, Andrew had also lost his eldest daughter, Margaret King Currie, just a few months earlier, in June 1875. She died of tuberculosis, aged 32. Margaret had taken a keen interest in his antiquarian work. He mourned her passing, and the fact that she would would not be there to read his notes to when he returned. In the Magdalen Fields, he picked flowers to put in her wreath.

*

On this melancholy note, Andrew's holiday ended. As he journeyed home, however, there was at least one happy event to which he could look forward. His third daughter, Helen, was about to be married. The wedding took place at St Patrick's Roman Catholic Church in Edinburgh on 1 November 1875.

Helen's husband was James Hume Nisbet (b 1849), a colourful character. Born in Stirling, the son of a painter and decorator, he had emigrated as a teenager with his family to Melbourne. In Australia, among other things, he had tried his hand at acting. On his return, Nisbet studied art in London, taking up a position as a teacher of freehand drawing at the Watt Institute in Edinburgh. He met Helen in 1874 on a trip to the Borders where he painted romantic landscapes, including one entitled *Ettrick Brig*.

After eight "eventful" years of teaching, Nisbet resigned to concentrate on painting. A commission took him back to Australasia and New Guinea to provide illustrations for a travel book. Unable to make a living from such work, he became a writer, cranking out four volumes of poetry, five books on art, several collections of horror stories and some forty-six novels. Many of the latter were set in Australia, including several that feature a Chinese criminal mastermind called Wung-Ti, who was based on an individual Nisbet had met in Melbourne. In 1887 the family moved down from Edinburgh to London.

The Nisbets had five children. Having inherited artistic genes from both parents, two of their daughters trained at Clapham School of Art. The eldest, Margaret Henrietta Nisbet (b 1876), became a portrait painter who exhibited at the Royal Academy. The youngest, Noel Laura Nisbet (b 1887), became a well-known illustrator. She specialized in brightly coloured mythical scenes of warriors and princesses done in watercolour in the Pre-Raphaelite style. Hume Nisbet bought both his daughters houses in the same street in Merton Park in southwest London, adding studios with large windows to their top floors. An extrovert, Noel Laura married a fellow artist, Harry Bush, a quiet man who painted in oil in the Dutch style mostly local street scenes, earning him the epithet "the painter of the suburbs." Opposites evidently attracted.

Whether Andrew and his son-in-law got on well is unknown. Hume Nisbet's 1890 novel *Ashes* is supposedly semi-autobiographical (the main character's wife is named Nell, short for Helen, the couple have five children). Judging by the way Nisbet complains about in-laws in this novel, it would seem that they did not.

*

In Australia, as we have seen, Andrew's younger brother, John Lang Currie, had prospered mightily as a pastoralist in the Western District of Victoria. He ultimately owned five farms, on which he bred prize-winning merino sheep. They produced fine, lustrous wool that commanded premium prices at auction in London and elsewhere. In 1871, with an eye on retirement, John acquired a mansion in St Kilda, a prestigious beachside part of Melbourne. Naming it Eildon, after the Border hills he had known in his youth, he hired an architect and set about remodeling and extending the house, adding two symmetrical wings. The improvements were completed in 1877.

Also in 1871, John returned to Scotland taking with him his eldest daughter, yet another Henrietta (known in the family as Etta, b 1853). In Selkirk, Etta met Patrick Sellar Lang, second son of her father's cousin John Lang. A handsome chap with a dry wit and a lusty singing voice, Patrick had several years previously, aged

22, taken over from his father as Sheriff-Clerk of Selkirkshire, becoming the fourth of his family in succession to hold that office. The cousins fell in love. Patrick followed Etta back to Melbourne where, in August 1873, they were married. The reception was held in the ballroom at Eildon. In 1879, Patrick moved to Australia permanently, taking with him various Currie family documents. They included four volumes of handwritten reminiscences and diaries that Andrew had entrusted to him for safekeeping.

In 1874, undeterred by having been shipwrecked off Ceylon on his previous voyage, John Lang Currie returned to Scotland. It was likely on this trip that he commissioned his older brother to carve an elaborate wooden fireplace-surround and over-mantle for the receiving room in the west wing of his new mansion. For this large piece, which would take Andrew six years to complete, John would pay him the princely sum of five hundred pounds.[54] No doubt his brother had seen and been impressed by the enormous wooden bookcase that Andrew had carved many years earlier for Ladhope, the farm where their elder sister Jean and her husband William Scott lived. A "leisure-time work," the bookcase was "full of unexpected cupboards and drawers, the figures carved upon it seem to have been chosen as the humour seized the wood carver, and include such diverse characters as Father Neptune, Moses and his tables of stone, and Robbie Burns."[55]

---

[54] According to the National Archives calculator, £500 would be worth about £22,850 in 2005 money.

[55] Oddly enough, this too ended up in Australia. The bookcase was sold in 1939 by Jean Scott's grand-daughter to Sir Alan Currie, one of John Lang Currie's sons, who donated it to his old school, Geelong College. The bookcase was removed from the college library in the early 1970s. It is thought to have been destroyed by a fire while in storage.

The over-mantle and fireplace-surround that Andrew carved for his brother is the most extraordinary of his wooden pieces. All his previous works had treated predominantly Scottish subjects. Here his task was to commemorate his brother's life and accomplishments in Australia. Working from photographs and illustrations, Andrew carved figures, flora and fauna that he had never himself seen with his own eyes. This tested his skill, but it also allowed his imagination free rein. The resultant piece is imposing, "his finest work in wood-carving."

Made out of dark-amber-coloured oak, the work is about fifteen feet high. Its salient feature is two one-third life-size figures of aboriginal warriors. They stand guard on either side of the fireplace; one holding a spear, the other a boomerang. Above them, in a frieze running across the mantle, four scenes outline the history of the squatters. They fight with native inhabitants, plough the land, sheer sheep. Facing sideways at the corners are two contrasting figures, on the right a blacksmith busily hammering on his anvil and on the left a shepherd in repose with his flock. In the central panel on the next level, a winged human-faced chimera stands astride a globe around which is draped a streamer bearing the legend: "Thy Kingdom Come." To the right a raptor clutches a snake in its beak; to the left a lyre bird displays its tail feathers. On either side stand figures, a settler with a rifle in one hand and a boomerang in the other, and a classically-attired woman holding a scroll. The fourth level mounts an Australian coat of arms, a kangaroo to the right of the shield, an emu to the left, with the motto *prorsum et sursum* ("onwards and upwards"). The ensemble is capped by a winged angel, with figures sitting on either side. In addition to these main features, overall the piece is richly decorated, with carvings of rams' heads, kangaroos, platypuses, foliage and other exotic details. It was reportedly exhibited at the International Exhibition of Melbourne in 1880 (though the official catalog makes no mention of it) where the piece was "universally admired."

*

Another late work, date unknown, is the larger-than-life red sandstone figure of a warrior that stands in an alcove to the right of the front door at Netherby Hall, just across the border in Cumberland. It was a commission from the owner of Netherby, Sir Frederick Ulric Graham, a retired soldier. Netherby Hall was famously the house to which Young Lochinvar rode out of the west to claim the fair Ellen in Canto V of Sir Walter Scott's epic poem *Marmion*. The statue was referred to in *The Scotsman* as "a moss-trooper." But the suit of armour he wears looks much older than mid seventeenth century, the period when moss troopers were active. As we know, Andrew did careful research for his historical subjects. According to Graham family legend, the figure is that of a Border reiver who fought in the Battle of Solway Moss (1542). A humiliating defeat for the Scots, this paved the way for a treaty which defined where the border between Scotland and England should lie. The Grahams were one of the most notorious families of reivers, "fighting men who earned their living on the battlefield and when they weren't soldiers, would make a living by robbery." But it is also conceivable that the figure is intended to represent Sir John of the Bright Sword, a thirteenth century Graham ancestor, who fought with William Wallace and was renowned for his valour. The face appears to be that of a real person: Sir Frederick Graham himself perhaps?

Either way, this was Andrew's last major work. The only other sculptures he is known to have produced in the late 1870s and early 1880s are both small pieces, busts of children. One, the model for a marble bust of Arthur Dalrymple Forbes Gordon, was lent by James Dalrymple, laird of Langlee, an estate in Roxburghshire, for the Royal Scottish Academy's exhibition of 1877, when Arthur was four years old.

In 1881 Andrew assisted Sir William Ramsay Fairfax in restoring Maxton Cross, Roxburghshire, a rallying point for armed men in ancient times. The shaft of the old cross had been displaced to "a hedge at some distance from where it originally stood," in front of the village smithy, while the rampant lion which formerly crowned it had ended up in the rockery at Maxton House. The restoration, it was felt, would be "as enduring a monument to Sir William's fine antiquarian taste as ... representative of Mr Currie's well-known skill as a sculptor."[56]

Andrew's ultimate work - and his only known sculpture carved in marble - is an exquisite bust depicting a little girl holding a bunch of flowers. It was probably commissioned by a wealthy individual in memory of his daughter. Frustratingly, other than its date - 1882- we know nothing about this elegiac piece. It brings to an end Andrew Currie's career as a sculptor.

* * *

---

[56] Alas, the restored cross turns out to be a very plain affair, without a rampant lion or indeed any decoration at all. By a curious coincidence, the village smithy outside which it stands is now the home and workshop of Jake Harvey, a well-known Border sculptor.

Eleven

Singularly Dilatory? (1882~1891)

In 1882 Andrew turned 70. During the final decade of his life, in retirement, he participated in the activities of the Berwickshire Naturalists' Club, which he had joined in 1876. Founded in 1831, the stated purpose of this club was to examine the flora, fauna and antiquities of Berwickshire and vicinity. Members, who were all men, met five times a year, went on outings and published annual reports of their findings. Andrew acted as guide and instructor on at least one outing, and submitted detailed written follow-ups for another. He also provided drawings of antique artifacts like bronze axe-heads and stone graves, as well as the plan of an excavation.

In August 1881, Andrew led a party of forty members on an excursion to St Mary's Loch, passing by his old home at Howford. They alighted first at Yarrow Kirk, built in 1640, which he had attended as a boy. Andrew was a mine of local knowledge. He pointed out a deep hollow in which there was a shepherd's house, at a place named Kershope. "I can recall a common remark in my young days that in the shorter days of winter, the sun did not shine on Kershope for three weeks," he told the group, adding that this wisdom no longer held true.

From there, the party moved on to Tibbie Shiel's Inn, where the Ettrick Shepherd, John Wilson, and other famous conversationalists had formerly congregated for evenings of alcohol-fueled eloquence. "We had Mr Andrew Currie with us," the report notes, "who knew personally several of the participators in those conventions." The company walked up to Andrew's statue of James Hogg, erected with such ceremony more than twenty years before. Then, as now, graffiti and vandalism were a problem. "The members felt indignant at the profanation that Mr Currie's work was undergoing from the thoughtless public and covetous visitors. They have commenced cutting their names, and scribbling their ribaldry on the pedestal, and have even knocked off and appropriated one of the horns of the ornamental ram's heads ... that terminate each corner. Several [members] subsequently subscribed to the fund for erecting an iron railing to preserve the statue from further spoilation."[57]

Two years later, in August 1883, the club went on an excursion up the Yarrow. This time the focus was the battle of Philiphaugh, outside Selkirk, where in September 1645 a Covenanter army led by Sir David Leslie routed the Royalist forces of the Marquis of Montrose. A conical, stone-cobbled cairn commemorated the Covenanters' victory. Twenty feet high, it had been raised in 1848 by the laird of Philiphaugh, Sir John Murray, on the site of Montrose's camp. Andrew had assisted in its design and erection.

Montrose's men attempted to stop Leslie's forces crossing Ettrick Water at a ford in the river. The people of Selkirk flocked to watch the fighting from the vantage point of an overhanging bank. A royalist piper stationed nearby was shot dead in mid skirl. He tumbled "like a shot rabbit down the brae into the water," which was thenceforth known as Piper's Pool. Andrew heard this story from his mother, whose ancestor had been one of the onlookers. More than a century later, in February 1752, Andrew's great-grandfather Andrew Lang accidently drowned in this same pool.[58]

---

[57] Old photographs show that a railing was indeed erected, but it is no longer there. It was probably removed and melted down during World War II.
[58] Andrew believed that the ancestor who witnessed the battle was the same as the one who drowned. Since the latter was born in 1712 and the battle took place in 1645, this is obviously impossible. His confusion is however understandable, given that there seems to have been an Andrew in each generation of the Lang family.

Around 1760 a bridge had been constructed across Ettrick Water. Known as
the General's Brig after its builder, Lieutenant-General Mackay, it was now broken
down. As a man who had worked with stone most of his life, Andrew knew a thing
or two about bridges. "I have always in my professional capacity been curious
about bridges as regards their mechanical structure at different periods," he wrote,
adding dismissively, "I may tell you that this one has been very badly built."

By contrast, Andrew approved of the construction of Deuchar Bridge at
Yarrow Kirk. This was a gothic structure, now a picturesque ruin. Only one of its
two arches still stood, "stretched, like the stump of a maimed arm, toward the
further shore of Yarrow." He believed the bridge dated back to the thirteenth or
fourteenth century. Andrew had examined several other bridges of this vintage, at
Stirling, Ayr and Twizel. "All of them have been very carefully and strongly
constructed and founded, with hot lime poured in as the structures were built up,
and when finished forming like a concrete mass," he noted. "[H]ence their great
endurance through the tear and wear of centuries to the present day."

A highlight of the Yarrow excursion was a visit to the grave, on the site of a
vanished chapel at Henderland, of Piers Cockburn, a fourteenth-century Border
chieftain. The sandstone slab was marked with a sword, shield, cross and an
inscription. The tomb had been repaired in 1841. At that time a fragment of human
skull had been dug up, purloined and sold to "a gentleman in Edinburgh."
Andrew learned of this when he went back that December to make a drawing of
the tomb for the club's report. His youngest brother George, visiting from
Australia, told him what had happened. "That [the tomb] was desecrated I have on
the authority of my own brother ... to whom the thief confessed the foul deed, and
indicated the party to whom he had sold it. I am glad to find now from my brother,
that this same party had the good taste to restore the skull to its tomb at
Henderland."

Andrew reported that the gravestone was "in a very bad condition, being
scrawled with names. One of these has been *recently* cut along the sword, and so
deeply that the only way to restore it to the original state would be to fill the letters
in with hard cement; also to clean the whole stone of its moss, and enclose it by an

iron railing. If this is not done, it promises fair to be destroyed, and unintelligible in a few years." What with the wretched state of the slab and the darkness of the winter's day, Andrew had been unable to decipher the letters. Happily, he was able to turn for assistance to his "nephew," Andrew Lang - in fact his cousin John's eldest son - a well-known poet, novelist, literary critic and collector of folklore, who knew the inscription:

HERE LYIS PERYS OF COKBURNE AND HYS WYFE MARJORY

*

Andrew Currie himself had literary aspirations. In his sixties, he compiled memoirs of his childhood and edited the diary he had kept during his apprenticeship. His account of his 1875 holiday to Berwick contains references to "my book on Selkirk," and an article about Flodden on which he appears to have been working at the time. One of his friends, the Galashiels woodcarver and antiquary Francis Lynn, believed that Andrew "had a fine literary gift, which would have carried him far if he had persevered in that direction." Another friend, George Desson of Paisley, also an antiquary, wrote in a posthumous appreciation that Andrew had "contributed many racy and interesting articles and stories to Border newspapers and magazines, but the fact that they were generally unsigned, or only initials used, prevented him from getting full credit for the delight he gave to the readers."

"Newspapers and magazines" may be an exaggeration. Andrew's main outlet for his writings was the *Border Counties' Magazine*, which billed itself as "a popular monthly miscellany of the history, biography, poetry, folklore, etc, of the Border Districts." It cannot have been that popular: published in Galashiels, the magazine lasted only from July 1880 to December 1881. At tuppence an issue, it was felt to be too expensive. For the section of the magazine entitled *Tales and Traits of the Border*, Andrew worked up several of the best yarns from his diary and reminiscences. They include two ghost stories, *The Spectre Seen at the Bishop's Stone* and *The Gruesome Sight My Father Saw*.

Another tale, *William Murray's Secret*, is a first-person narrative about a treasure trove. William Murray was a servant lad at Howford who, while helping his aunt to cut peat, stumbled across the grave of a Roman soldier which contained a cache of silver coins. Much to William's chagrin, the treasure had to be handed over to the owner of the land, Lord Polwarth. Under cover of night, he went back to the spot, eventually discovering a stone slab much larger than the first. He kept this knowledge a secret, confiding its location only to his friend, Andrew. But the two youths could not agree on how to lift the huge stone by themselves. Eventually, Andrew was apprenticed and William went off to Australia with Andrew's brother, John, where he died shortly after landing. "Thus the secret was left with me," Andrew wrote.

"The late Lord Polwarth and I had once a conversation on the subject at Mertoun House; and he surmised that it was probably the tomb of a distinguished soldier, whose treasure might or might not have been buried with him. His Lordship offered to send labourers with me to the spot, to excavate the ground, whenever I gave them notice of being ready to set them to work. But, somehow, I never found a suitable time to go, and ere long his Lordship died, and, of course, there was an end to the matter. ... Often since then I have had grave reflections on what a singularly dilatory character I am!" Andrew concluded ruefully.

William Murray's Secret also appears in *North and South of the Tweed*, a 1913 book of Border legends compiled by Jean Lang, wife of John Lang, yet another "nephew." This collection includes Andrew's most memorable story, extracted from his diary of 1830. It records his encounter on his way home from Denholm to Howford with the extraordinary gypsy woman, Madge Gordon, on whom Sir Walter Scott had based the character Meg Merrilies in his 1815 novel, *Guy Mannering*. Almost six feet tall, this "gigantic Amazon" with her "yellow hair streaming behind her like the pennon of some Border chief" must have been a formidable sight.[59]

*

---

[59] See Part III.

On 7 July 1888, disaster struck. Andrew's beloved wife Belle died, of heart failure, aged 72. The couple had been married for almost 49 years. Andrew was devastated. He had been utterly dependent on Belle. "His dear practical wife suffered from his mutable moods of genius, but understood them well," wrote Lillias Cotesworth, "and to the day of her death was a ministering angel to her husband, never worrying him, never insisting on punctuality, setting his food on the hob to keep warm until he chose to take it, and studying his material comfort and varying humours in a manner worthy of high praise, for they must have seemed to her strangely unnecessary and incomprehensible. ... Her loss was irreparable, and he daily and hourly missed her love and care. Feeling lonely and lost without someone to look after him, he married again."

His second wife was Agnes Miller Greig, fourteen years his junior, the widow of a railway clerk. How and where they met is not known. Their wedding took place on 29 April 1889, "according to the forms of the Roman Catholic church," at the Church of the Sacred Heart in Lauriston Street, Edinburgh. Andrew left Darnick to live with Agnes at her flat on Leven Terrace. It was pleasantly situated, across the road from The Meadows, a large park, near the university library. But he did not like the hustle and bustle of urban living. A friend who ran into Andrew in Edinburgh records that "he lamented having forsaken a pastoral quietude like Darnick - fit shrine for a man of his literary and artistic temperament - for the comparative distractions of city life."

Andrew did not long survive his relocation. He died suddenly of a heart attack while walking down Melville Drive, not far from his new home, on 28 February 1891, aged 78. The death certificate was signed by Sir Henry Littlejohn, a famous Edinburgh physician. His funeral took place in Melrose, where he was buried, next to Belle, in Weirhill Cemetery.

"Many who had known the old man and missed his well-known figure, gathered to pay a last tribute to his memory, and to see him laid to rest in the Border country he loved and understood as few can understand it in these roving days, when the spirit of nature finds no resting place amidst the busy ceaseless rush for notoriety and self-advertisement."

*

What sort of man was Andrew Currie? To get some idea, we must rely on obituaries and fragmentary accounts written by those who knew him. The obituary in *The Scotsman* does not tell us much: "Physically as well as mentally he was a man of marked individuality." In a memorial address delivered to the Berwickshire Naturalists' Club ten years after Andrew's death, the Border writer Sir George Brisbane Douglas (b 1856) of Springwood Park, Kelso, had a stab at defining the physical individuality.

"Currie, to judge from his appearance," Douglas speculated, "had probably a strain of the gypsy." This is a bit rich, coming from someone who was born in Gibraltar and whose mother was a native of the Rock, a territory known for its ethnic diversity. Judging by what Douglas said, he was only slightly acquainted with his subject. He was aware for example that Andrew had been a tradesman, but mistakenly believed him to have been a wheelwright, not a millwright. "That he belonged to the order of the peasant genius admits of no doubt whatever," Douglas went on to assert, wrongly. (Andrew, as we have seen, came from a family of farmers and lawyers.) Doubtless the baronet equated the sculptor with "his gamekeepers and other worthies," who were the sources for the Border tales he recorded.

Though a snob, Douglas does offer some insights into Andrew's personality: "All that he did ... commanded attention, wonder, admiration. But a simple, dreamy, unpractical nature prevented his making the most of his talent and opportunities. Perhaps his character rather gains than loses from this defect." To explain what he means, Douglas cites an example: "[W]hen the design for the Byron memorial was thrown open to public competition [in 1880], he declined to enter for it, alleging as his reason that he '*did not care much about the man*'! And no one who knew anything of Currie personally will suspect him of affectation. It was very different when he had a task which appealed to him, such as the carving of figures to represent the characters in the Waverley novels. Nothing could then exceed his keenness ... . His life was passed in a world of his own, above the range of ordinary mortals, and doubtless he failed to attain to those conditions under which his genius might have grown to its full stature. His wife ... would sometimes thank the Lord that none of her children had inherited anything of his talent."[60]

George Desson was an antiquarian who came to know Andrew in later life. In a detailed, carefully-researched appreciation of "this gifted knight of the chisel" for *The Border Magazine* in 1906, he wrote that "[i]t was while in quest of Border folk-lore that I became acquainted with the genial, warm-hearted and gifted artist, and it is with pleasure that I look back on the many pleasant and profitable hours that I spent within his art sanctum in the quiet little old-fashioned village of Darnick. ... Mr Currie never looked on his art as a means of gain, but simply as a pure labour of love."

By far the best, certainly the most intimate, portrait we have of Andrew comes from Lillias Cotesworth, the daughter of his first patron, who as a girl used to ride over to Darnick from her home at Cowdenknowes once or twice a week to take clay modelling lessons. This, too, was published in *The Border Magazine*, in 1902:

"When I first remember him, he was a vigorous man of about sixty [ie, circa 1872], with bright brown eyes in which fun and humour lurked ... . I always considered his friendship a privilege and no one could have been a pleasanter or more sympathetic companion. He was a gentleman in the true sense of the word, and his sweetness of character and simplicity endowed him with great charm; when quietly working in his studio he would give his thoughts rein, and allow those who listened a glimpse into the world of dreams which

---

[60] In his writings, Andrew Currie makes no mention of his three sons. The eldest, George Hardie, emigrated to New Zealand; William John became a weaver; the youngest, Andrew Lang, the current writer's great-grandfather, a commercial traveller.

was his possession, and where selfish emulation, disturbing envy, or even ambition had no place. ...

"I sometimes think sadly that much must have been lost when he died, for he gathered his stories from the old people of his boyhood, but, like so many, kept them mostly in his head, whence in quiet moments they would come forth, apropos of some subject on hand, for a certain diffidence or shyness made him unwilling to tell a story when asked to do so, or to give information on any particular subject, in which circumstances he would reply in his slow, reflective way: 'Well, I'm sure I can't say.' ...

"I often regret that I did not write down all I heard from him at that time, quaint tales of fellow-villagers, that would have filled a volume, and legends of Old Melrose, "Gladswood with its milk-white ewes," the Leader Haughs, the Black Hill [Earlston], where St Cuthbert as a boy herded his sheep ... .[61]

"Far too unpractical and without ambition to succeed in the world ... he never made money, and it went to my heart to see him working at the first rough chipping and the plaster casts himself, when he should only have superintended and put finishing touches. However, it all interested him, and if a cast was good he experienced

---

[61] The reference is to the sixteenth-century ballad, *Leader Haughs and Yarrow*:

> Sing Ercildoune and Cowdenknowes,
> Where Humes had aince commanding,
> And Drygrange, wi' its milk-white ewes,
> 'Twixt Tweed and Leader standing.
> The bird that flees through Redpath trees
> And Gladswood banks ilk morrow
> May chant and sing sweet Leader Haugh,
> And bonnie howms of Yarrow.

genuine pleasure and would work up the fine plaster till it looked like marble.

"Now and then for pastime ... he would model grotesque little faces; his sense of humour was strong, and though never spiteful, he would have his joke in a quiet way against artists whose ideas were greater than their powers, and who depended for success on the modern fashion of booming [self-promotion]. Alas, most of them prospered while he stayed behind, but none will be remembered for the childlike charm and single-hearted selflessness that were characteristic in the old sculptor."

* * *

ANDREW CURRIE.

PART II: BORDER SCULPTOR

Andrew Currie (c 1875?)

[Above] Howford farm (extended since AC lived there) © John Reiach

[Right] The artist's mother, Henrietta Currie, by her son (private collection)

[Above] Viewfield, Selkirk © John Reiach

[Right] AC's aunt, Margaret Lang (artist unknown, private collection)

[Above] Leyden's Cottage, Denholm, where AC trained as a millwright © John Reiach

[Below Right] Darnick Tower © John Reiach

[Above Right] Fisher's Tower, Darnick © John Reiach

[Above Left] AC in his workshop at Darnick 1867 © Tom Little Collection

(Melrose Historical Association)

[Above] First commission: Cotesworth bookcase (private collection)

[Top Right] Detail

[Above] Cotesworth bookcase extension (private collection)

[Mid Right] Detail II: Thomas the Rhymer (self portrait?)

[Bottom Right] Detail I: King David holding model and

charter of Melrose Abbey

[Above] First sale: Dead Partridge (Abbotsford) © Mara Johnstone

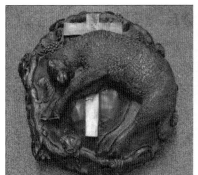 

[Above Left] Paschal Lamb (Abbotsford) © Mara Johnstone

[Above Right] Inspiration: Lamb, boss from ceiling of chapter house at Dryburgh Abbey, where Sir Walter Scott is buried © John Reiach

[Above] "He lived in Yarrow." An Ettrick Shepherd (Abbotsford) © Mara Johnstone

Mungo Park monument, Selkirk, c 1859 Robert Clapperton © Clapperton Trust

Mungo Park monument, Selkirk, 2012 © John Reiach

[Above Left & Right] Mungo Park © Walter McLaren

[Above Left] King David (?) Detail from gravestone of Robert Bower at Melrose Abbey, 1860

[Above Right] Deerhounds outside front door at Abbotsford © Scotiana

James Hogg, the Ettrick Shepherd © Walter McLaren

"My beloved Shepherd ... your effigy will be seen on some bonny green knowe in the forest, with its honest face looking across St Mary's Loch ..." © Walter McLaren

Masterpiece in Stone: The Ettick Shepherd © Walter McLaren

[Above] Detail of altar © Walter McLaren

[Left] Altar of St Patrick, Our Lady &
St Andrew, Galashiels © Walter McLaren

[Above] Pulpit, Our Lady & St Andrew, Galashiels © Walter McLaren

[Right] James Hope-Scott looks down from on high, Our Lady & St Andrew © Walter McLaren

[Above] Edie Ochiltree on Scott Monument © John Reiach
[Left] Edie Ochitree in 1872 © City of Edinburgh Council

[Above] Old Mortality on Scott Monument © John Reiach

[Right] Old Mortality in 1872 © City of Edinburgh Council

[Above] "An aged but strongly marked and expressive countenance"

Edie Ochiltree at Abbotsford © John Reiach

[Above Left] Jock the Ladle and [Below Right] the Ewe Milker: AC made multiple plaster

casts of such genre figures to sell to tourists (private collection)

[Left] King Robert the Bruce monument, Stirling Castle Esplanade © Historic Scotland

[Below] Making the point: "Designed and Executed by A. Currie, Sculptor

[Above Right] King's Head © John Reiach

[Above Left] Mugshot: Govancroft Potteries, after AC's statue of Robert the Bruce © Stirling Smith Art Gallery & Museum

Border Reiver/Sir John of the Bright Sword, Netherby Hall © John Reiach

"Rest in the Lord" cathedra (?) chair (date unknown, private collection) © John Reiach

[Above] Overmantle/Fireplace-surround, commissioned by John Lang Currie for Eildon, his St Kilda, Melbourne mansion (private collection)

[Above Left] Detail: Aboriginal warrior in possum-skin cloak (note kangaroo at below left)

[Centre] Detail: Shepherd at rest [Above Right] Detail: Blacksmith at work

Last work: "Girl Holding Flowers" © David Patterson, City Art Centre, Edinburgh

Gravestone of Andrew & Belle Currie, Weirhill Cemetery, Melrose © Walter McLaren

PART III: BORDER WRITER

INTRODUCTION TO WRITINGS

Andrew Currie had a good ear for the spoken word. Starting in his late teens, he would write down stories that local people told him. Later on, he would put this talent to good use in his antiquarian research, collecting oral histories from the old folk he met. Andrew also had a keen eye, as portraitists must, and a retentive memory. In his sixties he was able to recall scenes from his youth and bring them to life on the page. And he had a fine sense of humour, often making jokes at his own expense.

Andrew wrote in standard English embellished with the odd dialect word. When transcribing speech, however, he almost always switched to broad Lowlands Scots. Some of his friends thought he could have been a writer. But he lacked the opportunities and, until late in life, the time. Andrew published very little, just a handful of stories in an obscure, short-lived Border magazine in 1880~1881. Gathered here under the heading *Miscellaneous Writings*, these are typically somewhat polished versions of originals he wrote as a young man. The stories carry no byline, just the initial "C" or sometimes "AC."[62]

The bulk of the material that follows has never been published before. It consists of (lightly edited) transcripts from four exercise books that Andrew wrote, in his own hand, in 1874 and '75.[63] For safekeeping he gave them to Patrick Sellar Lang, the son of his cousin and childhood chum John Lang, and his nephew by

---

[62] I have included only pieces that I am convinced are by Andrew Currie. There are others that may also be by him, notably a long story entitled *The Laird of Harden's Escape From Oakwood: A Tale of the '45*.

[63] Andrew numbered the last two volumes of his reminiscences 5 and 6. If we make the initial volume number 1 and the diary number 2, that means at least two volumes are missing.

marriage. In 1879, Patrick Lang emigrated to Australia taking family documents including the exercise books with him. They have been there ever since.

*

The first of the four volumes is dated 1825, when Andrew was aged thirteen. It is written from the perspective of a man in his sixties looking back on his boyhood. He begins by describing the circumstances that ultimately led him to be apprenticed as a millwright. And why, despite him having shown signs of artistic talent, this early promise was not followed up.

Much of this volume consists of recollections of people and places from Andrew's youth. Places include Yarrow Kirk, where he worshipped with the Ettrick Shepherd. Andrew describes with amusement the scenes of canine chaos that took place there every Sunday. He also sketches two of the eccentric characters who attended the church. There is an affectionate description of his father, and how he would get together with his cronies on neighbouring farms for a blether over a whisky or two. Most interesting of all from a biographical point of view is a depiction of the charming scene of domestic bliss at Howford, the farm where Andrew was born. The volume concludes with a humorous ghost story, *The Gruesome Sight My Father Saw*, which he later recycled in *Border Counties Magazine*.

*

By far the longest of the four volumes is a "selection of leaves" from the diary Andrew kept while an apprentice millwright in Denholm, 1830~1834. It purports to be "the history of a day," one Saturday in June 1830. The diary describes events that occurred and the 18-year-old Andrew's reflections on the seven-hour, fifteen-mile walk from Denholm to his home at Howford. In fact, as becomes immediately clear, this is not a single day, but a composite. In the very first entry, Andrew mentions that he has "laid in a stock of literature to beguile the time." This includes the latest issues of two magazines that did not begin publication until 1832. Later on, he alludes to an article that was published in 1834. Thus, the single day and the journey are actually literary devices that enable him to cobble together multiple items from different times under a single heading.

Andrew illustrated his diary with sketches, mostly of animals - sheep, dogs and birds - but also of people and places. He cut these out of the original and pasted them into his transcription. The sketches include a self-portrait. Wearing a bonnet the young man strides jauntily barefoot, his shoes tied together Dick-Whittington-style on a stick over his shoulder.

The chosen day is significant because it occurs at a pivotal moment in young Andrew's life. He is about to be formally contracted as an apprentice millwright, something about which - as he makes abundantly clear - he is deeply unhappy. The day climaxes with a dramatic encounter between Andrew and the extraordinary gypsy woman, Madge Gordon. It begins with him initiating an ill-advised race with her and ends with her counseling him to accept his fate.

Andrew sets off on his journey musing on memories, still fresh in his mind, of his brief stay in Edinburgh. He includes a characteristically funny story about the then-current fad for phrenology which includes a dig at his dogmatic uncle William.

As Andrew goes along, he ruminates on philosophical matters like the meaning of life and the existence of God. These are precisely the kind of questions about which serious young men are prone to speculate. An interlude with a comic rogue on the run called Sandy Shiels serves to lighten things up.

Andrew visits the Bishop's Stone, the scene of an encounter between a miller and a ghost, a story he knows well. He considers the case for the Reform Bill, then much in the news, coming down in favour of the enfranchisement of the new working class. He comments on the similarities between the Newfoundland dog described in an article and his own family's Newfoundland, "the famous" Watch.

An encounter with two passing tramps prompts more philosophical speculation. This is followed by the meeting with Madge Gordon, in which Andrew learns from the gypsy much that he did not know about his parents and grandparents, including some unsettling items. From there he moves on to a lengthy description of an exciting incident from his childhood: being chased and almost caught by Highland herdsmen while out rabbiting with his chums. Like the first volume the diary ends on a light note, with a funny story told at the expense of his master's aunt, a superstitious old hypochondriac.

*

The final volumes - numbered 5 & 6 - are very different from the first two. For one thing, they are contemporary records, describing a holiday Andrew took in 1875 to visit the battlefield at Flodden and the ruined monastery at Lindisfarne. (Both volumes deal with Flodden and Lindisfarne, so I have condensed them into a single narrative.) For another, while some parts of the text appear finished, others are very much a work in progress. Andrew goes into the events of the battle in great detail, transcribing large chunks of texts from other writers in order to comment on or refute them. He makes a passing reference to an article on which he was working: these may well be his notes. Since these passages are for the most part not original, I have deleted them. I have also cut a section on the early history of the church in England, which was copied from an 1845 article in *The Penny Magazine*. Another difference is that Andrew is now a devout and, let it be said, somewhat credulous Catholic and his world view has altered as a result. The text is peppered with references to his new faith.

The reminiscences divide into three parts. First, a wander with old friends around Selkirk and environs, taking in and discussing local landmarks. Second, the trip to see the battlefield of Flodden; and third, the visit to Holy Island. In these episodes, we see Andrew in different modes: as expert on local history; as antiquarian, inquiring about the history of his surroundings; and as bereaved father, lamenting the deaths of two of his daughters. In keeping with the melancholy mood, there are no funny stories here. But, as always, the text is enlivened with flashes of Andrew's characteristically self-deprecatory humour.

Ultimately, what we have in these reminiscences and diaries is a keenly-observed, intensely personal record. To read them is to get a good idea of what kind of man Andrew Currie was, and of the times and places in which he lived.

* * *

WRITINGS ONE

REMINISCENCES 1825

When I began these notes on the Howford old papers I had no intention otherwise than giving some of my own commentaries on their subject matter, as far as my recollection of any of the parties was concerned, or anecdotes by my father and others in the locality of Ettrick Brig-End [Ettrickbridge End], but somehow I find myself drifting into a biography of myself, which at first was far from my intentions, at least in connection with this subject.[64] Seeing however that I have already gone thus far in bringing my unimportant boyhood to the front, and in hope that there may yet be some passages that may prove instructive to others, especially to those of my own children after me, I shall just continue it ...

*

In the autumn of this year [1825, when AC was aged 13] I have mentioned making the acquaintance of an excellent man, Dr Paterson, whose friendship in after years till he left Galashiels, I always look back upon as to one of the pleasant passages of

---

[64] "Howford old papers" refers to family documents - letters, contracts and suchlike - held at Howford farm which AC gave in 1875 to Patrick Sellar Lang, his second cousin and nephew by marriage.

my young life, and from whom I learned much.[65] I have yet in my eye those never-to-be-forgot pleasant Sunday evening walks, starting from the Manse at Galashiels and making the circuit of Galashiels hill, by the old Selkirk road, thence eastward till we returned. But as these were three years after this date I shall only notice them and in the meantime refer to an incident at Howford which I am not sure, trifling though it was in its nature, but it had influence in shaping my after-life as a mechanic.

There was a threshing mill erected at Helmburn and, it being the first introduction of the threshing mill into this part of Ettrick, the event created no little sensation among the simple denizens of this part of the Forest. We - and when I say "we" I include my companion at this time, a clever cow-herd laddie - we found to our dismay that all at once our favourite burn, rising from Howford hill, where we derived no end of sport in girning [snaring] trout and eels, was at once dry, from the feeders being taken from it to supply the pond of this mill. Of course we were indignant and mourned the drying-up of the burn, but as we could not make better of it, we submitted with the best grace we could and determined to go and see the ill-starred thing that had caused the calamity and spoilt our sport. So off we set the next day to see the mill at work.

This was the first time that I had ever seen a piece of machinery in motion, different from the rickety wheezing old grinding meal mill of Howford Mill. There was something so grand and bewildering in the water dashing over the bucket wheel, and the array of strange little wheels and revolving rakes tossing the straw from them, that for some time the herd laddie and I were fairly lost in admiration and bewilderment. Coming home he remarked: "Faix [Indeed], I think you and me could make a water wheel like that — let's try this very day, and we we'll set it a-gaun [going] down the burn." And the upshot was that in a very few days, this part of the burn was studded with water wheels of all shapes and sizes and all in motion, and besides a cozy little rush-house against the bank arose where we sat

---

[65] Nathaniel Paterson (1787-1871), the minister at Galashiels Kirk from 1821 to 1834, was the grandson of Robert Paterson, the model for Old Mortality, and a regular guest of Sir Walter Scott at Abbotsford.

and admired our handiwork and criticized the working of our machinery. Some of them had the water laid on by a hemlock pipe [sic], and would go steadily and well while another - a breast wheel - would be exposed to the full flood of a fall of the burn, and get into such a delightful velocity as at last to leap out of its socket and decamp down the burn, like a thing in a paroxysm of joy.[66]

This was a new field of amusement and invention opened up to us all at once, and we wrought it up for a while with great enthusiasm. Soon we had a host of youthful imitations, but our mills always took the lead, and we were continually contriving improvements in the shape of cranks and pulleys, and then the doctor's knife [think Swiss Army] was a workshop in itself for mortising and boring holes and which with our own skill kept us far ahead of all competitors.

Our mechanical imitations in water wheels began to attract rather more than usual attention among the elders, and I think it was about this time that uncle William Lang [b 1791] came to hand on his holidays for some shooting and fishing. Now I had no great love to uncle William ever since he threw my pet hurchin [hedgehog] into the mill pool and made the dog worry it, myself crying piteously and pleading for its life, which he only made sport of. Besides, he was dogmatic in his ways, and continually telling you how to speak, and how to behave. A kind generous-hearted man in the main, however, if you took him in his own way, and he carried great weight with my mother in all his utterances.

Her three brothers and her sister Mrs [Jean] Blaikie were patterns of the brotherly love which should always exist in any family — always kind and considerate to each other, and to each other's welfare. This I frankly and with pleasure admit on a retrospective view, although to this day I have ever had the conviction that in their attitude and treatment of my kind-hearted erring father on his insolvency some years before this they committed a grave error, and one which left its mark further than I care to speak of. But on this I shall impartially state the case, and make some remarks by itself; at present, I confine myself to the

---

[66] A breast wheel is a type of water wheel into which water enters at the mid-point (breast) of the wheel and is kept in buckets until discharged at the lowest point of the wheel; the weight of the water in the buckets turns the wheel to provide power.

handiwork of myself and the herd laddie and uncle William's decisions on my after-path.

After a scrutiny of his nephew's mechanical gifts, says he: "That boy has a great turn for mechanics." "What's a mechanic?" says cousin Elizabeth [Lang, b 1811], who chanced to be among the group of youngsters around uncle William. "What's a mechanic! Well, I will tell you what a mechanic is: the man who makes these" - lifting the candlestick and snuffers - "is a mechanic; also the man who makes this table and these chairs is a mechanic; and the men who make mills and wheels are mechanics by the name of millwrights and engineers. And this is what the boy shows such a turn for that, after a year or two in the grammar school of Selkirk, I will have him with me in Edinburgh and put him into training for that line."

Says my mother: " I was thinking of by-and-by of getting him into Andrew [Lang, her brother]'s office - as he is no stout [not in good health] - and it's licht wark a writer [to the signet, ie, a solicitor], but he is very young yet - just gaun seven - but if ye ..."

"No such thing — he must be a mechanic, and we will just keep that in view hereafter." And from that day there was a tacit understanding in the family council that the "boy" was to be of some handicraft — uncle William had said it, and the thing was settled. He was pleased in having discovered it and proud of the "boy's" gifts, and the audience of the whole family, including the boy - his father, mother, sister and cousins - were pleased.

I said I did not like him at this time, but in after years when he kindly had me under his roof - No. 118 Princes Street [Edinburgh] - I altered my views and did have a strong attachment to him. And for all his seeming dogmatism, a trifling incident occurred in after years which showed me that, whatever views he formed and stood stoutly by them, he was yet open to conviction and would honestly confess his mistake, and the following is an instance. I might be about 13 or 14 when he and I went on the beginning of autumn to Howford loch to have some wild duck catching with [our] dog Watch. This was done in the lochs and mosses before the young brood took to flight, and required such a dog as this famous one, who could dive after them in the water.

So after some capital sport and success, we took a seat out of sight of the loch till the young ducks gathered again from their hiding places among the reeds. After our lunch, I commenced with a piece of soft bog oak to carve a wild duck shape, with the dog pursuing in the water. The softness of the material soon enabled me to bring out a rather spirited thing, which uncle William looked at for some time musingly, laid it down, then took it up again and had another look. Then says he, rather speaking as it were to himself: "Well, here is a something" - as Mr Dick [character in *David Copperfield*] says - and perhaps after all that something may be, not mechanics, but art. I think, Andrew, this is so very good - and like our sport today - besides a memorial of it, that I shall take it home with me, and put it on my mantlepiece." "With all my heart," says I. But Watch saved us the trouble, for having laid it down on the heather and, likely enough in a bad humour for want of his dinner, he demolished the picture of himself and the wild ducks, to my uncle's great mortification.

That night, however, he says to me, after a long talk between my mother and he by themselves: "Andrew, I think you had better come in to me this winter and I will put you under some artist for freehand and perspective drawing before you go to your apprenticeship next summer — you can't be the worse for it, and who knows but something may [come of it]." I thanked him, and meant to avail myself of the offer, but some other arrangement in schooling at Selkirk [was made], I have forgot what, but I did not go, which I ever after regretted when apprenticed to a millwright at Denholm.

I took a back-ganging [had a relapse] in the autumn of this year [1825], and can yet recollect of the significant looks and shaking of heads of the old wives, besides the frequent finding of my pulse, and examining of my tongue by our old dominie, for he practised a little with simple prescriptions and blood letting. He was counted a rather "skeely" [skillful] man in trouble, and I believe he well merited the name, in that line was very useful in the place, the nearest doctor being seven miles off at Selkirk. By advice of Dr Anderson I was at length removed to my uncle [Andrew Lang]'s house at Selkirk, in order to be near him for the treatment of my trouble, which began at last to assume the appearance of a goitre below my chin. Long and severe was my illness, but at last it was successfully cut, although I bear the marks of it to this day, and, under the kind motherly nursing of aunt [Margaret] Lang, I was at length restored to health, and was ever afterward better in bodily condition. No one ever took hold in my youthful affections among all my relations as aunt Lang for her unwearied attention.

I remained at the grammar school under Mr [James Douglas] Oliver and, from this time, I may say I never afterwards was a resident at our Howford home, only in vacations. Before I relate my after-life and experiences at Selkirk, I shall, before taking leave of Ettrick Brig-End and its surroundings, take some notice of our mode of life, habits etc, and some odds and ends about our neighbours and their doings in this unsophisticated pastoral district of Ettrick, and first about our weekly attendance at the parish kirk of Yarrow.

*

I have often wondered how habit reconciles us to things, which people of a higher civilization in towns would consider an intolerable hardship, such as the travelling of five and more miles to church over bleak roads oftener without roads as with a single good one. Yet this was our case as well as all our neighbours in the outlying parts on the Ettrick side of Yarrow parish, and thought nothing of it. We were distant I think about four miles from Yarrow kirk, and summer and winter our family were pretty regular attenders there - generally in a cart with sacks of straw to sit on, and in fine weather the young took a nearer road on foot - except when the weather was stormy, and in those cases our Sunday observance was restricted by our pious mother to reading "gude books" from the family bookshelf.

As to our father, he was of a more liberal turn, and was more inclined to give the children some latitude in useful knowledge as natural history and astronomy, and this he often delighted to do, as well as our mother, for both were well-read and had got good education. My father, although without a single particle of music, was one of the finest readers I have ever heard; in fact, it was a treat of no ordinary kind to hear him read some of the sublime passages in the Old Testament as the Book of Job or the prophesies of Isaiah, but he hated cant, and the putting-on of that sanctimonious air on Sundays so common with Calvinists. On the contrary he always inclined to do his religion in works of charity to his neighbours, but I am afraid latterly he got into a habit about this time of preferring a quiet stroll on Sundays and studying the works of the great Creator to sitting from two to three hours in Yarrow kirk listening to the prosy [dull] old doctor. I think there were a few others in the congregation of the same way of thinking for I began to notice the absence of many of the familiar faces, and among these the Ettrick Shepherd.

I do not mean for a moment to disparage the venerable old Dr [Robert] Russell, who was as kindly and genial a man as you could meet in any parish minister on the Borders, but old age was dealing with him and at this time he was was lapsing into the prosy state so well described by Balwhidder in the *Annals of the Parish* when he did not know *when to stop*.[67] In this state was the doctor about this last year of my attendance — the sermon and lecture were delivered without any interval, and it was so long a diet to the young, that there were few who were not wearied out before the termination if they were not sound asleep. A joyful event was the end of the service, and was always heralded by the barking of the shepherds' dogs, who thus expressed their sense of the happy conclusion.

The doctor always pronounced the blessing with the congregation keeping their seats, and I believe this plan was begun by him for the purpose of cheating the dogs. But the dogs were not to be cheated, the first solitary bark got up about the end of the sermon, then it was taken up by others till the blessing, when it had

---

[67] 1821 novel by John Galt, narrated by the Reverend Micah Balwhidder, a vain, deluded and self-important minister.

In *Reminiscences of Yarrow*, James Russell, who succeeded Robert as minister, describes his father thus: "His commanding appearance and benevolent expression and dignified bearing at all times won the respect of his people; and when on a sacramental occasion he walked out in his court dress and cocked hat and powdered hair, there was something more striking and venerable in the eyes of his rural flock. I have often heard the Ettrick Shepherd speak of it with admiration ... ."

reached its climax in a grand general bark of jubilation all over the church from floor to galleries. Of course, the shepherds' dogs, who knew every word their masters said, knew also of the doctor's ending his sermon or lecture, and were not to be gulled by this maneuver. It was laughable to see some of the younger ones not even content with this, but they must also in a frolic of youth scour [rush about] the passages, leaping over one another and barking with all their might in the height of their glee. I always noticed the dogs were worse in the summertime — no doubt, in dog wisdom, they considered how much better they would have been on the hill-side, to sitting here listening to a decorous continual pouring forth, instead of the hearty "Yeo-he-yo-o" of their masters.

But there was sometimes a worse breach of decorum in the canine section of the congregation, and that was a free fight. The long passage of the church in front of the pulpit was always selected for this purpose by the dogs and so accustomed was the old doctor to this frolic of the dogs that he usually stopped his discourse and stood complacently till the fight was over and silence restored. As to putting the combatants out, it was never thought of, from the well-known fact that the shepherd and his dog could not be parted, even in church, and that, if once put out, the fray would be worse outside. So minister and people just resigned themselves to the least of the evils, altho it had an occasional skirmish.

The shepherd's dog in the main is not a fighting quarrelsome dog, on the contrary he is rather gentle and timid, but very sagacious and sensitive to any affront. Now as I used to loiter in the Churchyard like the herds[men] and their masters before the church went in, and a pleasant weekly gossip it was to them. I used to sit on a through-stone [flat gravestone] watching the gambols of the dogs and every fresh comer as he entered the gate. From studying the various groups of people and their dogs, I came to have a theory of my own about how the shepherds' dogs came to fight in the church, when it was so rare to see them fight anywhere else, and it is this.

The Sunday morning at church was a pleasant meeting place, fathers met sons and daughters, friends met friends who joined each other from the distant parts of this moorland parish laying in Ettrick and Yarrow. Hearty were the congratulations as they met each other in the churchyard and formed into groups to have a kindly crack till the minister made his appearance from the manse when, as he passed through among them, there was a friendly recognition on both sides.

Now while noticing this, I never failed at the same time to observe a somewhat familiar deportment among the dogs — they too recognized friends they had not seen since last Sunday. First, there was a brisk approach to each other, then in a upright posture of the neck as they approached each other, the head level till they were close enough to rub noses, the tail wagging in jerky fashion all the while; then a mutual snuffing of the hinder-end, and away they would scour around the church in great glee and friendship.

Another class would approach each other, not with such genial friendship, and out of this class came the fighting. You might observe two dogs making a slow approach to each other with their birses [hackles] gradually rising, as they with seeming reluctance grew nearer; then coming alongside, instead of the friendly kiss of peace by smelling noses, the heads would slowly slide along each others' broadsides till noses reached tails, when after a contemptuous snuff on both sides they would stop a yard apart, and vigorously spurt up the grass, then leg up and strone [pee] on a stone, eying each other wickedly at the same time uttering some savage growls, which is neither more nor less than fearful oaths "that, if it were not for certain circumstances, they would annihilate each other on the spot."

Now, very likely, at the clipping [sheep shearing] the other day the stranger has given mortal offense by showing his superiority on strange ground and humiliating him in the eyes of his master - and, it may be, his harem of ladies - and the dishonour can only be wiped out by the satisfaction of taking out of his skin, but not in this public place in the gaze of decent dogs and men. No, "stop till I catch him below the pews in the church out of sight and see if I don't teach the audacious mongrel better manners." Such was my theory of how they came to fight in church, although the weekly meeting was generally pleasant and peaceful among the shepherds' dogs, yet there were more or less a few individuals who had accounts of their weekday transactions to square. I remember one of these fights being almost attended with something serious, but as it turned out there was no harm done.[68]

*

There was a half-wit, and a very regular attender he was at the kirk summer and winter; his name was "Daft Jock" — not the Jock Gray of whom I have mentioned for his musical gifts, but John Scott, one of three bachelor brothers who were in the lease of Gilmanscleuch farm, and who was also known by the popular name of "Daft Jock o' Gilmanscleuch." Jock was a man of portentous stature and strength — I should say he must have measured at least 6-6 in his stockings. He would sit pretty fair and decent for some time till he tired, and then there was no end to Jock's "mollops" [mannerisms]. Sometimes he would take his knife out of his pocket and open and shut it a hundred times till he caught the eye of perhaps us youngsters watching him, then the fun began. Jock would carefully gather his auld plaid about him and over his head, leaving a small hole to keek out of, then you got a peep of the knife now and then - drawn back and forwards, sometimes shut, sometimes open - and at times a halfpenny for the [collection] box stuck into the handle. Then he would take a keek out to see if you were paying attention and thus Jock wiled away the time, till something else took his fancy, such as turning himself hind-side foremost and taking a seat composedly on the pew, to take stock of who and what was behind him. But of all Jock's recreations in church, watching the dogs formed always the principal share, and I daresay it might be to accommodate

---

[68] In *Reminiscences of Yarrow*, James Russell gives a corroboratory account of canine chaos in the kirk:
"... the strife was free and furious, the noise became deafening, the voice of the minister was literally drowned, and he was fain to pause, whether in preaching or in prayer. Two or three shepherds had to leave their places and use their nibbies [sticks] unmercifully before the rout was quelled, and the service of the sanctuary resumed. ... Old Mr Scott of Eldinhope used to relate how Dr Cramond bade the old beadle, Sandy Rae, put out the noisy delinquents and got for an answer, "I dinna like to meddle wi' the folks' dogs, sir;" somewhat more polite than another rejoinder, "I'm no gaun to get mysel bitten: they may put them out that brought them in."

Jock in his foibles and give more freedom to his huge body that he always got the open end of the seat to himself.

Now it was evident from Jock's bearing to the different dogs who were constantly sliding up and down the passage that he not only knew every one of them, but that he had strong sympathies and antipathies to sundry of them. This would be expressed by a sudden knitting of his shaggy eyebrows and a grasping of his kent [crook] as the dog passed him, while another - a favourite - would catch Jock's eye, gazing with a comical smile at him. Of course Tyne or Help understood the sign and would respond with a perceptible movement of his tail as he passed, but when a fight took place, then Jock was in his glory — his interest in the combatants was intense as he then rose from the sitting posture and, kent in hand, reared his bulk half over the next pew. It was to such a fight as this that I have alluded and when Jock in this posture was watching the fray of some four or six dogs worrying and rolling along the passage towards him, the ominous kent now raised aloft to punish some dog he did not like, then lowered and raised again, till at last down it came with a whack, not on the dogs but on the opposite pew, slightly grazing the shoulder of a decent-looking old man, who might very easily have been felled on the spot, but who fortunately escaped by a hair breadth. Jock assumed a comical air of amazement and sat down, but ever afterwards he was confined in the other end of the Gilmanscleuch seat.

*

There was another "oddity" in the Yarrow congregation at this time, who seemed to be a never-failing centre of amusement to all the lads and lasses, whom you might have seen grouped around him in the Churchyard till the bell rang. This was Adam Dalgleish of Glowerowen or, as he was commonly called, "Sir Adam."

Sir Adam and his brother were small farmers in this peculiar-named place and I believe, altho both were competent enough in all business transactions and work on the farm, yet both had a "craze" like Don Quixote. Particularly Adam, who kept up a great correspondence with the princesses of the royal family, in the firm belief that there was rivalry for his hand and that he was destined, if not for king or prince consort, to be at least a great personage by marriage. Hence the weekly gatherings round Sir Adam in the churchyard to hear the news and progress of his latest negotiations — generally conveyed to him by good-sized letters with large red seals on them. Of course the lads and lasses of the Watergate were the authors of the correspondence and a never-failing fund of amusement.

Adam once went to Dr Russell for advice as to which royal princess he should take, he having received in the same week two remarkable-looking letters - gilt edges and something like royal arms on the seals - and each letter professing the same ardent love and overtures of marriage. The doctor, after carefully looking over the letters, inside and outside, and hearing Sir Adam's object in seeking his advice thus delivered himself, rather as it were soliloquising: "Poor deluded creature! And what a shame for a parcel of idle fellows to write these letters and impose on one who is just a maniac!"

"What d'ye say sir?" seizing his documents out of the doctor's hand and rushing to the door, "What d'ye mean by ca'aing [calling] me a mad man? My faith, but the first thing I'll du - after ah'm married - wull be to send doon a regiment and pit you oot o' Yarrow manse and clap ye up in a verra different place — that'll learn ye better manners, than to speak evil o' dignitaries — ye'll believe it than whan it's oot o' time." Exit Sir Adam in great wrath and the doctor never after meddled with him.

The last time I saw Sir Adam was about the year 1839 while a party of friends were on a "pic-nic" to St Mary's and I then made a pretty good sketch of him which I afterwards transferred to oil. As the incident has a comic feature, as well as showing the ruling passion of the man to the last, I shall relate it. We were a party of some nine or ten, four being ladies. As we got to to Yarrow Yews, one of the party wished us to stop for a few minutes till he made a call on a friend who lived in a house by the roadside. Presently the woman of the house came out and invited us all in, particularly the ladies to get a drink of milk, and so after the refreshment as we were preparing to re-mount, says this woman: "Wad ye no like to see Sir Adam afore ye leave?"

"Who is Sir Adam?" says one of our party. Suddenly I minded the days of old in Yarrow kirkyard, and says I: "By all means, we must see Sir Adam" - I had no thought that he still lived - "does he still believe in letters from great personages?" "The same as ever — he got one, he says, the other day from Lady Ann Hamilton [claimant to the throne of Scotland]. Shall I ask him down? says this woman. Yes, says we, and she bawls upstairs: "Sir Adam — cum down: Here is a lot o' fine leddies hae cum to see ye — and among them is Leddy Ann and the Duchess."

"Aye-aye — ah'll be doun enow [just now]" cried a voice, coming, to judge from the voice, from some faraway place or from the chimney above. "He is seeking his papers, oot the barrel where he keeps them," says our host — "and here he comes." My friends I observed were puzzled what to make of this, till the door opens and enter Sir Adam, a little squat old man carrying a mass of papers below his arm, not so tidy in his dress as I minded him. He had knee-breeks but no straps to them in the usual way, and the consequence of that was that a goodly margin of shirt was shown around his middle. After Sir Adam had made a shambling sort of bow to the ladies, he thus introduced himself: "Now leddies, although ah've been expekting ye — ye've taen me unawares this morning for ah've been away wi a cow to the bull and haena gotten masel changed yet, sae ye maun excuse ma appearance i' the first place, on that account ..."

*

When the kirk at length "skailed" [broke up] there was a mustering of horses and carts at the common stable, besides which there was also stone steps for the accommodation of ladies who rode on a pillion behind the gudemen [farmers]. This fashion has been long disused, but was quite common at country kirks in those days. In our haste to get home we only took the use of the cart across the narrow gothic bridge below the kirk and then footed it up Kershope hollow, till we got to the top of the "Swire" [hollow between hills] from which we took a near-cut by footpath past Kirkhope Tower to Ettrick Brig-End, leaving the old people to come on at their leisure in the slower conveyance of the old mare and cart.

I never was partial to Yarrow in my young days. There were no trees like we had in Ettrick, and besides there was a silence and a melancholy aspect about it that you felt as soon as you descended from Kershope Swire. I recollect a peculiar aspect I often noticed in the summer and autumn months, as we looked from the height, and that was the whole valley shrouded in mist — Deuchar Law and Lewingshope rising out of it like islands in a "waveless sea" and the stillness, only broken now and then by the bleating of sheep, which you heard afar off but could not see. The scene never failed to impress me with its weird supernatural character, and years after, when I came to read Hogg's *Kilmeny* [1813] I recognised how he may have got the image and its perfect truth in the lines:

> As still was her look and as still was her e'e
> As the floweret that grows on the emerant lea
> Or the mist that hands over a waveless sea[69]

*

Our immediate neighbours among the farmers were two Patersons - Thomas and John - in Helmburn; Mr Gibson of Shaws, who was my father's fast friend and bosom crony; Mr Scott of Kirkhope; Mr Gideon Scott of Singlee; Cunningham of Newhouse and Mr Beattie of Oakwood who farmed also Hutherburn and Whitehillbrae, and Dalgliesh of Fauldshope.

In this pastoral district where there was no more corn grown than what served for home use, the farms being principally for sheep, there was of course a good deal of idle time on the masters' hands. Lambing time, clipping, smearing

---

[69] Evidently quoting the lines from memory, AC gets them slightly wrong. They should read:

> As the stillness that lay on the emerant lea,
> Or the mist that sleeps on a waveless sea

The mistake is rectified in the version of the paragraph that ran under the heading *The Melancholy of Yarrow* in the *Border Counties' Magazine*.

[treating the fleece with a tar-and-grease compound to protect it from damp and pests] and attending the sale market being the only stirring events and special times which demanded superintendence. There was consequently a good deal of spare time, generally filled up by a shot of the "grews" [grouse] occasionally, for mostly all took out the license, fishing, reading - there were few who had not a share in Selkirk library and got their books up weekly or fortnightly - and chiefly of all, visiting at each other's houses to get a crack over the news of the week and over the indispensable tumbler.

These meetings would often look like mere accident or business, such as: "I think I will take a step up and see if Shaws has heard ony thing o' Lockerbie mercat [market], and I daresay I may tak the gun — maybe get a shot i' the hame coming." So "Shaws" would be met on his own hillside - and mutual expressions of how fortunate - and they were just wearying [longing] to see each other. As to the business, very likely it was never at the time mentioned or, if it was, it would be settled in five minutes, but "Ye wull just gang in a get a bit denner, and than we will gang oer to the loch and hae a shot among the wild ducks or blackgame [black grouse]." The house is gained, the success and the tramp through the heath putting both parties in the best of spirits and appetite, and "We maun [must] hae a tumbler and a crack afore ye take the road." So, after a little haggling, the neighbour is prevailed on to take "just ane", and presently Singlee lands by the merest accident to enquire when "ye're gaun to smear" as he can spare his hands, so this leads on to a lively talk about tar — its price and where to get it, and how to "meng" [mix?] it, etc, etc. Then ensues some remarks about "crocks" [old ewes] it might be, or "are ye gaun to eat yer turnips" — "what's the price o' them eenow?"

This was all very business-like but, by the time of the second tumbler, the crack got more lively and took a higher range than "crocks" and "tar" — droll anecdotes, politics, literature and the last new novel, presently it would be, "Hae seen the last *Blackwood*?" for they were all Conservative and read *Blackwood*.[70]

---

[70] *Blackwood's Magazine*, first published 1817, Tory counterpart to the Whig-supported *Edinburgh Review*.

"Lord man! What a bitch they are making o' Jamie Hogg i' the *Noctes*. I can weel beleeve that — they say that the Mrs [the Shepherd's wife, Margaret] is perfectly wild." Here would follow the quotation from the *Noctes*.[71]

"Ma hind [herdsman] cam frae him at Mt Yerra, and he gie's me a puir account o' Mount Benger stock — besides, the man's eaten up wi' visitors, no to speak o' his time taen up — he never saw his clipping this year!"[72]

"Weel, if he doesna do it by his buiks [books] — it'll no be the lambs and the woo'"

"Let's drink his health gentlemen - in a bumper - "for he is a famous gudefellow."[73]

By the fourth tumbler, there would be great glee and elevation of the spirits — nothing they could not accomplish, from the office of prime minister and managing the affairs of the nation, down to the Selkirkshire Yeomanry or clearing off the burgh debt, when at last they would disperse with a tryst [appointment] for another nicht — which was pretty sure to be in no great length of time after, only varied by a similar nicht at a different place.

*

Our long winter evenings — I love to dwell on the pleasant memory of them, as we sat in the little cosy parlour around the table, piled with books, mother at one side of the fire with her little work-table knitting stockings for the little feet of Jean, Andrew and Henrietta - for John, William and George had not yet entered on the stage of life – our father opening up the green bag with the new-come batch of books from Selkirk library, and preparing to read aloud something very interesting

---

[71] *Noctes Ambrosianae*, Ambrosian Nights, a series of 71 fictional conversations, published in *Blackwood's Magazine* from 1823 to 1835, in which James Hogg appears in the character of The Ettrick Shepherd, "an enthusiastic drinker and a man of supreme social tactlessness" who "utters various nuggets of pawky wisdom."

[72] Mount Benger was the farm on which Hogg was the tenant, "a most disastrous speculation ... involving the poet in difficulties at his very outset, and ending in ruin ..."

[73] A bumper is defined as "a generous glassful of an alcoholic drink, typically one drunk as a toast."

till supper-time, when the mill ford has to be burned [ie, lit up at night, to attract fish] and there is sure to be fish, which mother dearly loves and is longing for; the men saw them at the darkening when they were watering the horses. He sits on his favourite homely sofa, not a haircloth, but stuffed with hay, and covered with something of a dark red colour, which can stand a little rough usage and look none the worse. Occasionally he takes a nap on it with the plaid drawn over him, but not now, for the excitement of seeing the new books and pictures keeps everyone lively.

Between the old couple is the cheery peat fire, and the hearth rug has its little wood chairs and baby Henrietta; beside her, the old grey cat brought by our mother after her marriage. Above the plain mantlepiece hangs a picture in a round gilt frame not of large size, but beautifully executed; it is Melrose Abbey, nearby is a tree, and among the foliage a small bird singing. The work is cut in white paper on a grey ground, and the artist is our mother; another and larger work by her hangs on the side wall facing the front window and above a folding tea-table. This is the two halves of the terrestrial globe, at a little distance it looks like a large engraving with the letterpress even to very small words neatly and sharply printed. Yet it is not an engraving but a piece of sewed work of various colors showing land and sea - equator lines - the whole work on a ground of light fawn-coloured silk and well executed.

Between this picture at the extremities of the wall are two closets, the one nearest the fire father's bedroom, the other with shelves for jugs and crockery, candle box and an old army shelved press for sundries. Above all, the family collection of books, which comprise Josephus [Jewish historian whose works were more widely read than any book other than the Bible], Mathew Henry's commentaries [on the Bible], Blair's sermons, Guthrie's [Geographical] Grammar, [Isaac] Newton on the Prophesies, Pilgrim's Progress, etc, etc, perhaps 150 books altogether.

On the wall at the door hung an engraving of Duke Henry [probably Henry Scott, Duke of Buccleuch, their landlord], and this completed the pictures of our parlour at Howford. First among our juvenile books - which never failed to interest and amuse - were three very small but neat and substantial volumes, a present from uncle William to each of us and having our names on the fly-leaf. These were the little pictorial Bible, with short bible stories, costumes of all the nations in the world, and the third Animated Nature or pictures of beasts, birds and fishes [*A History of the Earth and Animated Nature, Oliver Goldsmith, 1774*].

When we tired of the parlour, we took a spell in the kitchen, where the entertainment was of a different but equally interesting sort, for as a buxom lass plied the muckle wheel while her neighbour was carding by the peat fire, she would start in song, sometimes some favourite by Hogg as "When the King comes home," but oftener something more local and by some humbler bard — such as "the Carterhaugh la'", or "the bachelors of Gilmanscleuch":

> Led on by haverel [foolish] John
> May count their fingers o'er and o'er
> The bonny lassie's gone ...

Then it would be ghost stories and the last wraith. This was perhaps the most common subject of the winter evenings of these days for superstition had yet a strong hold on all classes, and many a place near by us had its ghost, brownie [goblin] or fairies, to disbelieve these was the mark of a regardless man. I can remember yet of the number of stories of Boston and the Deil [Devil], and how he laid [exorcised] the pedlar's ghost of Thirlestane Mill.[74] The Deil was always worsted in these encounters with Boston, I have seen us get into mortal terror - durst not go to bed alone - after these stories of ghosts and goblins.

*

Our father would often come dropping ben [ie, into the inner part of the house] to get his smoke and, by some witty remark, would spoil a good story about ghosts,

---

[74] Rev. Thomas Boston, 1676-1732, author and minister of the parish of Ettrick for quarter of a century.

for he professed to be above superstition, and always to make good game out of the subject. On one of these occasions I mind of an old crone remonstrating with him something like this: "I didna say ah've saw it masel, but I had it frae decent John Richardson o' Singlee, wha had it frae the man a't saw it atween Hope House and Tushielaw, it canna be doubted, an awesome sicht atweel [indeed], and hanna been seen afore, sin' the days of the sainted Boston, ah've heard he laid it — but ye ken maister, it's no sae lang sin yersel saw a coffin at the Boggle burn ... ."

Here, my father would hastily knock the ashes out of his pipe, and beat a retreat with some jocular remark. When he was out of earshot you might have heard a chuckle, and some such remark as "I hae pitten a flea in his lug, I jalbose [suppose]."

In after years I learned from my father himself about this ghost, which he encountered on Huntly Loan. It was one of his good stories, which he could afterwards afford to laugh at then, altho at the time it occurred I have no doubt that there would be a good laugh at his cost. It happened as follows:

My father had walked down to Selkirk market, sometime about the Martinmas [11 November]. After doing his business he prepared to take the road home immediately, as the days were short and the nights at that time very dark. However, he happened to encounter his old friend and crony Mr Grieve of Howden, who pressed him to take tea and maybe a tumbler, which was at once agreed to. Now, gentle reader, I am not altogether sure whether the tumbler part of the story did not extend to more than one, seeing that when my father encountered this ghost after he left Mr Grieve's hospitable board, the time turned out to be on the borders of twelve midnight, whereas the two worthies had their tea at the usual hour about five. I used to ponder in my own mind thus: Here are about seven hours, and it is absurd - at least in my way of reasoning - to suppose that there was only one tumbler and an animated crack all this time. But be this as it may, and I leave others to form their own opinion about this, my father would never admit there was any more than "a tumbler."

Well, at last Mr Grieve lighted him out to the door with a candle: "If ye wunna be prevailed on to tak a bed," said he, "gude nicht, but "tak tent o' [watch out for] the gutter [mud] syne [after] the midden - haud [keep] to the left when ye're through the yett [gate], aince ye're fairly on the hill road — Lord, but it's derk, derk!" And so, with a hearty shake of the hand, my father found himself on the road home over the old Ettrick road by Huntly Loan, as it is yet called, a road running in a bee-line up one brae and down another, in contempt of the modern system.

Dark indeed and a dreich [dreary] road at midnight, not to speak of the Boggle Burn to cross, which all decent kirk-gaun folk avoided after dark. But my father scouted [scoffed at] such nonsense. Moreover, he was a stout bold man and in his prime, and he had with him a mastiff dog, his constant companion, which he used to boast "wad face the deil himsel."

When he was fairly on the road, however, he picked his way much better as the wind began to rise and to dispel to some extent the pitch darkness. By the time he got to take the incline down to the deep hollow of the Boggle Burn it was lighter and he thought he would take a seat for a few minutes on the old substantial stile at the march of Middlestead. And so, as he sat and enjoyed his ease very comfortably, he took out his frizzel [flint] and match with the intention of having a smoke, laughing heartily the while at some of Mr Grieve's droll stories. Click! click! went the frizzle, and the sparks flew about, just enough to make the gloom more profound, when suddenly the mastiff, which had been running on before, rushed behind his master as if he were chased for his life, and uttered a stifled growl of terror.

"What the deil's the matter wi the dog?" said my father, as he put down his hand on the dog and felt it trembling behind him, its birses [hackles] all on end. "Watch! — You that's sic a brave dog, what ails ye? Is is beast or body?

"Growl-owl!" replied Watch, in a low tremulous tone, at the same time licking his master's hand, and whining in a coaxing way at intervals.

"Na, na Watch, I wunna gang back till I ken better what it is. Sae if ye are feared, I'll gae forward mysel'."

My father straightened himself up and, grasping his stout staff, steps boldly down the brae, the old dog dropping behind some yards, with the same plaintive note of warning or remonstrance. "I can't comprehend this by any means," said my father to himself; "that there is a something before us is without a doot, and that this something is no canny [ie, is unnatural] is another fact, else sic a wise and brave dog wad never gie this warning and, Faith! now I think on't, this place gets a bad name. Tuts! auld wife's clavers [tales]! I wish it may be — ahem!"

The little insignificant rivulet was at length reached without scaith. My father stood before crossing it, to consider the situation ere he went further. The mastiff has now dropped considerably behind, still keeping up the same plaintive whining.

"That's curious," thought my father, "but the nicht's a good deal lichter, and if there is anything I will see it now between me and the sky, up that straight road." So he boldly stepped across the brook and lies down on his belly on the grassy path, having a tolerable view against the leaden sky, of any object not of very small size on the road before him, and the vizzy [view] as he slowly rose from his posture was *not satisfactory*.

My father, I may mention, was a man of the sharpest vision: indeed, I often thought those grey eyes of his had a double power of most people, whether in daylight or dark. Often have I seen him point out a fish in rough water, when no on else could see it, and he would tell you its weight to a pound, which would be wonderfully verified after he had thrown his liester [pronged spear used for fishing] through it and brought it to bank. So, when he had carefully scanned this uphill road, his bold bearing all at once gives way to some symptoms of fear and uncertainty, as he soliliquised:

"I kenned there must be something - the dog's richt - but what's to be done? Lord, lord, I wish I had never come to this road the nicht! *Shall I go back?* Maybe ah'm mista'en and ma imagination at o'er great a distance, gars [makes] me think — it's a-a coffin! But it looks awfully like ane, and there is naebody dead i' the place — that's waur [worse]! Afore I turn, I'll step forret [forward] a bit and get a better vizzy at the horrid thing — if I dinna ..."

Now my father, a man who was, as phrenologists say, high in size and weight, committed here a great mistake, which I can only account for from the excitement of the occasion. As for the toddy, it must have been quite evaporated. But the fact is, he had miscalculated his distance and no sooner had he squatted down to reconnoitre than - oh horror! - he is within five yards of the coffin! And a coffin it surely is, of gigantic size; more, it has a man's head projecting from it.

At this moment the dog Watch, in the distance, utters another melancholy howl and my father's hair almost raises the very hat on his head. At this crisis, I rather think my father took to his prayers; at any rate I inferred so, for, imagining that the coffin was going to overwhelm him, he sprang to his feet, and with uplifted staff and invoking the name of the Almighty, demanded of the gruesome sight who and what it was.

The coffin turned sharply round, a white shape like a man's face staring from it, and said:

"Lord keep me! Mr Cuther — is that your voice?"

Now I have protested all my life against my father's taste in changing the good old family name of Curror to Currie, which the old people - and the coffin among them - had corrupted into what he could not endure, viz, Cuther. But as that would doubtless be the last of his thoughts at the time and lead me to diverge from my tale, I shall let it drop.

"Who or what are ye?" roared my father.

"Mey? Ah'm Wat Grieve o' the Brig-End," answered the other. "The stupid cadger [pedlar] brought up the warks o' ma knock [ie, the workings of my (grandfather) clock] frae Selkirk, but he forgot the case — sae ah just set off i' the darkening for't and here ah'm wi't on ma shouther [shoulder]!"[75]

*   *   *

---

[75] The *Border Counties' Magazine* contains a very similar version of this story, entitled *The Gruesome Sight My Father Saw*.

WRITINGS TWO

DIARY 1830

To Patrick S. Lang Esq. This selection of leaves from my diary showing the history of a day forty-four years ago in its incidents, recreations and reflections is inscribed with much esteem and respect by Andrew Currie, June 1874.

Saturday June __ 1830 [when AC was aged 18]

From Denholm to Howford, a matter of 15 lang dreich [dreary] miles. The route this time is by Hornshole Brig, Appletree Hall, Grindstone Edge, Ashkirk, Woolrig

[Woll Rig], Outer Huntly, home to Howford — resting places for my notes or pencillings as inclination directs. True, the road is long but what of it, the day is fine and calm and haven't I laid in a stock of literature to beguile the time — last issue of *Chambers's Journal, Penny Mag.,* etc.[76]

Hornshole, my first resting place

A pedestrian, especially if he rambles alone, as has been my practice and preference since my young days with dominie Morton of the "Brig-End" [Ettrickbridge End], should in particular places "be unto himself good company." I think I must have seen that in old Walton [Izaak Walton (1593-1683), author of *The Compleat Angler*], but whoever is the author of the sentiment, it suits my nature - morbid you may call it reader - but if he, a solitary pedestrian on a long journey, does thus learn to depend on himself for society, he will soon care little for the want of any other. To parody a saying of some old sage, "You must for yourself, to be company for yourself, prepare to entertain yourself." And this is best done by learning to draw all the entertainment possible out of present circumstances, be they ever so uninviting; besides, it imparts a cheerfulness and lightens the way.

There is wisdom in the old English ditty [from Shakespeare's *The Winter's Tale*]

> Jog on, jog on the footpath way
> And merrily hent [jump] the stile-a
> A merry heart goes all the way
> Your sad tires in a mile-a

[76] *Chambers's Edinburgh Journal* was a weekly magazine started by William Chambers in 1832, price one penny. Topics covered included history, religion, language, and science. *The Penny Magazine* was an illustrated weekly aimed at the working class. Charles Knight created it for the Society for the Diffusion of Useful Knowledge in response to *Chambers's Edinburgh Journal*, which started two months earlier. This means that the diary, or at least parts of it, were written later than the stated date.

Hornshole Brig and the How Mill

I believe that story about the "Heroes of Hawick" and the taking of a flag from the English at this spot is all rubbish and moonshine — can't find any notice of it in history.[77] It is different with Selkirk and the "weavers' dishclout" or Flodden flag.

But to my reading of *Chamber's*: this seems a capital number, the first article being about Sir W[alter] Scott & William Laidlaw [poet, son of a border farmer, steward and amanuensis to Scott], "Laidlaw's acquaintance with Scott in the Autumn of 1802."

Blackhouse, a solitary and interesting spot is, with its complement of traditions - ruined tower, or the Tower of Douglas - the scene of the tragedy.[78]

Laidlaw prepared for Scott's mission. He had heard it from a Selkirk man in Edinburgh, Mr Andrew Mercer. I knew him very well, cousin Robert [Park?] used at school to mimic his auctioneering expressions: "going at six-and-six — any ... man ... more bid." He had a brother, a fine miniature painter whom I hear my mother spoke much about as having been at Lorrimer's school in the Kirkwynd with him.[79]

But to my article: "Hogg and his Uncle Will [Laidlaw] of Shawhope — Scott and Leyden duly appeared at Blackhouse."[80]

---

[77] The story goes that in 1514, the year after the crushing defeat of the Scots at Flodden, a large party of English raiders were wreaking havoc in the Borders. At Hornshole, less than a mile east of Hawick, the young men of the town fell on the English as they slept. The lads captured the battle standard of their enemy, and rode back into town, the banner proudly held aloft in defiance.

[78] The tragic story is told in a ballad in Scott's *Minstrelsy of the Scottish Border*. Lady Margaret Douglas fell in love with Lord William Douglas, a man disliked by her family. The couple escaped to Blackhouse Tower, but were pursued there by her father and his seven sons. William defeated them one by one and, though he survived, he was seriously hurt and died in his lover's arms. Lady Margaret, unable to bear the loss of her lover and her family, died of grief and was buried alongside William in St Mary's churchyard.

[79] Andrew Mercer was born in Selkirk in 1775. At Edinburgh University he was the classmate and friend of John Leyden, also numbering among his early associates Mungo Park. Mercer attempted to establish himself in the capital as a miniature-painter and a man of letters but was unsuccessful at both.

[80] Laidlaw met Sir Walter Scott in 1801. Looking for material for his *Minstrelsy* Scott went to Ettrick. John Leyden directed him to Blackhouse farm. There, Laidlaw introduced Scott to

How curious when I think that I am at present working at millwright's work in the house where Leyden was born — an interesting article truly. I must read the remainder as I descend Grindstone Edge, for the day is getting on and only two miles made.

Appletree-hall village

There is nothing of any consequence here, except a picturesque creeshie [crushing] mill on a bank of fine trees — a wheel of what I heard called "bevel" keeps constantly running outside the gable: what can be the meaning of this wheel kept running and doing nothing?[81]

Memo to enquire: This bank and its burn winding below the green trees is just one of these spots which it is refreshing to fall in with on a long dusty road. I like the spot. But about wheels, this reminds me of my master's message to my father "to see if it is convenient to him to meet at Selkirk on Wednesday next to sign my indenture."

Ah, this is the skeleton in my house, the lion in the path to mar my enjoyment of this beautiful June day. I suppose the thing is too far gone now to retract — can't see how I can do it. Cousin John [Lang] tells me last Sunday that "he has it written out," he is going on with his, so is Jonny Anderson with his Uncle Henry and so, as our hunting days seem to be over, and the realities of life coming on I may as well. No I can't, but must do nothing rash. Meantime I will resign myself, although I have a qualm of regret in not taking old Mr Dalgleish's offer when at Campsie [Stirlingshire]. "Go over all the shops in the yard, I will apprentice you to any you like, but I think the pattern shop for designs would suit you best". Well, well, the past can't be helped, I accept the situation and will make the most of it, wrong vocation though it be, so I will shelve this disagreeable subject by recording a laughable mater in connection.

James Hogg, the Ettrick Shepherd. Laidlaw took down a ballad from Will, the Shepherd's uncle. Leyden (1775–1811) was an orientalist who helped Scott collect materials.
[81] A bevel wheel is a toothed wheel whose working face is oblique to the axis.

Last winter, when domiciled with uncle William, our family - and these were happy days - consisted of my bachelor uncle, his strong-minded virago of a housekeeper, Jenny Cranston from Teviotside, myself and dog Peter. Says uncle one night: "Andrew, a good idea strikes me — to go down to Dr John Scott's with you tomorrow and have your head examined. This phrenology is getting to be a wonderful science and the doctor has it all at his finger-ends. Without a doubt his verdict will confirm us all in making you an engineer, I am sure you have constructiveness much developed."[82]

I had a few days before found among lumber in a closet, a curious old clock with an alarm apparatus. The thing had probably been bought at a sale among other lumber, but I noticed that it was of superior workmanship and only needed a few simple repairs to set a-going. So by dint of a little patience and ingenuity, I had it in order and put up in Jenny's kitchen. It went beautifully and I attached the alarm apparatus for 12 midnight, but at midnight, what an unearthly sound! I was startled myself and it would not cease — at any rate, I believe it carried on for 15 minutes. I heard uncle ringing the bell and crying "What the Devil is that?" Certainly the old thing uttered a sound like a shriek, which I never heard imitated before or since. The best of it was Jenny made my uncle believe that I had contrived this apparatus, and he was evidently proud of my gifts of construction.

In due course next morning we called on Dr Scott, he examined my head carefully and long. Uncle, a little anxious, says: "You will find constructiveness large, doctor?" "Not particularly," says he. "Indeed — what profession do you think he is best fitted for?" "Well, I should say a soldier." "God help me — What? We intend him to be an engineer!" I believe we both collapsed some, and I noticed from a remark he made that it was "possible phrenology might yet be [proved] wrong."

---

[82] "Constructiveness" in phrenology - the study of the shape and size of the cranium as a supposed indication of character and mental abilities - was said to be the seat of initiative, creativity and originality. Located on the temples, it supposedly confers "the capacity to plan and construct, to design and invent, to organise and devise ways and means of carrying out projects with ingenuity and dexterity." Edinburgh was a centre of phrenological expertise: the Edinburgh Phrenological Society was established in 1820.

What a change from the refined society of No 118 Princess Street to Denholm and its radical stocking makers.[83] There we had books from the advocate's library - Chateaubriand was the last I read - *Blackwood's Mag*, as it came out, and then the jolly bachelor parties and the capital anecdotes.[84]

I liked Graeme Bell the best as he and I never tired of a fishing crack. Even dog Peter had his share of enjoyment on these occasions and mounted the sofa, despite the warning fist of Jenny as she went out and in, when you might have heard Peter's curses uttered in a very low growl. Of course he knew that, for the time being, he was a petted and privileged member of the party, but the revengeful Jenny never failed to let him know at time convenient her opinion on the subject by such convincing arguments as drove him usually to me for protection.

What a number of men of note there are just now and many of them in Edinburgh, Sir Walter in the height of his fame, often I saw him last winter sitting listless in the Court of Session. John Wilson, professor of moral philosophy, I never tired of seeing and hearing him, truly in physique a grand man.

---

[83] The stocking industry was introduced to Denholm village at the end of the eighteenth century. It prospered and by 1837 it is recorded that most of the inhabitants were stocking makers. Hosiers included AC's future father-in-law, George Hardie.

[84] François-René de Chateaubriand (1768–1848), French writer, politician, diplomat and historian. Although AC had learned schoolboy French, this would likely have been the English translation of *Travels in Greece, Palestine, Egypt and Barbary, during the years 1806 and 1807*, published in 1814.

Sir W[illiam] Hamilton in Metaphisicks, [Francis] Jeffrey and his maintaining the cause of intellectual progress in the *Edin[burgh] Review*, [Thomas] De Quincey, dreaming strange dreams, Dr [David McBeth] Moir, the "Delta" of Maga, James Hogg, Professor [John] Leslie, with his short dumpy figure and piebald hair, [Robert] Jameson, professor of mineralogy and natural history, it was a pleasure to listen to him, especially as I heard him one day last winter when James Sibbald and Alex Anderson smuggled me in to hear a lecture on meteorology and the homely old Scotch sayings on weather prognostications. All round the walls were ranged in boxes his stuffed birds and animals, among these were all our own home birds like familiar friends. And now for a rest under the refreshing shade of this old thorn and fail [turf] dyke.[85]

*

Suppose now that we had never seen or heard of a butterfly, could we conceive that this beautiful creature was once a crawling voracious worm, and then a torpid being like a mummy in a case, whence it sprung in newness of life, graceful in every movement and amazed in beauty as it flits before me. And though I know this to be a fact, from my mother's teaching and often her pointing to it as the symbol of the resurrection, yet when we look at the contrast of the sluggish leaf-eating caterpillar and this beautiful creature, one feels involuntary emotions of wonder. Well might the Greeks, elegant and poetical in their mythology, apply the term psyche to the soul, and to the butterfly the latter being the mystical emblem of power: I possess little knowledge as yet in the insect world, but this much I know, that the butterfly lays its egg and always on the particular plant fitted for the future

---

[85] *The Edinburgh Review* was an influential Whig magazine; Jeffrey was its editor and a leading literary critic, also a judge. Hamilton contributed a series of articles to the *Review* that were later published under the title *Discussions in Philosophy, Literature and Education*. Doubtless De Quincy's dreams, which he describes in his writings, were opium-derived; he moved to Edinburgh in 1830. Moir was a poet and medical doctor who wrote for *Blackwood's Magazine* - "Maga" - under the nom-de-plume Delta. James Hogg also wrote for *Blackwood's*. Leslie was a well-known mathematician and scientist.

caterpillar. The egg is firmly glued on to its leaf: in due time it produces the caterpillar, of course of small size at first. Its growth however soon commences and is as rapid as its appetite is voracious. In course of time the caterpillar has arrived at maturity and appears to have lost its vitality and, with a shrivelled skin, to be in a dying state. Another skin is however forming below and in a short time the creature appears in a shining casing like armour, soft at first and showing through it the wings, eyes and legs of the perfect insect. It is now during the winter in a torpid state, till the time arrives for its exit of a perfect butterfly. The rest of the tale is soon told. Bright things must fade, for all things perish and decay, such is the doom of all created life: the butterfly enjoys its brief summer, deposits its eggs on the plants which Providence teaches it by instinct are the the suitable nourishment of the future caterpillar and passes out of existence.

[At this point, AC encountered some sheep]

O my brothers, don't be alarmed, I see your curiosity has got the better of your timid natures, and you want to know what your biped brother is about. Well I am just - bah - musing on the doom of all animal life, sheep as well, and thinking aloud, but there's no occasion for me giving you pain in forecasting the future of your life. No, enjoy your innocent life my friends while you may, and this is a pleasant spot to enjoy yourselves among the green pastures — you look very contented. I am tempted to ask, O aged patriarch with the horns and black face —

how old art thou? And is this your native [place]? You look of the genuine sort, fresh from the wilds about Ettrick head and like [James Fenimore] Cooper's Natty Bumppo [warrior hero of a series of novels, notably *Last of the Mohicans*, 1826] "without a cross" [ie, with no native blood]. For my sake, don't run away till I take an interesting memorial [sketch] of your phisog [physiognomy] however rude, in after days it will remind me of our pleasant meeting on this green hillside - ba-bah - well, goodbye, goodbye, good-bah ...

Top of Grindstone Edge

Here, at last, after a long climb under a burning sun & feet glowing with heat too hot to be pleasant. But now, since I am getting to the wilds among unprofaned Nature, I have a good mind after a comfortable rest to strip shoes and stockings in the fashion of old Morton's [school] and do it barefoot.

O! There is a joy in the moorland with such a scene as this far away to the south, with the blue sky smiling above, the green earth waving beneath in mountain & stream, and the merry summer breeze passing right cheerily. The song of the lark, the distant cry of plover and whaup [curlew], the happy hum of the "busy bee" and insect world all tend to elevate the mind to high and holier thoughts than the world in which mankind tear & wear their lives out in pursuit of riches.

At least for myself, I feel as if I could sit and gaze for hours on this picture of loveliness, for never have I seen a finer. The lofty Cheviot on the horizon, the peaked blue summit before me, with its varied grassy slopes, the Teviot stretching far away, the river showing silver till it is lost to sight by Minto Crags and woods, insects buzz on the wing, flocks bleat in the distant pastures, and all Nature seems to enjoy the quiet stillness of the hour. The scene is one of calm repose over the earth, prompting by sympathy a joy and holy peace in the heart. There is, however, a shade to disturb the harmony around me — "If a man die, shall he live again?" We put the question to the heaven above, the smiling earth around. Alas, they reply not. Their own work is enough for them and man must work out the problem for himself. In the day, he gazes on the sun while in its meridian brightness it makes merry the bird on the wing, the browsing sheep on the hill, the flowers in the beauty of their summer hue, the rolling waves of the eternal ocean, and the tiniest insect at my feet. Again I would press my enquiry: "If a man die, shall he live again?" and, once more, there is no response, all nature is dumb in answering this momentous question.

Science deals in what is material, and no information can be gained from this source — air pumps, electric machines, galvanic batteries can tell us nothing of the immortality of the soul. We may dissent and examine every part minutely, but no extent of convolutions will furnish us with the faintest indiction of the life beyond the tomb. Turning to the moral world, we get nearer the solution of the problem but even here there is no definite proof, no doubt we have aspirations after immortality but this is not proof — a stronger case exists in a feeling implanted in us, and I believe it is universal, of a hatred of injustice. How comes this if it is not implanted by God? All history of peoples shows that it has ever prevailed more or less amongst mankind: the literature of the Greeks ...

*

A rough voice joined with the rumble of a cart over the fail [turf] dyke behind me have put an end to my reverie: "Hilloa — wha' are ye?" I turned around and a rough-looking man with a very red face down which the perspiration was trickling, an auld white horse and cart and some chuckies [chickens] in a hutch below, stood before me.

"Sandie Shiel cadger [pedlar] Ettrick Brig-End! Lordsake callant [lad] is't yow? What are ye doing here?"

"I am resting a bit, Sandie, after that I'm gaun hame."

"Gude now, I'll just gie a liff and take ye alang we mi — ye'll sit fine and soff on the top o' the skins."

"Where are ye gaun Sandie? I mean, what road?"

Here Sandie took his hat off and, after looking thoughtfully in the direction of Hawick where we had occasional glimpses of the long stretch of road, scratching his head, responded:

"Weel, ah'm no very sure, whaten road to gang yet — is yon twa black specks we seen the far road folk, think ye? or is it dogs?"

"It is two or three men Sandie, and suppose it be — some mischief ye're into again?"

"Weel, the fac is I sold a famous gem [game] cock for a decent price to some Hawick chields [young men]. They agreed on the price but on condition that they had it on trial till the day [today], when they would pay me. Sae I saw them on the

Tower Knowe the day, an they wadna pay me a farthing till the cock was tried on Monday when some famous match comes off. I get naething but impudence and, ma passion being up, I was just on the point o' knocking him down when I heard ane of the squad at ma back asking, Where was the cock? And the answer was, Appletree Hall, wi Tam. Brawly [well] I kenned the house for I've often gotten their eggs, sae I neer says a word but yokit Nannie [his horse] at the Black Bull, and takes the road, finds ma game cock in a cavey [hen coop] at the back o' the house. And here ah'm wi' it but pursued without a doot, and I'm no safe till I put Ale Water atween me and them, and a friend like yersel to help me. Now ye see how ah'm set, ye'll no be yer faither's son if ye see me beat in a pingle [fight]."

Here, all at once, was a piece of business I had not bargained for nor dreamt of in my holiday programme. So at once I protested against being mixed up with his quarrels with cocks and cockfighters. I urged him to "cut his stick" [run away] without a moment's delay to Sinton or Sinton Mop-end where he would find plenty of friends, and I began to resume my pencillings.

Quoth Sandie (aside) "Lord, but it's true what his father says after all, he is no like other folk.

"Na, na, I ken a better trick than that — Ye'll just sit still till the Hawick birkies [youths] come up, and be sure and tell them there's a cadger on the road afore them to Ashkirk. I'll push down this road, Hermiston to Sinton Mill to Aedie Niel, an' that'll throw them off the scent."

"Get away Sandie and out of sight — they will be here in fifteen minutes, I see them running."

Exit Sandie Shiel, down the Lillieslee road and out of sight, round a plantation in a few minutes.

Thinks I to myself: I have just a minute to spare for Ashkirk, downhill, barefoot, in fine running order and fifteen minutes start, for I have a vision of mischief in remaining longer here. And, after the shaking-up by a little excitement, I'll resume my studies when I get to the ancient heather by Bishop Stane. Once there, what a pleasure in the privacy of the moor and a long rest, and some reading — "sweet is the pleasure after pain," says some poet.[86]

I have, however, gleaned some good from your troublesome presence, Sandie Shiel, in that expression of yours about "no being like other folk" of which it behooves me to be wary in any exhibition of my tastes, which the common herd do not understand. Although their company may be an infliction, yet prudence prompts it better to be a clod among clodhoppers.

Woolrig

I have not got the length of [can't afford] a watch yet - wish I had one - but to the best of my reckoning I have done my five miles an hour, and the suppler and better of it, so no rest here but jog on quietly. How true it is that "the spirit supports a man."[87] In another hour I shall meet my father, whom I adore, despite all his failings, above any other being on earth, and next to him my aunt [Margaret] Lang. In that awful fever which prostrated our house, and took from us that dark-haired pensive boy William [1820~1825], myself escaping only by a hairbreadth, she was a ministering angel. Can I ever forget her kindness, affection & consideration in sending up so many comforts, not forgetting pencils and a box of colours, to amuse me when I got the fever? No, never, and thus it is that affection begets affection, long life to them both. This was the first incident in my life which created my feeling for art, which is daily gaining strength.

And now, about my reflections on the top of the Edge so sadly ended by that confounded cadger and his gem cock. By the way, he is never out of mischief since I first knew him, and that was when a very small boy at old Morton's school. Father and mother gave me in charge of Sandie Shiel to go and see Thirlstone Fair, and he was "never to lose sight of me," but bring me safe home in his cart afore bedtime. Alack a'day I lost him ere I was well in the fair, and when I did find him late in the summer night, my playmates and myself ran to see a great ring of folk,

---

[86] John Dryden
[87] "The spirit of a man will sustain his infirmity," *Proverbs* 18:14

in the centre of which there was a fight going on, and one of the combatants, the victorious one, was Sandie. After [an]other two bottles that night he managed to deliver his charge about two in the morning, since when I always give him a wide berth — spoils meditation rather.

I shall not study more on this subject of evidences of the soul's immortality at present further than to record this much: it is beyond reason, at least my reason, and I believe it on God's word, the Apostle's creed, I therefore confess to. I am sorry now that I had hurt my poor mother's feelings by some rash expressions in that argument on religion when she sent for old Morton to quash me. How confused the old man became when I asked him to explain the Trinity! "It's a mystery," says he, "which we cannot explain, ye must receive it by faith." Says my mother: "Try and put him right Mr Morton, I fear he has been among infidels when in Edinburgh, he has gotten some awful notions." "He will gang to the Deil," says he, "if he disnae change." Now the fact is, both of these good well-meaning folk, viz, my mother and Morton, misunderstand me.

I believe in Christianity, but not through the medium of Calvinism and its exponent, the single catechism, of which I have a mortal horror. Not that it is connected with tears and tawse [strap, ie, punishment] and bubbly noses, but from its revolting principles, at which my nature rebels and, I will add, its sophistry:

Master: What is the chief end of human life?

Scholar: To know God by whom men were created.

M: What reason have you for saying so?

S: Because he created us and placed us in this world to be glorified in us. And it is indeed right that our life, of which himself is the beginning, should be devoted to his glory.

M: What is the highest good of man?

S: The very same thing.[88]

---

[88] Catechizing was a part of life in the Scottish church with itinerant catechists being employed to instruct the people, a practice that continued into the nineteenth century. The

My dear old dominie, who taught me my ABC and under difficulties, you say, being a weakly boy and so often absent through that, and idleness, that it took you three months' hard labour before I mastered these rudiments of knowledge. I believe I used that word [sophistry] in our late argument and it hurt your feelings, I saw. I respect you for it and declined to give you, as you asked, one single instance. Well I did not do it, and I had my reasons, one of them was that you at least identified the "Single Questions" with the Bible, that my quotation and proof would have still further grieved you, which I had no wish to do, but out of mercy instances of the sophistry of Calvinism I could have begun with — "God fore-ordains every thing that comes to pass." Now I would say, explain it away as you may — sin comes to pass and, by logical sequence, you make God the author of sin, much more I could have said. But I am glad that I did not, for it would have grieved your honest heart, more than my mother, for she has grave doubts, though not so openly expressed as myself, on the same subject.

Somehow or other, whenever I come in contact with these extreme Calvinists or Cameronians, we seem instinctively to know and repel each other, I suppose by some unknown principle of sympathy and antipathy.[89]

My first impression was at their camp meeting on Howford Croft, a long sederunt [gathering] it was, and a goodly collection of dour-looking carles [men] in faded tartan cloaks and plaids. My wonder was, where did they come from? How they scowled at a few of us youths who were profane enough to do a little bit of romping between the rows of sitters on the green brae side! The wood tent stood at the foot; some wicked boy stole the bawbees [coins] out of the wood dish mounted on a stool alongside of the dyke. He - Jemmy Fletcher, my then-comrade under the

---

catechism is composed of 107 questions and answers. The most famous of the questions is the first:
> What is the chief end of man?
> Man's chief end is to glorify God.

[89] The Cameronians were a Calvinist sect. The name derives from Richard Cameron (1648~1680) a presbyterian preacher. Robert Paterson - "Old Mortality" - was a fervent Cameronian.

dominie, I think to this day was the guilty culprit. Didn't unknown pennies long after come out of his pockets, [which] I spent on clagum [treacle toffee] and sugar alla [sic] at Jenny Feather's. But then how could he be guilty of such a heinous sin, being the son of "oor ain folk" a sma' but elect band [ie, of Calvinists]? No, the thing was impossible, and so the blame was laid at my door. In vain, I protested my innocence; first, a sound thrashing from father and mother and lecture on the enormity of my crime; next, the dose repeated by dominie Morton with supplementary lecture and fearful tawse; then, old wives in the Brig-End taking, with pursed-up mouth and contracted brow, a stern look at the sinner as he passed their door. Old John Anderson I believe was the only believer in my innocence, and by-and-by managed to clear my reputation.

*

But here now is the Bishop's Stone and the scene of Jamie Murray's ghost. I have heard the decent old man tell the story twice now, forgetting that he had told me the same awesome story some years back. Last winter, however, I sauntered down to the mill to have the same story over, partly in case I might have taken him up wrong, and partly to find if he made any deviation. The old man was lighting in at the kiln, seated very comfortably on a half-empty bag by the kiln and, after various enquiries about what lair [learning] I had been getting in Edinburgh, Burke & Hare and the hanging of Burke, which I gave him an account of, and also of having seen [Burke] lying on Dr Monro's dissecting table in the College, I gradually brought him on to the subject of the supernatural and his ghost in particular.[90]

I found to my surprise that he did not deviate a hair-breadth from his first narration. James Murray, miller in Howford mill, I have always looked on as a sagacious, thoughtful, matter-of-fact, but unimaginative man — very reticent and

---

[90] Burke was hanged in the Lawnmarket on 28 January 1829, after which he was publicly dissected at the Edinburgh Medical College. The dissecting professor, Alexander Monro, dipped his quill pen into Burke's blood and wrote "This is written with the blood of Wm Burke, who was hanged at Edinburgh. This blood was taken from his head."

secretive though. So much so that, according to his own showing, he never divulged this ghost story for a dozen years after and then only to his wife, whom he had been courting at the time of its occurrence.

My curiosity is excited to see the spot of ground and to compare the reality to the ideal called up by recital and, as ghosts don't appear at noon-day, only at some mysterious hour of night, I suppose I need not be afraid. No, but what about the dark winter nights that you will probably be found wandering by here, homeward? And who knows but you, like Jamie Murray, may have been intruding on hallowed or unhallowed ground, and a punishment sent for a warning to others. So beware, young man, in time, and check your wayward willful fancies. Oh bosh and superstition! Besides, I only want to see the nature of the ground and the little hill or hillock rising from the flat, all this I must see to test the truth of the story, and lo! — there it rises. Well, I think, as I need not give myself unnecessary travel and these burrs from last year's heather are not pleasant to bare feet, I will not go further. I see it all before me, quite distinct.

How truthful, after all, is the old man's description! He asked me to explain it by my lair [learning], for he was open to conviction, and now when I cast my eyes on the situation I confess I am more bewildered than ever to find a natural solution. I have the satisfaction however of having seen the place and finding my picture pretty correct - the imaginary to the real - bushy heather being the only discrepancy, but that may have been changed in the course of fifty years.

I have made enquiry of my fellow apprentice, who is the son of Jesse Elliot, schoolmaster and session clerk of Ashkirk, to get me information regarding the meaning and origin of the name of this spot, "Bishop's Stane." Jesse Elliot's reply was, "in old times, a Catholic bishop was murdered here and an annual [game of] football was played here in commemoration and only fell into disuse in the last generation." The information is scant and only whets my appetite for more, but how he should have appeared here, to a young man, on a good and harmless errand, in clear moonlight, and so frightened him as to lay for months after under the doctor's care is more than I can make out.[91]

I have paid a little attention to the supernatural, listened in winter evenings to stories of ghosts, wraiths and warnings told by Peggy Lovat and others while spinning or carding wool, heard my mother on the same subject. Father is sceptical and laughs them down. Tibby Bell of the Woodend before she died is striking, to say the least of it, she was a singularly good woman who went into the wood every night to say her prayers, and the last time she was there it was midnight when a voice called three times, "Tibby Bell — come away," she died a few days after. On the other hand, I have read Sir Walter Scott's demonology [*Letters on Demonology and Witchcraft, 1830*] and the optical illusions explanatory of the hallucinations people are sometimes subject to, but while I admit a good deal of that, and one of my father's ghost stories is to the point showing how from a very simple and ludicrous cause a ghost story may arise, yet there is a vast amount of instances in all ages and well-attested, which cannot be explained except by supernatural influence, and we have the authority of Holy Writ for ministering angels, spirits of the departed.

Taking all into consideration I conclude in the belief that Providence sees fit at times to manifest himself to men by supernatural agencies and for wise purposes unknown to us. I believe that these manifestations are confined to an age of great faith and not to an age of excessive worldliness. So I leave the subject to others better qualified and welcome again the parish road and some other musings to lighten the way — but not ghosts.

*

The Penny Magazine: I like the publication, with its short articles on every sort of useful knowledge, and the woodcuts so cleverly done. *Blackwood's* runs it down

---

[91] For the story of "The Spectre Seen at the Bishop's Stone," see *Miscellaneous Writings* below.

unmercifully and, in a late number, there is a satirical poem on [Lord] Broughham, in which occurs the following lines:

> Oh this wondrous, wondrous man
> Who planned our great machine
> The London University
> And the *Penny Magazine*[92]

Now, Professor Wilson, this is too strong and, from a working man's point of view - as I must now rank myself as such - I think your satire, clever though it be, is unjustifiable and uncalled-for. We want knowledge at a cheap rate, and here is a weekly sheet for 1p which supplies the want, and we hail the donors - Lord Brougham and the Society for the Diffusion of Useful Knowledge - as the people's friend. Your party says that it is "confounded whiggery"- by-the-by, this is just the expression Uncle Andrew [Lang] used about it lately - and you urge that it is part of a political engine to excite the Mobocracy and prepare the way for this much-talked-of Reform Bill.[93]

And what for no? I would ask, why should the mass of workers in the kingdom, the sinews of the nation, not be elevated in the social scale and have a voice in the squandering of their hard-earned money, often in expensive wares and increased taxes? I think they ask for no more than what is just and reasonable, although I am not at all inclined to go to the lengths of the Denholm stocking makers — give them rope and we would have a repetition of the horrors of the French Revolution. I see that the Iron Duke [of Wellington] foreshadows a similar fate in store for us, but then these extreme radicals are luckily a small section of the

---

[92] As a young lawyer in Scotland Henry Brougham (1778-1868) helped found the *Edinburgh Review* in 1802 and contributed many articles to it. In parliament Brougham fought against the slave trade and opposed restrictions on trade with Europe. He proposed educational reforms and also was one of the founders of the Society for the Diffusion of Useful Knowledge in 1825 and of University College London in 1828.

[93] Presented in 1831 and passed into law in 1832, the Reform Act widened the electorate to enfranchise the new cities that had sprung up during the Industrial Revolution.

community and do not represent the good sense of the working classes. Earl Grey and Brougham repudiate all such levelling as would destroy our famous constitution.[94] They hold by the golden mean in that, and the increasing of the trade and resources of the country, so that we shall soon be paying off the national debt and without wars, our taxes from reduced expenditure will by-and-by be very light, almost nominal. Such is the programme, as far as I can learn from these famous speeches of Brougham's. But about the *Penny Mag*, you look in vain for anything in the shape of politics.

*

There is an article on the dog of Newfoundland, from "Juke's Tour in Newfoundland."[95] I must read this first as being connected with our [dog] Watch, or rather I should say his mother. She was brought from there by Lord Napier, [Francis Scott Napier (1758 ~ 1823), Lord Lieutenant of Selkirkshire from 1797] and one of her pups sent to my father after his two servants were drowned in the mill pool. His education in the water has been carefully attended to by my father and John Anderson. As yet there has been no repetition of that tragedy in Ettrick, but there can be no doubt he would bring a drowning person out, even were he to dive 20 feet for him. A noble dog is Watch but now past his best and his teeth terribly worn down by our own folly in making him dive for stones. But to this article:

> "They are more intelligent and useful to the natives than any other
> species of dog. This one caught his own fish. He sat on a projecting
> rock beneath a fishflake or stage, where the fish are laid to dry,

---

[94] Earl Grey, one of the primary architects of the Reform Act, was Whig prime minister, 1830~1834.

[95] Some confusion here. The first article on the Newfoundland Dog in the *Penny Magazine*, extracted from *Jukes's Excursions in and about Newfoundland*, is from the 11 January 1834 edition. However, the article from which AC quotes is much later, from the 3 September 1842 edition.

watching the water, which had a depth of six or eight feet, and the bottom of which was white with fish-bones."

This is a very interesting article indeed and reminds me of Watch's favourite pastime of leaping up on the parapet of the bridge at Brig-End to vizzy [view] the trout below. Once he lost his balance in a fit of excitement and down he flew, spreading all his legs out like a flying squirrel, came out after a swim round and about and not a bit the worse ...

I see a cart in the distance — can that be the hero of the gem cock again, to inflict me once more with his company? Let me see, if it be the same man, I must contrive another path else my meditations are ended. No, I see the horse is black and his was white and that looks like a man and a woman ...

The Dog of Newfoundland

"Every now and then, three or four clumsy-looking fish called sculpins, with great heads and mouths and many spines upon them would take a sweep from the deep water to near the side looking for bait. Then all of a sudden this dog would set attentively, and the moment one turned broadside to him, down he darted like a fish-hawk, and very rarely came up without his fish and his grip of them was always the same — behind the head or region of the heart, which made them powerless."

Now Mr Juke, I would just remark that had Watch sat for his portrait, instead of this dog, it could not have been more truthful. He darts at a salmon, be it in the mill pond or the mill dam, just in the same way — invariably his grip is behind the gills, and I never once saw a fish big or little give a single wallop when in his jaws, thus showing that his instinct taught him to paralyze them, by the grip over the heart, poor fellow! I have no doubt his mother sat in her heyday on the prow of some Indian canoe catching fish in the same fashion.

"As he caught them, he carried them regularly to a place a few yards off, and they told us that he sometimes made a pile of fifty fish in a day just at this place. He never attempted to eat them."

Ah stop! Our comparison is at fault here, you may trust to Watch's fidelity in keeping ward over your gudes and gear and even everything eatable but always excepting raw fish, probably a weakness he has inherited from parents living with the Indians from hand to mouth. Certain it is however that at this time of day the old habit is not yet cured with Watch, and it behooves one to look sharp when he gets hold of either trout of salmon.

I remember once catching a good-sized trout in the Linns after a considerable run. Watch was in his teens then and, after helping me to land it, I was intending to put it in a pool as my father used to do in his education, but he saved me the trouble, for the last sight I got of that trout was when it disappeared in his capacious jaws, and fly hook as well.

I wish I had seen him with that 30-lb pike caught by my father and Mr Gibson in Helmer Loch. Of course he was beat with it, being unused with a fish of such rapid movements, and then the monster leaping out of the water and fetching the line round his neck. But then the two old worthies confused the dog with their swearing and noise, at least knowing as I do the nature of them both, I can understand as well as if I had been there, the excitable state they would be in, all three in the water splashing and tugging the cord.

"When the fish did not come, I observed he put his right foot in the water and paddled it about — his feet were white to the first joint and inside his legs as were his breast and ring around his neck, with a lozenge-shape white from his nose to the crown of his head."

Body o' me, Mr Juke, this is our dog to a shaving, who knows but your dog may have been Watch's father, your portrait is so faithful. I must read it to the old man and hold a council on it.

*

Two gangrel [tramp] bodies I am going to meet, a feeble old man and woman somewhat younger supporting him, both in rags — what a state of misery that must be! No, puir bodies, I have not a copper coin upon me, else you should have had it.

"A bit tobacco?"

No, nor that, either, for I don't smoke.

"Weel, sir, we're no that hungry yet, we got some parritch frae Mr Limson where we put up a' nicht, but me gudeman misses his smoke.

"Whaur do we belong? "Weel, we come oot o' Galloway, Balmaghie parish an' we are just fechting [fighting] oor way hame again."

People blame beggars for their unsettled vagabond lives, they tell them that their poverty and wretchedness are of their own making, and when they do give them a trifle they often do it as if they bought a right to insult them. But take this poor creature for instance — if the lowliness of his state had not bridled his tongue with shame, I fancy I hear him speak out thus:

"What do you reproach me with, a lazy wandering vagabond? And what are the cares which employ you amid your wealth? Ambition, money-making, your passions and your pleasures. Perhaps I am a useless servant, but are you a faithful one with the goods God entrusts you with? You find fault that my strength is not employed in labour — how do you employ yours? You say I have no right to food because I don't work — does the same law not apply to you? Are you only rich that you may live in sloth or to pamper and glorify yourself? There is a Lord will one day judge between us — and it will be seen if your pleasures and extravagances were more lawful in you, than the little artifices I employ to get a bit of bread in my abject state."

Yes, it behooves us to look at both sides of the matter; besides, if we have nothing to give them we may at least lighten them their heavy yoke by a kind word. Shall we drive him from us harshly, or even set the dogs on him, as I know some do, and so add to the sorrows of his heart? Unfeeling souls that we are! And yet we can give our tears to the fancied trials of a hero or heroine in a well-spun novel.

Talking of beggars, the wanderer like myself if he wishes to know his brother man in the poorest state of life should beware of haughtiness. The secret of gaining the confidence of the poor, as it is of everyone else, is to respect their way of thought, habits and expression. And, there be sincerity, that feeling will not be wanting. The surest way to shut out knowledge as well as happiness is to let the heart and lip carry an everlasting sneer — stand out of my way, thou mouldiewart [mole] for I am ashamed of thee. I am a mole of a clear vision and the salt of the earth, while thou art a poor blind abject mouldiewart. And it ought never to be forgotten that every man, however humble and ignorant he may, be has feelings, affections and sympathies, and these should be treated with respect as Holy things. He therefore who cannot descend from his proud pedestal to respect his brother's joys and sorrows had better far avoid intercourse with him.

*

I mentioned having seen a horse and cart at some distance moving Ettrick way on the Parish road. I now found myself within a couple of hundred yards of it, a man and a woman walking behind. I was reminded of a great gathering of these mugger [tinker] folk a few days before on Denholm's "level green" which ended in a fight of no ordinary character. A gigantic Amazon rushed into the melee, at first evidently with the object of acting the "redder's" part [ie, trying to stop the fight] and making peace, but having got the "redder's lick" [blow received by someone trying to stop the fight] and hampered besides by a child she carried on her left arm, she slewed it at once behind on her left hip and struck like a hero with her right for some time. It would not do, numbers and one hand were fearful odds, and feeling the odds against her and her blood being up, she tossed the child like an old bundle some yards behind her, bounded among her foes like a tigress let loose. Down went old and young like nine pins till her sole antagonist was a great hulking fellow, who had the cowardliness to seize hold of a staff, but as good luck would have it, just as he was fetching a sweeping blow, he toppled and fell and before he could right himself, it was wrenched from his hand, then with a whack on his posterior, tossed through the air like the child.

The screaming and crying of children was a thing to be remembered, but on the principle of the old proverb, "the hotter the war, the sooner the peace", this fray settled the series of skirmishing which had lasted for hours, and calmness forthwith was over the camps on Denholm Green and the tinkers [were] hob-nobbing by the evening by their bright fires just as if nothing of bloodshed had ever happened.

But to my present introduction with these singular people, which not only put an end to my reveries and changed my thoughts into a different channel, but gave me a wholesome lesson in prudence which it behooves me to act upon in all time coming — lucky for me that I escaped as I did without sharing the fate of the vanquished on Denholm Green.

I noticed the woman before me to lift a good-sized basket of crockery from the cart and set off on a footpath which went across a level marshy flat which, after about a quarter of a mile or so, again joined the cart road, the road making a considerable bend to west and then doubling to east. I had felt chilled with loitering and made up my mind for a sharp walk. In an evil moment, the thought struck me to match myself against the big wife and her basket in a walking race to that point where she struck the parish road.

She was carrying weight, I had none but my shoes over my shoulder and that was nothing but then she had something like half the distance and a good start, while I had uphill for the half of my way. The chances looked against me but, knowing my ability and endurance in walking and running, I decided in a moment; so off like an arrow, but fair-play, no running, nothing but a straight-out walk. I quickly passed the cart, just had a glimpse of a stout lumpish fellow in a battered white hat, whom I recollected having seen before somewhere, and my eye took in at the same time a large shaggy greyhound below the cart, but I had no time to give anything but a passing glance at these, for the steam was up and I was making wonderful leeway. The hasty glance I took down the flat at my antagonist to measure our progress showed, to my surprise, that she fully understood the challenge and accepted it by straining every nerve. Thinks I to myself, this is capital sport, beats rabbit hunting to sticks.

Three minutes more, it's to be a dead heat if I don't make more speed. Another three minutes, I am doubled the bend and now downhill — still doubtful though, my enemy making a noble effort. Further on I am gaining rapidly, the enemy seems fagging and her ground rougher, but stop a moment — mercy on us, as I am a sinner, that is no other than the hero of the battle, there is the same yellow hair streaming behind her like the pennon of some Border chief, and if I win I am without a doubt in for dule [grief] and sorrow and maybe all the same if I don't win. So if this be that awful woman, which I hope it won't - it's as broad as it's long - our distance is shortened and I could go in and win. But I had better not, my worst fears are a certainty, my instinct tells me also that there is mischief in that very red face and determined air of her who used her fists so well in the battle. So go in to your doom and punishment young man, for the mischief you have fairly brought on your own head — nice job to go home to your mother all battered and bruised, perhaps with a pair of black eyes.

A few minutes more and my enemy is nearing the goal of the road, I have wisely slackened speed. There is a hundred yards between us, and I can see distinctly now, that there is no doubt of the Amazon. What is to be done? To be sure I may bolt across the moor, but then that fellow would to a certainty let loose the hound, and I would be worried ere I had made a hundred yards, and I hear him thrashing in his haste to be in at the death. Besides, the plan is unmanly; no, I will face it out and make the best of my impudence. Now the enemy has gained the winning post, tossed her heavy basket on the green sward, planted her arms on her hips and turning her face to the fore, straight and erect with head thrown back looks the very personification of something or somebody I have heard of in the classics — what is it, let me see, ah yes, I have it — Ajax defying the thunder or, to come down to our own times, Helen MacGregor [wife of Rob Roy]. I wish to goodness Morris' fate is not in store for me, only there is no water.[96] What an attitude and what a model! If I had only the power and, I must add, though with bated breath, the composure to transfer you to canvas as you stand with your erect sinewy frame, streaming yellow hair, wouldn't it make a picture? But the day may come: till then you are stamped on the tablets of my memory and will not be effaced. How I wish that I had been among Sandie Shiels' sheepskins, or even run chance of waiting with the ghost on Bishop's Stane, but now all the reflections are ended by Amazon loquitur [ie, speaking], myself cautiously keeping the breadth of the road between us as a base for a masterly retreat, should the enemy mean fight.

"So, younker [youngster]! An' ye'll be thinking nae doot that ye've dune a grit [great] stroke o' manhood in racing an auld woman gaun seventy an' carrying a heavy basket!"

Myself: "It ne'er entered my head gudewife by the race ye've run, that ye could be sic an age as seventy and vexed and that ye should hae paid ony heed to ma foolish freak [whim], but ye've won the race, and weel deserve a' the honour, sae I can only add forgie [forgive]."

"Afore I say another world to ye, come here and feel the weight o' this basket."

---

[96] In Sir Walter Scott's novel *Rob Roy* (1817), the cowardly character Morris is thrown from a cliff into a loch.

Here, the enemy cut off the only means of escape by bringing me within range of her powerful arms, my bending below her in the very posture of the victim to be beheaded and his executioner. But there was nothing for it but obey the victor, so I stepped across and grasped the basket with both hands and, mercy! what a weight, as I lifted it breast high. My surprise and respect were uttered in unfeigned terms as I replaced it on the ground.

"Now what do ye think of yersel and yer feat, e'en supposing ye had beat me?"

"Well, ye shall hae my answer and it is this: that had I known the odds against you, I would sooner have lost all I am worth than done you such an unmanly trick, but as a sma' amends, I will carry this heavy basket of yours as far as we may gang thegither [together]."

"But ye shall do nothing o' the kind - I'll carry ma basket mysel - but while we travel thegither on the road till ma son Matthew comes up, ye'll answer me some questions: In the first place, whae are ye, and where do ye come frae?"

"Well, then, gudewife, I have come from Denholm."

"Ane whae do ye belong to at Denholm? Ah ken everybody in Denholm — there's baith gude and bad in't, frae auld Duncan to Sergeant Houston. Tell me at aince, whae is yer folk?"

"Hae patience, mistress: I only said I had come from Denholm, I have only stayed there since last Whitsunday [15 May], and I wish to goodness I had never seen it. My native place is in Ettrick, about the Brig-End."

"Weel I ken the Brig-End and everybody in't as weel as I ken Denholm — and whae has the misfortune to own ye there? Be quick, and nane o' yer dodging wi me, for ah'll hae't oot o' ye, and something else, afore I part wi' ye."

Myself: "Well, well, mistress — ye have a perfect right, for ye're the victor, and can impose what terms ye like on me that ye've vanquished, and so as I have no reason to deny my parents, but of whom ye can know nothing about, after I have made ye that wise. I was born at Howford, I am Andrew Currie, the son of the oldest one, of William Currie, who again was the son ..."

"What's that you say, younker?" Here the enemy stopped short all of a sudden, put down her basket slowly on the road, and thus addressed me: "Say nae mair, younker, I ken yer forbears, baith father and mother's side far better than ye do yersel, and the Lord be thankit that I ken whae ye are, for to be plain wi' ye, I intended to have gi'en you a thrashing that ye wad hae minded to the langest day o' yer life, but sin' ye're the grandson o' those gude men that aince did me and mine a gude turn, saved me and weans frae starvation i' the dear years, that of course alters the case entirely and I freely forgive ye on their account yer impudent trick on an auld wife ... Weel, weel, eneuch said, I see ye're sorry for it, and ye wadna be yer gude-hairted father's bairn if ye wasna. But here's Matthew ma son, an I see he has been knotting his whup for yer back, but fearna, he shall ne'er lay a finger on ye."

Here the old woman stepped between Matthew and me with, "Haud yer hand Matthew, it was his grandfather that saved your life when ye was a sucking infant and fed and clad yer faither and mother at Brownmuir! You and him will stop and crack here till I gae down and hawk the herd's hoose [ie, sell something at the herdsman's house], syne I want to hae a crack wi' him as far as we gang thegither, and that will be to Hartwoodmyres, I guess, sae be freends."

These words acted like a charm on Matthew, whose countenance changed at once from saturnine to as bemused an aspect as his nature was capable of. I at once seated myself on the roadside, while he put the pin below the cart and threw a bunch of grass before the auld yaudi [mare]. I was a little puzzled on what to speak with Matthew but at a random guess tried — dogs.

"That's a grand dog of yours, Matthew!"

"Aye, Billy is a good tyke but getting past the best."

"What breed is he? He's larger than an ordinary greyhound?"

"Weel, he is a cross between a staghound and a greyhound bitch, his father is the Shirra's dog Maidey, nae dog wull beat him for speed and keeping it up, and o'er and aboon [above] he has a gude nose and carries — ah wudna take £5 for him although he is getting past the best."[97]

I was not surprised at Matthew's rejection of the price, considering the dog's capabilities of supplying the larder. I remarked on his resemblance to the haining [guard] dog which Harry Bailie kept muzzled at the lodge on the green.

"Na, na, I kent that dog weel, and a fierce bad brute he was but nae kith nor kin to mine, that was a bloodhound frae foreign pairts, he was far bigger than that dog, but the same colour o' greying hair."

Matthew and I got on famously on this subject of dogs, in which I found he possessed more than ordinary lore, till I saw he mother coming up the bent [hillock] to rejoin us. I was interested to hear something more from her about friends, otherwise I would not have waited. Before she came to hand, I spoke to her son about the fight on Denholm Green which I had witnessed and remarked his mother's prowess and share in the fray.

"Aye faith, lad! She is no canny [natural] when her bluid's up, although she is gaun 70, but mind ye, they were maistly a' her ain kith and used to get a cuffing frae her, of course they just let her knock them down without ever lifting hand again her. Ma mother's vera muckle respeckit an sae was her mither, Eppie Faa, among oor folk and even by mony o' the gentry. The Shirra [Sir Walter Scott] when he was at Ashteil and huz camped about Thornilee, wad hae had grannie cracking

---

[97] Maida was Sir Walter Scott's favourite dog, "a stag-hound of the old Highland breed, and one of the handsomest dogs that could be found; it was a present to me from the chief of Glengary, and was highly valued, both on account of his beauty, his fidelity, and the great rarity of the breed." Scott named him after the Battle of Maida, which took place in Italy in 1806. Maida is immortalized in the white marble statue of Scott in the Scott Monument, sitting beside his beloved master.

wi' him for hours about auld world things, and weel read she was in a kind o' lair [lore] and spaeing [fortune telling]. They tell me he made a buik aboot her, weel I dinna ken what it was about or what they ca'ad the buik, ma mither will likely ken. But ah ken this, that he tauld her never to gang by Abbotsford wi'oot cawing in an' getting a drink o' yill [ale] and a feed to the yaud. He is awfu' gude is the Shirra to huz puir bodies ..."

Our discourse was here ended by his mother joining us.

"Here Matthew, pit the basket in the cart and ca' [drive] on I've selt half a crown's worth, and now ma bonny lad - for ye *are* bonny, although it wad just tak aboot twa o' ye to make ane o' yer grandfaither for buik's pairt [?]. I hae just been wondering i' ma mind what way ye're leeving at Denholm, what ye're doing there when ye should be a help to yer faither at hame – ye hae nae friends there? I kent yer faither's cousins in Ha'rule and Whitriggs, that was George in Whitriggs aboon Denholm, but they are a' off the place now."

"My father has been out of the lease of Howford for the best part of his life and his brothers-in-law have had it till now for the family, my father having debt to contend with and little means to carry on with, is doubtful of succeeding, and so thought it mair prudent to put me to a trade, and that is why I am a millwright apprentice there."

"Aye, aye — I see it a' now as plain as a pikestaff, although I dinna see the force o' pitting you to a tredd instead o' helping him when he needs it, puir man in his auld days, and sae muckle sair wark beginning the world o'er again. Ohon! Ohon! [Alas!] had yer faither but ta'en care o' his hand when he had plenty, instead o' getting it wiled [cheated] off him by that polished cousin o' his in the Kirk house wi' his law plea, for I ken aw aboot it, ye wadna hae needed to gang to ony dirty tredd, my man. But I hope it will come aw richt i' the end, and that he wull get his head aboon the water, and hae aince mair the means as he has aye had the heart to help his neighbour — mony is the pickle strae [quantity of straw] and turnips I hae gotten frae him, though I gang very seldom now to the hoose."

"What for?"

"Weel, there is a' sorts o' questions, young man, that ye micht ask me, but it's no every ane that I may see wise in me to answer, for ye micht tell o'er again to them that I wadna like to hear, and sae make needless mischief, folk may do muckle ill in saying o'er muckle but never in saying o'er little."

What all this meant, I was at a loss to know but tried another tack, so as I might come back to something this woman knew. Thinks I to myself, she is queer ane and no to "creel eggs wi'" [ie, mess about with].

"Wha' was the gude turn you said my grandfather did to you?" says I.

"Aye, well, I will tell ye about that. Afore ye was born, there was a famine and I daresay mony ane perished o' want that winter, what wi' cauld and hunger, and this plight nearly happened to huz. That is, faither and mother - mysel and three bairns - till hunger drove us to take means to save our lives, and for that we was marched up to Selkirk Cross wi' our bits o' cuddies [donkeys] and my auld faither far gaun wi' the trouble that ended his days, harled [dragged] through the snow wi' the handcuffs on him to the jail, and I had to stand at the cross wi' ma greeting bairns, till our bits o' gudes was selt to pay the expense o' poinding us [ie, as debtors, their goods were sold to pay for their impoundment].

"I believe I had it on my lips to invoke a fearful curse on some that shall be nameless, when auld John Lang stepped up to me, and says kindly, like a ministering angel: Ma gude woman, ye're at liberty to gang away wi' yer gudes, a friend has paid the fine for ye, and here is five shillings to get some meat for yersel and bairns; after that, ye will get lodging at Mr Curror's, Brownmoor.

"My heart was afore this steeled but at thae words I fairly lost the field and grat [cried] till I thocht it wad break, and I saw the gude-hearted auld man turn his back and tak oot his pocket napkin to dicht [wipe] his een. I invoked a blessing on him and his, and yer faither's faither who kept us and fed us and set us a-gaun again, and that blessing wull be felt for time to come — I dinna say in this generation, for atween us, this son o' his may be a just enough man for a lawyer, but I doot he has but a cauld heart; but tent [mark] ma words – Providence will yet reward that good deed.

"I have a kindly interest in baith the families and keepit mysel acquaint, through my cousin Rachel at the fit [foot] o' the Kirkwynd o' the welfare o' their young family, and I can tell ye I was very wae [sorry] when that young lad [John Sibbald Lang, 1783~1812] ga'ed a-sodjering to Spain (some say he took the rue [ie, regretted it] at the last, but that's maybe hearsay); but mair by token, they used to come aboot the camp to get their fortunes spaed [told] wi' my minnie [mother], for she was wonderfu' at the glamory [magic], and I mind aince when we were campet on Bullshaugh brae, and i' the Sunday afternoon, yer grandfaither and his wife Jean Sibbald and a' the young folk cam oot for their walk and I said to my mither, Did ye ever see sic a bonny family? So they are, so they are, says she, but there's dule, dule [sorrow] to the best and bonniest o' them. I didna ken what she meant and didna take muckle heed at the time, but ah often thocht o't after, when the sodjer ane was shot through the head — Ye cannae mind him, do ye?"

"No, but I lay in his little camp bed, I mind weel of that at Howford, when I was a dwining [pining] brashy [sickly] bairn."

"Aye, I think I aince saw ye, when I was hawking the Brockhill, yer nurse, I think they ca'ad her Betty Glen, cam into the house wi' ye in her airms. Ah'm thinking, ye wadna be nursed wi' yer mither's milk? Likely enough, I never heard, but what the matter if I was nursed wi' somebody's milk and thriving at this time a day? Hur puir outlandish bodies thinks different anent that, but let me ask ye about Margaret [Lang]'s family, the Parks — her and Archie gaed to the Highlands and died there. I kenned them baith weel, he was as bang [good?] a man as ever steppit in shoe leather, and she was the best o' the three dochters. They were aye kind to me when I cam about Lewingshope and fine he liked a bit banter and a joke. Did your mother ever speak to ye about a brother o' his that bolted frae Selkirk and gaed south?"

"Oh aye, often — that was Mungo the traveller."

"Na, na — I see ye ken naething about it. This Park was a doctor as weel as the traveller, and slighted yer mother, puir woman, I have heard say that she was never like hersel after, and then the auld folk got yer faither like the cat o' nine tails wi' his siller left him [ie, inherited money], they gat them buckled [married] to mak up [set (her) up], but I trow he turned oot the cat wi nae tail at a' — now I have maybe said o'er muckle, my man, but if ye are a discreet lad, ye'll *keep this to yersel*. I have a warm side to them baith for the sake of their faithers, but ah doot, ah doot they are no well yokit [not happily married] ..."

"Well, this is the first time I ever heard of such matters gudewife, and likely enough it may be all true, but this last part is rather painful, and we shall drop it for something else."

"Dinna ye imagine for a moment that ma words to you were without a better motive than idle clash [chatter] — Na, na, what I've tauld you is for yer ain especial benefit, whilk is just this: granting that yer pawrents dinna 'gree [get along] weel, and draw opposite ways in everything, e'en to their vera bairns, the tane [one] hating or at best treating wi' negleck the bairn the other ane likes, mind ah dinna say this is your case, ma man, but if ever it should be it behuves you to consider that ye're in a very critick situation, for ye've duties to them baith and bund to honour and obey them, e'en suppose ye should be treated like a dowg — du ye understand me? Verra weel then, let an auld wife gie you the advice, to take heed to yer ways, and never du ony thing, e'en suppose it should be running a race wi' that auld wife carrying weight, till ye've well considered the end and upshot — I mean ye weel, for I see ye're a gude-hearted chield, but vera wilful and thoughtless and has that about ye that'll bring ye into muckle mischief in after-life, and that's ma reason for gie'ing ye some wholesome advice. Du ye take to yer tredd, I mean du ye like it?"

"No, I think I will 'Burke' it [chuck it in] and run away."

"Aye, aye — there again now: and where will ye run to? Whae wull pay yer caution, yer faither has had enough to vex him already without his son adding to his bitter draught.[98] There's some bees in your bonnet youngster that, had I the guiding o' ye, I wad soon pike out, and mak ye strechter [straighter] in yer work — be advised by me, and do nae sic thing, but stick till't like a man, and whene'er we

---

[98] In Scottish law, a cautioner is a guarantor.

camp on the Green, ye'll come aye o'er and tell me how ye are coming on — wull ye?"

"That I will, gude wife and, what is mair, I will take it, for it is sound and wholesome tho a wee [bit] sharp — I think you must have second sight."

"Na, na, I make nae pretense to that, only ordinary wit in reading human nature for sixty and odd years. And now here's our different roads, where we maun pairt i' the meantime, but I houp we will sune meet again at Denholm for I wull look after ye, and mak enquiries. I hae mair to say to ye that I will say then sae — ye dinna take it amiss what I've said to ye?"

"Not a bit, but thank ye for it, in token here is my hand — farewell."

"Fare ye weel, and mind me to yer faither, I wull be at the Brig-End on Monday and gie him a ca' — but dinna be feared, ah'll no speak a word out o' joint. Fare ye weel."

*

As I went down the slope of Huntly Loan, with the opening view of home and its surroundings before me, my mind was filled with the above adventure and its lessons, changing the whole current of my thoughts into a graver cast and forecasting some rules or mode of life in the forthcoming five years of my imprisonment, rather smarting though, under that old woman's remarks — "bees" indeed. Yet there is truth in them, which makes it the more necessary to keep a sharp look-out over myself, and subject myself to some discipline of a severe nature, so as to train the mind to concentration on one subject at a time and one only till it is mastered.

1st Then I would say, 10 hours to business among wheels and spindles, that of course with all my might.

2nd To seek a quiet nook in Denholm Dean for study[99]

---

[99] Denholm Dean was a beautiful woodland garden, with fine trees and a wealth of wild flowers. It belonged to the Laird of Cavers, but was open to all.

3rd What shall I study? Let me see, and beware of "bees." To begin with, Locke on the human understanding, Bacon and Paley on moral philosophy, also Reid. All these I see are in the village library and quite handy, besides the Edinburgh Encyclopedia for reference on any subject. And, by way of recreation after such severe reading, say a spell at drawing, or *The Pleasures of Hope*, my mother's copy being carried mostly in my side pocket. This is pretty well chalked out and looks feasible.[100]

I must not forget my diary and to note down progress in my studies and any daily incidents worth writing. There is a difficulty here, tho it looks a small matter, I have no privacy in this garret room of my master's which is common to all the men. Lately, after some writing it was put under lock and key, but next day in the workshop, A[ndrew] formed the subject of much mirth, but about this I shall contrive so as to prevent the like recurring again.

I think I must not indulge in poetry, it dissipates the mind — I am intensely fond of it and yet never could put two lines together in my life. But if ever I should make a poem, my subject shall be the scene now before me, bringing in all that the eye rests on, with those mostly of the present generation about Brig-End and its surroundings of Helmburn, Howford, Kirkhope and the auld Meal Mill of Howford with the Brookhill. Something of the kind I began to lately, suggested by a similar subject by a local poet, and should ever it be finished, it will at least be a curiosity, although devoid of poetic merit. So be it on record to those of a future day that they only poem ever I made was "Our Howford Hame" and the opening of it, let the ending of it be when it may, is as follows:

Oh our pleasant Howford hame, how dear it is to me

Wi' its "bonny bush" and plantation and the auld boontry [elder] tree

---

[100] John Locke's *Essay Concerning Human Understanding* (1690); Francis Bacon, originator of the scientific method; William Paley, author of *Natural Theology* and proponent of the argument from design; Thomas Reid, moral philosopher who founded of the Scottish school of Common Sense; David Brewster's *Edinburgh Encyclopedia*, published in 18 volumes between 1802 and 1830. *The Pleasures of Hope* was a didactic poem published in 1799 by the Scottish poet Thomas Campbell.

Wi' their branches bending o'er in all seasons still the same

Summer shade and winter shelter to our bonny Howford hame

And the murmur of the Millford making music evermore

And the burn and the byre wi' the peat stack at the back

The very hens make music wi' their cheery noisy clack

Our couthy [comfortable] house at hame when the winter nichts were cauld

We sat roun' the blazing peets when the storm blew sae bauld

And we listened to the tale of ghosts in Ettrick's haunted vale

Till we thought we felt their presence in the moaning o' the gale ...

To be continued, some other day.[101]

*

I must apply to Tom Anderson my old schoolmate and dear companion to help me along with this subject, very dear to us both, for we have the same intense love for all the nooks and glens and picturesque spots between Selkirk and Howford. How often we have rambled up Colin's brig burn and taken note of every old root, fern and flower on our way to Howford of a Saturday, then up the waterside past Huntly Cliffs and the Cat Haugh, taking stock of everything as we sauntered upwards.

Here then is Huntly and, looking upward toward Howford back o' the hill, I see a clump of whins [gorse] which I think I had better walk out of my road to have a look at. It is a long time since I was on the spot and to you, my reader, it can have no interest, but to me it has been stamped on my mind as this adventure today will be in all time coming, with vividness of detail which some six or seven years have not effaced. As it is connected with another race like this day's one, I think I can't do better than sit again on the spot and do what I have oft intended — that is,

---

101 According to a reference from 1881, AC was a member of the Border Bards Association and "a frequent contributor of verses." None of these have come to hand, which if the above juvenilia is anything to go by is perhaps a mercy.

commit the battle wi' the herds[men] to writing, but first let me make a sketch of the ground — here it is:

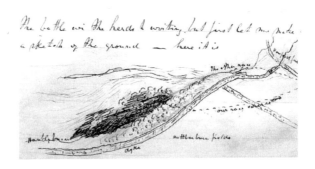

And now to the story. One day in the autumn vacation found my cousins Robert and John Lang hunting rabbits on Kirkhope hill.[102] They were staying then at Kirkhope and I spied them above the Brockhill plantation among some famous ferns along a dyke which runs up the hill. Father sent me through to them with Watch, then a young dog scarcely a year old, to tell them to be through to dinner [ie, lunch], after which he would set us on to a capital place he knew of where he had lately seen lots of rabbits. So off I set up the Brockhill wood and joined them.

First-rate sport we had in those ferns, but not one killed, for while the dogs - that is, Pepper and a collie - were hunting the brackens, the rabbits now and again managed to slip out to the westward where they had a series of holes about 300 yards off. Well, there was an old ash, I think it is there yet, and we ran about six rabbits into their hole below this tree. We decided to dig but had nothing to dig with, so it was agreed to go through to Howford for some tools and return after dinner. We therefore closed up the hole and went over to Howford in great spirits and anticipations of our forthcoming haul. But father had a different scheme and that was to practice our young dog on the green slopes about Huttlerburn whins. I recollect how I demurred at this, so did my mother because as she said, Mr Beattie -

---

[102] John Lang, b 1812, was AC's exact contemporary. Since there are no Langs of that generation named Robert, this may be Robert "Robbie" Park.

as he was popularly called, "Nezzar" Beattie - had not long before sent up an ill-natured message about the boys stopping up the drains about the March dyke, and that if ever we were caught on his ground again he would have "an example made of us".

I heartily backed up my mother, especially as I had a mortal fear of Nezzar's men, a wild-looking uncouth race were his herds, not men of the district but from the Highlands mostly, and at this time Huttlerburn was stocking with droves of Highland cattle and ponies. Not so Robert and John, they were rather fond of any event where there was the additional excitement of danger, especially Robert. And so, as they formed the majority, the thing was decided, to hunt Nezzar's whins and take our herd laddie along with us to act as a look-out from some knowe [hill] top in case of danger.

An hour afterwards found us on the south end of Howford hill in view of the said whins, which formed a dense mass on each bank of the little burn running to east on the base of Huttlerburn hill. We were feeling our way cautiously and having a vizzy [look]. Not a herd[sman] was to be seen, unless they were denned [hidden] about Huttlerburn, and there everything seemed quiet enough. So our General Robert organised the plan or the campaign, and at once put it in motion downwards to our ground: herd laddie to be sentry on the dyke top, where he had a view of Huttlerburn and north, Robert and John to beat the whins with Pepper and the collie, myself to keep outside with young Watch in hand and slip him as soon as a rabbit took the green hillside.

The plan was unexceptional in theory but in practice turned out unworkable for in the first place, the rabbits, instead of taking the hill, just ran from one whin bank to the other; in the second place, Watch had a mind of his own on the subject and, after a tremendous struggle with me, he dashed in among the whins and, shortly after, many were the rabbit death squeals we heard among these dense masses, tho ne'er a one we got. To complete the confusion of our general's well-planned programme, the sentry deserted his post, seeing no danger, and joined the melee among us, and for a time the sport and excitement were something to be remembered.

Ah luckless boys! Little did we know as we sat on the green hill end of Howford, that the enemy were watching our every movement from the window of Huttlerburn, saw us plant our sentry, the only thing that bothered him in how to circumvent us. In vain Robert ordered the sentry back to his post, but he was too much engaged with his collie in a solitary bush and too excited to obey orders. I myself had managed to wade up the north bank where Pepper had killed a rabbit; John and the herd laddie were down at the burn side on the open surrounding a small culvert in which were the collie and a rabbit.

Robert with a prudent forethought climbed the dyke top on the north bank and, next moment, jumped down with a cry: "Run, callants [lads], run, dogs and a' for yer lives - run - we're chased - run, run - up the burn — halloo!"

Now John and the herd, from the situation they had in the level bed of the burn, with all the dogs around them, had a fair start, for themselves and dogs, viz, Watch, Pepper and the collie. Luckily it turned out in the ensuing chase that, out of the squad of four of us, these two were by far the strongest and the fleetest. Especially John Lang, who had a wonderful power of endurance in a race or in any severe experience, and I believe ever after the following chase, Robert bestowed on him the soubriquet of "Cogou," a name that was meaningless to outsiders but well understood by ourselves.

When Robert uttered his cry and jumped so quickly down, I had had my eye upon him from a sense of danger. He had stumbled halfway down the bank after his jump and like myself, we found ourselves in a bad fix for a run.

"Dive down at once!"

"Where are they?" says I.

"Close on, coming through the hollow o'er the dyke - nae time for us - dive close in against this hag [ledge].

"There," he whispers, "five men strippit [stripped, ie, for action] wi' dogs ..."

Here, he was interrupted by a rushing sound of men and dogs, a rattling of stanes as they vaulted the drystane dyke. Then, all at once, a swearing and barking of dogs, as the two youths with all our dogs were seen swiftly making way with a fair start, as I saw from my peephole of, I would say, 200 yards. In fact, I see from this spot where I sit, the whole affair even to the spot where Robert and I were jammed up, although nowadays the whins have been partly burnt down.

Well, we were snug enough below an impenetrable mass of whins tho bleeding sadly from many a cruel prong. From our situation pretty well up the bank, we saw a part of this exciting chase. All the herds appeared to us to be in pursuit, a mistake on our part, for one had been set right on the dyke top above us to watch us while the rest pursued, and a mistake we had nearly paid dear for.

What a state of suspense Robert and I endured! The noise of dogs barking and these uncouth men halloo-ing and swearing, getting gradually fainter, Robert listening intently.

"They wull be catched," says he, "O Lord, ma puir Pepper, it canna run I doot ... nae fear o' the other dogs, they canna run again thae muckle yauld [vigorous] fellows up the hill — they are sure to be ta'en. But now is our time — I'll slip oot first, ye bide still, till I come back ... I think a' is quiet, and if they are a' away, you and me, cut doon the burn, by the west end o' the moss – take the west o' Huntly and through the water to the clints [cliffs] afore they come back, for they will be back ere lang, so I'll not be a minute in seeing if the coast is clear."

All this was uttered in a whisper and Robert crept softly up the bank, as a hedgehog might do through the grass. I don't think he was absent above three or at most five minutes when he returned with a frightened look, rather unusual in his bold manly nature.

"What is it?" says I.

"O Lord, how near I was catched! Crap [crept] up afore ever I kenned, to the verra heels o' a man set to watch us, but he is so intent on the race to the west, and him standing wi' his back to me, that he never noticed me. What will we do? He has nae dog — shall we take chance and bolt as long as the play is gude afore they come back? For back they are sure to come and worry us wi' thae fierce collies."

Now it is always with me, although naturally timid, to rise with adversities when better men are despairing and losing heart. I believe, all at once, I felt myself rising from a state of abject fear to heroism: I rose right up through the whins, with

"Let us bolt — it's the least of the two ways," but Robert pulled me down, "No, no, it's o'er late now."

I daresay he was right, for in the short time I stood, I saw his man with his back to me still standing in the same position, but I heard voices coming towards us along the side of the dyke, though unseen from a crack yet I knew that they were near, too near indeed to alter our situation. Still I was resolute to run, and pretty conscious I was of my superiority in a foot race. But Robert let me know that he could not attempt it, so we two dived once more into our hurchin [hedgehog]'s nest and waited the course of events.

Says he: "Hae yer gully?" [knife]

"Yes, but we will not use that way wi' their dogs if we can help it — besides I don't think their dogs will take the whins."

"Dinna delude yersel wi' that, they will hunt us oot like twae hurchins if they should fire the whins, and we must be ta'en."

"Then had we no better be ta'en at aince?"

"No, no — something will may be."

Here our parley was brought to a close by, all at once, a terrible noise of loud talk and swearing. But this time the swearing seemed to be directed at each other, each blaming his neighbour. From our peephole we had a glimpse of four strapping fellows, each with a stick in his hand and stript to shirt and breeches, all very red in the face, and coming along the bank top.

Says one: "Ye're a useless soul or ye might at least hae killed the little dowg, if ye couldna catch its maister."

No.2: "And what the deevil was ye doing wi' yer michtiness, ye gude-for-naething lazy hallion [clown], aye baith o' ye sitting down blown out, and leaving me to run them up that hill, ah've a gude mind ..."

No.3: "Nae mair now lads, eneuch o' that, the dog got the cundy [ie, reached the drain entrance] i' the dyke just as it was gaun to get its death blow, I saw that wi' a glance ... Dad! But he's a fell ane that laddie its maister! He was mair concerned about the bit dawg than himsel. But now for the other twae, we are sure of them ony way, if Swan hasna let them slip, and ye can take yer ill nature and disappointment out on them lads instead o' ane anither ... Here, Cheviot, here Yo-ho ... Where are they Swan — they are no away, ah houp [hope]?"

Swan: "Nae fear o' that — ye'll find them i' the bank i' the ither side. I saw them down there."

Here commenced a smashing with sticks among the whins, three of them wading all the way along, dogs barking, tho only one of them could be induced to venture in. But on reaching the end of the whins and no game found, their ill nature was now vented on Swan, for letting us escape. He had kept his stance above us until now, when all at once with an oath he jumped down through the whins within three feet of us. We saw his staff and thought it was all over, but luckily he went striding away to the east, while another at the bottom came along the contrary way, but as yet was clear of us. After a thorough beating of this bank, the whole party seemed convinced that we must have slipt away unseen by Swan. But this he resolutely denied as "impossible," vowing that he never kept his eyes off the spot, but for a few minutes in watching the chase, "and even had they slippet away, where could they run without me seeing them?" The whole five seemed perplexed and began to speculate on the event as they stood on the south-east side of the burn.

"Ah counted four and three dowgs as they cam down Howford hill."

"So did ah," says another, "and mair than that, a third ane close by the twae we chased set his head o'er the dyke as we cam forret — now where is that third ane?"

"They are among the whins to a certainty."

"Set the dogs in."

Says Robert: "Didna I tell now? Sit close and never fear — I begin to think we may have chance yet, the dogs will not take the whins except that we're faced ane, and if comes on us and barks, we're done, unless we run for it."

This prediction was correct, for although there was plenty of noise among the dogs, it was evident that they had no liking to venture much among the bushes. Only one of them, the wiry-faced one, persevered below us and was very busy on his own hook [?] on the rabbits. After a while, the herds began to saunter eastward on the hillside, with all their dogs at their heels, every now and then calling a halt and looking as if they were half-inclined to have another try at the find.

They had just turned, however, on their eastward route when one of them - the owner of the wiry-faced dog - turned about and commenced whistling on his dog. Now as bad luck would have it, this dog had been worming his way upward when, all at once, he comes in contact with us — his wicked eyes for a while speaking, as he steadily vizzied us for a minute, of startled wonder and wrath. At this moment, his master's whistle seemed to make him comprehend the situation all at once, for he set up a loud angry bark, without a doubt intended for his master's ears as "Tally ho, master, here they are, tally-yow-yow-yow."

Says Robert: "Lordsake make o' him, puir fellow, puir fellow, hae, hae, gude dog," clapping his leg to coax the brute. But the response was "Tally yow-ow-ow" in louder and fiercer accents. "Take that and be — to ye then," says Robert as he dashed his foot in the grizzly face, while I did something of the same with my pocket-knife, and down the hill went the brute, yelling murder, down the burn he ran, seemingly cowed. But there was not a moment to be lost now, for the enemy, warned by the dog, were in full chase back.

Now, says Robert, o'er the dyke at once, better ground, better foot — run, run. Only three of the herds gave chase, and it was good one. I think, but for the excellent start of, I would say, some 400 yards or so, we would have lost it and come to grief, for the herds gained for a while upon us, no doubt owing to our numbed state. I began to think that Robert at least was lagging behind me, would fail. I began to get suppled and better on, all the while wondering where the fierce collies were, for when we made our start we heard them hounded on in full mouth. We learned after from our friends who were watching our chase from Howford hill end, that two of the herds ran up on the south side of the dyke for a gate higher up the burn and so to get ahead and come athwart us before we could reach our marsh dyke and the dogs with them, while the one herd took our track, and that a providential hare or rabbit had been started, which took up the burn with the dogs in full pursuit, in spite of all the roaring of their masters. All at once I espied our friends jump up from behind the marsh dyke now only some 400 yards up the hill, they hailed us with a ringing cheer and began to hound on young Watch who was not slack in bounding like a young giant down the brae to us, with such-like cries from our friends: "Take a hand o' him, Watch - at him, at him - come on, come on, he's fagging [tiring]."

The lads in their anxiety now leapt the dyke and ran towards us, and whether the herd was done up and felt he was losing ground or whether there was in him a lurking fear of the big dog or both combined I know not, but certain it was that all at once he gave in when, within some 200 yards of us, he strode away eastward amid some jeers and another ringing cheer from John and the herd laddie. As for Robert and I, we were for some time too knocked-up and panting with our terrible run up the hill to be able to utter a word. At last, Robert said: "Lordsake callants, we'll mind this as lang as we leeve — how did you chaps escape, and Pepper?"

John: "A terrible race we had, waur than yours for they were fresh; we got a gude start when ye cried, and the vera dogs seemed to ken, for they keepit afore us up the dyke side till we cam to that yett [gate], and than we cut across for the the March dyke. It was than that puir Pepper began to fag ahint the other dogs and I was concerned how to get him o'er the dyke which we neared at last, wi' the herd only a wee bit ahint — all at aince he began to chase Pepper as it ran along the dyke side, I lap [leapt] to the top o' the dyke, waling [choosing] some gude stanes to gie him a fell, had he killed Pepper. Well, just as he was on Pepper, the kent [crook] raised to fell him, Pepper found that cundy and disappeared as the stick played smash where his tail had been a moment afore. We gave him a pairting salute wi' stanes and cut up the hill, and I believe he wad hae followed us, but all at aince Watch began to growl savage at him, and I think he got a paik [thump] on the fet wi' ane o' our stanes, or something else, for he set off crippling [limping], and we saw him pit his hand down to his foot twae or three times as he gaed back to his neighbours at the yell.

Now tell us your story — where was ye a' the time? And how did ye get sic a start oot o' the whins and ane left to watch ye, for we saw him and them begin to hunt ye?"

Hereupon Robert told the whole of our part much as I have related it, ending with "Now callants, let this be a lesson — him that's set to watch, on no account he leaves his post, for if ye had keepit on the dyke tap where ah've put ye" - I have forgot our herd's name - "we wad hae had plenty o' time to run up by the mass on level ground instead o' running this up brae road. But I think we may for time to come say gude day to Huttlerburn whins, I for ane will no forget them and this famous chase. Let's hame now, and have a bit of fun telling it o'er to our uncle — I think I see him laughing when I tell him about Andrew and me doubled up a rabbit hole like twae hurchins. And aunt, she will say "Aye, I kenned how it would turn oot but ye wull take nane o' my notice."

And thus ended this famous chase, which is yet a stock story and likely to be when we three meet in after years.

*

And now I must think of getting home myself. This rest is delicious and I could sit long enough but there is a gnawing at the stomach. Which way? To go down to where I started is against the grain; to go across, I will be seen by somebody who will tell my father, or likely enough I will stumble on him either at Whitehillbrae or about the road, and then the question: What were ye doing there? What road was that to come from Denholm? Tell the truth is doubtless the best always, but then it might either be "Gowk" [Fool] or perhaps Sandie Shiels commentary. So, as I have met a wise woman today, and got a wise maxim, to "take heed to my ways", excellent advice which I must at once set about acting on, even in small matters like this.

Let me see then — suppose I go up to the March dyke, come down it to the road and skip Whitehillbrae altogether? That's it, so *allons* [let's go], as we used to say in the French class. I will call at Whitehillbrae tomorrow and see Willie Mitchell's wife as I promised my master. She is his aunt and a Moodie, and all belonging to the Auld Licht or Cameronian body [ie, Calvinist fundamentalists] — so strict that they will not speak on worldly matters on Sunday. My master I see is so much that way that Sunday is likely with me to be the most uncomfortable day of the week - a day of gloom - I must contrive to make some congenial acquaintance, eg, Barrie the librarian or this Jamieson the naturalist, who I have heard my shopmates speak of as "a genius' - he seems a modest, unassuming man - and joins none of the athletic jumpings on Denholm "level green." I often meet him on a literary walk like myself, poking among the bushes; can't make out what he is after, but shall make his acquaintance and learn something.

Speaking of Jennie Moodie, I heard Dr Anderson tell a capital story about her lately. I think I shall just finish this day's rambling proceeding by recording it, and a hearty laugh, for a better one I never heard, so true in the acting of the two characters:

Jenny it seems is subject to periodical fits of the nerves and takes to her bed, out of which she will lay for weeks, holding out that she is "done now" and "will never rise again" has "no power in her body, etc." So a year or two back Dr Anderson had been sent for, and he found there was nothing the matter, but she insisted that she was very bad, far worse than he kenned, O and couldna rise if it was to save her life. He wanted her to try and get up just for a half hour, it was no avail and the doctor rode away.

The next morning was Sunday, and Dr Anderson is again riding up Ettrick when he minded Jenny Moodie's case, and began turning it over in his mind when, all at once, a bright idea struck him, which he would just put into practice. So at Whitehillbrae he ties his horse at the door and walks in - patient in bed of course - the doctor feels her pulse, says he: "Jenny ye are better the day" — "I am waurs," says she. Hereupon the doctor takes a seat before the fire, stretches out his legs and begins a lively conversation, and well he could do it, but all the response was only some smothered monosyllables from under the bedclothes. At last says the doctor, "Jenny, I heard a capital auld song last nicht — faith and it's been running i' ma head on the way up, I believe I will have to sing it, they ca' it "Doun the Burn, Davie".[103]

---

[103] "Doun the Burn, Davie" was written by Robert Burns in 1793.

Jenny, bolting up: "What's that ye say?"

Doctor, clearing his voice: "Ahem — Gang doun the burn, my Davie, love ..."

Jenny: "Ah, daun ye sing in ma house i' the Lord's day — are ye no feared it fa'as aboon [falls down]?"

(Louder) "Gang doun the burn my Davie love ..."

Jenny, very loud: "Gang oot wi' ye — will ye no take a telling afore the hoose sinks"

(Top of his voice) "And I will follow thee-ee-ee ..."

Exit Jenny, flying out of the door to the back of the house in flannel petticoats. I need not add that the medicine proved most effectual and all that could be desired in its results.

*

Here then is the end of this weary trail at last — seven hours on the road or about two miles an hour. Not that I have wearied in any other sense than from being a little foot-sore, and sundry gnawings of hunger which an hour's rest will remedy. But, upon the whole, I have had a most enjoyable day in my own company and resources, the only shade is that old wife. Her words seem like a nail driven home and yet I believe although I feel the smart yet, I will for time coming be the better to "take heed to my ways" in many other matters besides running a race with an old pig [pottery] wife. How strange that I should have saved my skin only by the accident of two benevolent grandfathers! And these are strange stories of hers, which I must have more of next time we meet, and must ask father all about her, but I think I shall be quiet about the race ...

* * *

WRITINGS THREE

REMINISCENCES 1875

My Holidays in the Autumn of 1875 and How I Spent Them

August 27 1875 [when AC was aged 63]

An old schoolfellow, James Henderson, called today with Mr Lewis to see me, and go to the scene of the monastery. He has been out 25 years in Canada and has come home for a visit of a few months to Selkirk. I find him a perfect repository of the old traditions of Selkirk, full of anecdotes of the people of the old burgh 50 years ago, and just the link I have felt the want of in my recollections of the auld town during my schooldays, from 1820 to 1826. I have been already much indebted to him for much information in many things I had but an indistinct recollection of, particularly for a little ms book of the names of every burgess and householder in Selkirk in the year 1817 — the whole population amounting then to 1,816: it is now 6,000.[104]

We have had an interesting walk and crack and, at parting, he told me that he had now seen all that he wanted before returning next week with the exception of

---

[104] *Catalogue, Containing the Number of Inhabitants in the Burgh of Selkirk*, 16th June 1817 (Communicated by James Henderson, Canada) Grand total: 1,816 *Border Counties' Magazine Vol. 1, 1880~1881*, p161.

the Peat Law, Three Brethren cairns and Tibby Tamson's Grave, and these "he meant to do tomorrow." It just struck me that, as I intended to visit my esteemed sister-in-law, lately come to hand to Viewfield, I might as well do this and go along with him to home ground I had not set foot on for 48 years. That was when a batch of us schoolboys went there to see a snow wreath that lay there all the summer of that year (1827). The winter of that year, or rather the spring, was the time of the greatest snow storm within the century. The sight of this huge patch of snow in the month of July determined us one Saturday to go and explore it and know all about it.[105]

And then the benefit of his company for further information towards my book on Selkirk with his own reminiscences, and his father before him. So, on proposing to accompany him, my plan was hailed with delight, and a fine finish to his holidays which my old friend S. Fisher and other south county Scotchmen in Canada would be glad to hear from him. Moreover, there was a remarkable old camp in the south which would remind Fisher of just such another holiday about 15 years ago, when old Kemp - and he with many others - made a raid on Cauldshiels hill camps and the Rink with the Catrail, and how we finished off our learned discussions over a tumbler in Maxwell's Inn.[106] I believe my usual bad luck with the weather followed us that same day — there was a ducking ere the otherwise pleasant holiday was over. I think I have recollection yet of some banter at my expense, in a proposal to a farmer in the company, Mr Elliott of Hollybush, "when he wanted rain, to just get me out on my travels and he would be sure of it." So I made some preparations for my holiday of tomorrow and anticipations of a pleasant tour to the Corbie Linn of our school days, and all the other interesting spots of the old burgh lands north of Ettrick.

---

[105] "The Snowstorm of Saturday, 3rd March, 1827. This remarkable snow-storm ... will be long remembered in this locality (Ayr). In several places of the town the snow was about twenty feet deep; and some of the country roads in the vicinity were so filled up, that the tops of the tall hedges with which they were skirted could scarcely be discerned."
[106] Native Picts built forts on the summits of local hills like Cauldshiels and the Rink in the first century BCE. The Catrail was once a large ditch, with a rampart on either side, constructed in the fifth century as a defence against the invading Saxons.

August 28

To Selkirk by 11 train and after a couple of hours with [cousin] John's wife and daughter [Jane & Helen] - Mr Lang himself away to Todrig to shoot - I found my way to Mr Lewis, the two Hendersons John and James waiting on me. We took the road by the Green, examined the old arch at Bogie's Close, anciently one of the ports of Selkirk, in the days when everyone had to be within the walls by a certain time at night and then they were barred. The strong crooks are yet on the sides, to which had been hung an iron gate or door. Crack about the old house on the other side, the head inn at the time of the battle of Philiphaugh and which, in our recollection, had a stone stair outside. Here Montrose slept on the night before the battle and General Leslie on the night after. We minded of Robert Chambers staying some days in Selkirk about 1822 before he published his *Picture of Scotland* [1827] and uncle Andrew Lang, then chief magistrate, showing him this house and the other places of note in the town, like the Pant Well, whose escutcheon is now sadly wasted and smeared over with a thick coat of paint.[107]

My recollection is of the beauty of this carving, the royal shield and Scottish lion emblazoned on the woman's knees with, here and there, bits of the original heraldic colouring, especially in the blue cloak of the Blessed Virgin. My friends were like all the other Selkirk folks, strangers to the meaning of the sitting woman, and had always thought that it had allusion to the dead woman and child who were found by the remnant of Flodden warriors at Ladylaw on their return. This has been the current belief in Selkirk since ever I knew it, whereas the symbol is the Blessed Virgin & Child with the royal arms of Scotland on a shield across her knees. In all probability the "Church in the wood" - Selcherche - was dedicated to her and embodied into the burgh arms, as Leith and Marseilles are, and the royal Scottish shield added, symbolical of the royal grant by James V for their gallantry in the ill-starred disaster of Flodden [1513]. I have no doubt that my uncle shared in

---

[107] The square Pant [covered] Well (rebuilt in 1898) marks the commercial centre of the medieval burgh.

this popular mistake about the town's arms, as he was Robert Chambers' authority on his visit to Selkirk and I find in his gazetteer [Chambers] says:

> "In memory of this latter event (the finding of the dead woman and child) the arms of the burgh bear a female, holding a child in her arms, and seated on a sarcophagus decorated with the Scottish lion, in the background a wood."

Now this is a mistake as far as the sarcophagus is concerned. As to the wood in the background I cannot speak, but I have a distinct recollection - and so has Henderson - that about 1820, the shield was neatly shown on her knees and [there were] even remains of gilding on the fleur-de-lis bordering the shield and the ancient symbolical blue of the Blessed Virgin's mantle. Besides, the origin of Selkirk was styled in the oldest charter *Seleschirche* - *Sele-chyre* or *Sel-chire* - which signify "the great or good church. Another church was built in the time of David I: the old church was called Selkirk Regis, the other one by the name of Selkirk Abbotis. Tradition is silent on these facts, and the curious fact is only preserved through the unerring records connected with church property.

It is different however about the castle, which tradition hands down as having stood somewhere near the present gardener's house on Haining ground, and of which some remains were visible 50 years ago.[108] Henderson says that an old tradition was that it was a royal residence, and used as a hunting seat by several of the Scottish kings; that it passed into the hands of the Riddells; and that the last of them had his son drowned by falling from the castle window into the loch; that from that circumstance, he drained the loch, which then extended to the castle walls. So much for the tradition, which I am sceptical about the truth of, as I can't see how the loch could from the nature of the ground and its other outlet extend to any such height.

---

[108] The Haining is a local estate, according to Robert Chambers, "the very elegant and ancient seat of John Pringle Esq. of Clifton."

So now we are descending the Green en route for the Peat Law, and the day is charming and cool. One house here is little changed in its outward aspect from the days of auld lang syne, and that is Julie Robertson's. This was a famous place then for the Ettrick and Yarrow lads at the Selkirk fairs, and also a decent house for a Sunday refreshment to these kirk-goers from the West who had walked their six miles.

We took stock of my uncle's old garden, which, till I got the explanation of the road having been altered, was often a puzzling subject to me. Now I see it all and the very site of the comfortable log house, and a famous apple tree before it. In all the ancient burgh there was not a finer garden for fruit, especially gooseberries, than this. A blue painted door opened at the angle of two wells, viz, the Haining and roadside one. Then a walk down the side of the former to the log house and round the garden, while another ran down the middle joining the one at the east well.

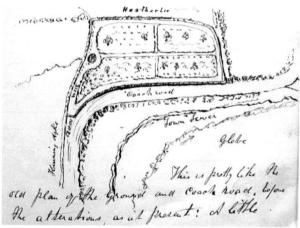

This is pretty like the old plan of the ground and coach road, before the alterations as at present. A little further down on the road leading to the Corn Mill was Deacon Emond's garden. It stood also on the north side of the Mill road and was a famous resort of the boys for gooseberries. The deacon kept up a constant sale in the season, besides giving the run of the garden for threepence, subject to his herding them in case they should fall on the nefarious plan of "pouching".

Bullsheugh: On comparing notes, the two Hendersons and I recollected of only two houses here, the one was a public house at the angle of the Ettrick road, the other was the house and workshop of John Shiel, joiner. I mind of it being built about 1821 or 1822, this used to be a pretty view looking down to the Mill dam, with its grassy slope and footpaths, while the flat on the other side of the dam was generally a busy resort for bleaching. It was here on a Sunday summer morning, when we were coming from Howford to church at Selkirk, that I first saw Robert Chambers.[109]

The "Piper's Pool": The origin of this name, as I have heard often told, is that at the battle of Philiphaugh, a piper who had been stationed up on the bank got a shot from the opposite side of the water and, as he rolled down into the pool, his pipes kept up a grunting till he and they were silenced by the water. It would appear from the stories of the battle we often heard in our young days, that numbers of Selkirk folk had come out to see the battle and stationed themselves on Lauriston bank where no doubt they would have a capital view, and be out of harm.

Lang Philip burn and the Corbie Linn: Quoth my old school mate James Henderson: "Oh! Then here is the Corbie Linn at last. But the old tree is gone, the tree where the falcons always had their nest — d'ye recollect it?"[110]

"No, I don't," says I. "Mind, James, that it is 48 years since I set foot on this spot, and that was in company of Walter and John Haldane — Robert Gibson and my cousin John Lang in the month of July 1827. Our object was to explore a large snow wreath that persisted in laying up in that hollow above us all the summer, although it was very hot. And when we did reach it, we found it a hard frozen mass, of a dingy colour, and a little trickling stream below it, while your memory is of some 20 years back. No, I don't mind your tree, but I have a vivid memory of these slaty precipices as well as the snow wreath, and Tibby's grave which we

---

[109] Robert Chambers (1802~1871) was an Edinburgh-based publisher and author of among other books, *The Picture of Scotland* (1827), a much-quoted work. It contained detailed descriptions of every county in the land, materials for which Chambers gathered by making tours of the districts he described.

[110] Circular enclosure, prehistoric monument

must be near, and to the west of us I think. How grand is the ancient heather, James, and in the full blow of the purple bells: how does it thrive in Canada?"

James: "Not at all — the frost kills both it and broom in the terrible winters of North America, only consider the thermometer standing last winter at 26 degrees."

High up on the Peat Law, across an ancient road on the Bleak Myres, the burgh lands form an angle with those of Philiphaugh and Yair. In this corner is a plantation of old weather-beaten and gloomy Scotch firs of stunted growth and in the extreme corner repose the remains of the suicide Tibbie Thomson. A rude boulder stone was put over her grave shortly after her burial here by a charitable dry stone dyker and bears the following inscription:

L.H.

I. THOMSON

F.S. — 1790

The meaning of this is: Lies Here Isobel Thomson From Selkirk —1790.[111]

I had but a dim memory of the story about Tibbie Thomson, which I had often heard in my school days at Selkirk, but had forgot the particulars. And as we sat by her lonely grave in the bleak moorland where three lairds' lands meet, I applied to my friend Henderson for information and he gave me the following account:

"Of course it was was out of my day and I have it from my father, who used to tell us, and, I think, was present at the unseemly proceedings of the poor creature's funeral in this unconsecrated spot. Tibbie or Isobel Thomson was a well-conducted young woman, who made her living by sewing, knitting and dressmaking. She was poor but always considered honest until the following incident of housebreaking and robbery was laid to her charge, for which she was laid in fact pending her trial but hanged herself before that day came. Public opinion was much divided in Selkirk as to her guilt or innocence, one party

---

[111] As AC was no doubt well aware, the initials *F.S.* do not stand for *From Selkirk*, but *Felo de Se*, "felon of self", an archaic legal term meaning suicide.

affirming that she was innocent and that no evidence could have brought forward to prove her guilt. To that belief I incline, but I will tell you the case as I have often heard it stated by different parties, and then you can the better form your own judgment on the matter."

*

Berwick, September 2 1875

There are two places of all others in the south of Scotland which I have ever had a particular wish to see, and these are Lindisfarne, or Holy Island, and Flodden field. I have seen the former more than once, when sailing past in the passage between it and the Farne Islands and made drawings of them on board ship. The first time was on board the Sir Walter Scott smack [ie, the boat in which Scott travelled] from Leith to London in 1835. Some years after, on board the ill-fated *Pegasus*, I amused myself with making sketches of it and the Farne group. I believe I then formed the intention of visiting them the first opportunity I might have in after times, an intention which unfortunately for the gratification of my own tastes I have never realised till now, in this month of September 1875.

Four of us set out from Berwick bridge in a wherry for a sail up the river as far as [the village of] Horncliffe on a pleasant afternoon, the distance is five miles. In the churchyard of Branxton, right before us to the south is a long ridge ending at the west in Moneylaws hill. The distance to the top, which is no great height, is maybe somewhere under half a mile, while between us and its base the ground is pretty level, with the exception of one of these knolls of ground which geologists term a moraine. This rises about 100 yards southwest of the church, and of a height about 12 to 20 feet. Here it was on this hill, called the Piper's hill, that the last stand was made by the Scottish host round the king, forming an impenetrable mass of spears which Earl Surrey tried in vain to break, but on which however the English arrows plied incessantly till night closed the scene. On the following morning, when Earl Surrey expected a renewal of the battle, not a living Scotsman was on it, all had departed under night after stripping the dead naked and no doubt burying the king, either there or in its neighborhood ere they departed. This has ever been my belief and now when I am on the ground with the parish schoolmaster giving me all traditionary information, this belief is strengthened that King James was stripped naked like others who fell around him and buried where they fell on the top of the Piper's hill.[112]

Looking to the north from where we stand on the Piper's hill is Cookham moor, where there is a large pillar-shaped stone, called "the King's stone," and there, according to tradition, King James was buried. I think this is very improbable: this stone was there ages before the battle and was known as "the gathering stone on Cookham moor." When England or Scotland intended to invade each other's country, the word was given to muster on such a day or night at "the gathering stone on Cookham moor." For this purpose it was made use of 32 years after the battle by the Earl of Hertford, and had it been known in these days by this name of "the King's stone" he would never have given it any other name. This fact alone shows that its position and antiquity support an origin that dates long prior to Flodden field. Besides, there could be no inducement to carry the dead body of the king across the English lines a mile to the north under night to bury him there. I think it is probable that the name may have originated from King James making some halt there on his march to Flodden hill, and hence the name of "the King's stone." I am more inclined to the conviction that the king would be buried on the spot where he fell, on this knoll, and under night before the worn-out warriors of the Scottish marathon departed. I think the tradition of the place is at fault about his place of burial, but correct about the state of this bloody spot on the morning after the battle - "a mire of blood on and around the Piper's hill" - "piled with ghastly naked corpses."

I lingered on this spot, hallowed with so many memories, especially with my own native Ettrick forest, when so many of her brave sons were "a' wede away."[113]

---

[112] "the parish schoolmaster" is Andrew's friend John Logan, the fourth member of the group.
[113] "carried off," ie, killed, from the well-known song about Flodden, written in 1756 by Jean Elliot, which contains the line, "The flowers o' the forest are a' wede away."

I took to looking about me for some little memorial of the battlefield of Flodden. Much to my surprise, while poking the soil with my walking stick on the knowe top, I turned up a stone ball about two inches in diameter and, a little further down, a human bone — a fragment of a thigh bone. At first I had some compunctions about removing the bone, but on being told that this field, at present in grass, would be ploughed next year, I decided to carry it home, and enshrine it among my sacred relics.[114]

We had been told when coming away from Berwick on the morning that this was a very hungry place, the small village having no public house and that we had better take our meat and drink with us. This prudent advice we had acted on in the purchase of a loaf and something else at Cornhill. We considered it full time now to have our lunch before taking another walk of one and a half miles to the top of Flodden hill. So we took our own seat beside a fine spring of water - the village well - where stood Surrey's waggons and tradition has it that on the morning after the battle it was *bloodstained*.

---

[114] AC took another relic from the battlefield, a flower, from "where the King fell," which he pressed in his book of reminiscences.

An old woman comes down with her pitcher for water and, as she happened to be the sexton's wife from whom we had got the church keys, these we handed to her when says she: "Ye wull be gaun to the 'Hill' gentlemen?

"We are intending that," says we.

"Then if ye will tell me when ye will be back, I will have some tea ready for ye — it will refresh ye after yer walk."

"Thanks, canny woman, your offer is too good to be declined in this wilderness, and we will accept with pleasure - say two hours hence - your well-timed charity to three forfauchlet [exhausted] pilgrims this hot day is beyond all praise. Surely you must be of the stock of Sybil Gray whom Sir Walter immortalises, a woman full of Christian charity.[115]

"And that she was, puir woman, her and me was cousins. But her name was Bell, no Sybil — how might ye come to ken her Sir, if I may ask?"

"How very strange — your cousin! How did I ken her, did you say? Oh well, it was the Laird of Abbotsford [ie, Sir Walter Scott] who informed me about her."

"Isna that strange! I didna ken him tho, but nae doot Bella Gray's been acquaint wi' him or he wadna hae spoken o' her. Then ye will find everything ready for ye twae hours after, when ye come back."

Our friend the schoolmaster here remarked that the most common of all names hereabouts is that of Gray. And when we arrive at Holy Island, more than half the population are Wilsons.

---

[115] The reference is to *Marmion: A Tale of Flodden Field*, Cantos XXX & XXXI:

> Where shall she turn?—behold her mark
> A little fountain cell,
> Where water, clear as diamond-spark,
> In a stone basin fell.
> Above some half-worn letters say,
> "Drink . weary . pilgrim . drink . and . pray .
> For . the . kind . soul . of . Sybil . Gray .
> Who . built . this . cross . and . well .

*

A pleasant walk southward brought us within fifty yards of the top of Flodden Hill. We halted on a level green spot, with a rugged ivy-clad rock rising some six feet from the level ground. Against this is a modern piece of sham gothic fountain and basin, supplanting the ancient well of Sybil Gray, which has been taken out and half-buried, upside down too, to form a seat in front of the well. This has all the appearance of a modern grate, with three angled faces in the recess and bears the following inscription:

> Rest weary pilgrim, rest and stay
> By the well of Sybil Gray

The ancient inscription on the buried stone, which we in vain tried to raise, runs thus:

> Rest weary pilgrim, rest and pray
> For the soul of Sybil Gray, who built
> This cross and well

The throwing down of this stone is significant of the Calvinistic tastes of the noble proprietor of Ford - the Marchioness of Waterford - but surely it is unfeeling to hamper and desecrate the ancient stone and inscription of its pious Catholic founder.[116]

A little higher up is "the King's chair" on which the marchioness has erected a neat rustic summer house, open all round with cutting of trees with the bark peeled for pillars to support the roof. Our temper got a little soured with the noble proprietor about the well, but here we had a double motive to get soothed and sing her praises. We had just a few minutes to see the most commanding view ever I

---

[116] Louisa, Marchioness of Waterford, "was a very Protestant lady who did not believe in prayers for the dead, and therefore substituted an invitation to rest for the second line."

had the good fortune to see in my life - Ettrick head, Lammermoor range to Abbotsford, the Merse, and the east coast of Northumberland - when down came a deluge of rain, that kept us fast within the little log house for fully half an hour. For amusement we took to reading the innumerable names cut and pencilled on the white parts of our house. A great proportion were from America, a good few from France and Germany, and scarcely a town or village on each side of the Border but was here represented. There is a good deal of poetry of the doggerel type, such as:

> From Coldstream's Town, of old renowned
> Four youthful pilgrims came (here followed the names)

and then:

> Three young men from Kirk-Yetholm hied
> On a warm July day to visit Flodden field
> Where their forefathers died — to be continued
> (on our next visit)

another:

> Some go walking tours and call it fame
> A smaller rout come to Flodden hill
> And write their name.

*

Holy Island, September 3 1875

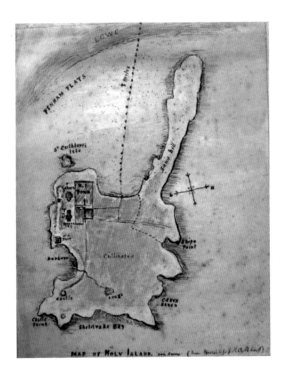

How beautiful to the eye and heart, by the side of the sea shore on a summer morning, the sheen of the morning sun on the ever-murmuring ocean, the glistening sands fringed with green sward clustering with wild flowers, and the hedgerows waving white with blossom. The mind beats in unison and our souls feel restored and happy. Thought becomes higher and nobler, while even sorrow catches a tinge of joy, and reposes itself on the loveliness of Earth and Ocean.

Take, however, a contrast to this day in September. A bright morning is suddenly changed to a drizzly rain, with a fog hanging like a shroud to your feet through which you see obscurely near-hand objects. You are glad of the shelter of a tree, from which you watch the pelting of the dreary rain, and the roadway deluged with a turgid mass of yellow water, while the dripping of the leafy shelter at last fairly makes you uncomfortable and wish you were under the shelter of a roof. But house there is none within miles, and the mind sinks in unison with the dreariness around you.

This was the sort of weather which overtook my companion John Logan and myself early on the morning of Friday Sept 3, just as we were within 50 yards of the beach which divided us from Holy Island, three miles across, and which loomed indistinctly through the misty rain. We managed to squeeze ourselves below a high quickset hedge which for some time afforded us dry shelter. And, as the tide was ebbing but yet too full water for wading what is called the "Lowe" or tide channel of some 40 yards width, which at ebb tide remains full of shallow water, we consoled ourselves that as time wore on it might be possible to get fair weather, in the course of another half hour when the long stretch of sands would be but ankle deep.

Says John: "This is dismal! What is to be done? Shall we go home again and get laughed at, or remain and get drenched, not to speak of starving of hunger in this dreary desert of sand and water?"

"No, John — we don't go back till we accomplish the praiseworthy object of our pilgrimage to the holy spot whence emanated the light of Christianity to the pagan tribes around, from Saint Aidan in 632; Eata, the founder of Melrose, and that truly great man, St Cuthbert the 6th Bishop; the learned Eadfrith the 8th Bishop in 700 whose beautiful manuscript of the four gospels you may yet see in the British Museum. No, shall we grudge a trifling inconvenience from a summer shower when St Cuthbert spent hours in his watery cell on yonder rock in prayer and meditation? Rather let us cast ourselves back in imagination some 800 years to these ages of faith when crowds of sandaled pilgrims joyously crossed that watery waste."

"Behold!" quoth John, "the wish is realized, we are in the days of St Cuthbert and yonder come three pilgrims - I am not sure yet about the sandals - I think they are barefoot and their garments are of the humblest type. Don't you speak, let me do the speaking. I was going to have some fun, but I will say instead some lively talk to raise our spirits. There is no doubt they are going across and, if they can do it, we may venture to follow. Should they fail, we are behind to assist; and they perish, why, it's only three old wives!"

Three wretched old women with small creels [baskets] on their backs, one bareheaded, another with a tattered round hat, while the third had a seal-skin cap and staff in her hand. They drew near to us to our side of the hedge and spoke:

1st Pilgrim: "Be the Lowe fordable yet, young man?"

Logan: "Oh! Mother pilgrim — how can I tell, a stranger from a far-off land, and wanting information about that stormy water ere we make our orisons [prayers] at St Cuthbert's shrine."

1st Pilgrim: "What? We be gaun across for cockles!"

2nd Pilgrim: "Ye be the schoolmeaster o' Scremerston [village in Northumbria]."

3rd Pilgrim: "An' we expeckit wad lead the way for us puir bodies — a't has oor merket to make at the ebb — wull ye no gang afore us?"

"O tempora, o mores [What times, what customs] — only fishwives who have not a soul above periwinkles and cockles, and I made sure you were ..."

"Stop yer nonsense and tell us if there is ony chance o' the brewer's cart frae Berwick coming to hand?"

Quoth my friend John: "Yes, I saw it leave Berwick this morning, and" - looking at his watch - "I am happy to tell you, it will be here in an hour. So you can either go across or take a comfortable seat and wait till it comes."

They passed on, and I thought I heard a giggle and one of them remarking, "I kenned him for to be the shipwright's brother - a solid sensible lad him - but that ane's *clean daft*."

In a short time and ere the old women were well through the Lowe, which we noticed scarce took them to the knee, the sun shone out bright and clear, the rain ceased, and in a very few minutes we had stript stockings and shoes and were fairly into the water. Very cold at first, we soon got used to it, and even liked it, especially as the bed was of the very finest level sand and a uniform depth, with exception of the deeper channel of the Lowe which, being narrow, was soon crossed and afterwards, the depth of our three mile wade might be 15 inches. A row of tall posts stretch all the way across, some 20 feet apart, with here and there some with cross-bars in ladder fashion, for the benefit of the unfortunate traveller who may be overtaken with the tide, which at times I am told sweeps round this island like a race-horse.

My companion John Logan here remarked about these posts that, although there would be a touch of the ludicrous in a couple of travellers such as ourselves and the old women before us being compelled, with a rising tide, to scramble up and perch ourselves like five demented clockers [broody hens] all in a row on these bare poles, yet that they had saved many lives, and witnessed many a sad death. "The fact is this — it requires one and a half hours to wade across, less, if the tide is ebb, when the sands are nearly dry by, say, quarter of an hour. But should you set out from either side at ebb tide, and that tide be a Spring one with a storm from the north or east, the probability is that you would be overtaken before you were half or three parts across. And then you are compelled and thankful for these poles even though it will be a seat of six hours while the water below you is 7 to 10 feet, a predicament that you and I must watch in our return in less than three hours hence. I think we can spare that, but no more unless we decide to stay all night, when we would get well posted up about the place from the fisher-folks' stovies and the Parish register, which I would like to see were it only to know the casualties on this dreary road."[117]

The extent of Holy Island is about two and a half miles from east to west, and from north to south about one and a half miles. It contains about 1,000 acres, about one half of which is covered with sand and produces nothing. The remainder is under crop and well cultivated. The principal proprietor is Mr Collingwood Selby who possesses nearly four-fifths of the island. The island is chiefly one continuous plain, inclining to the southwest; the village stands on an acclivity, which rises abruptly from the shore. At the southeast point is an abrupt rock which rises almost perpendicularly to the height of sixty feet and has on its lofty summit a small castle of ancient date. The village of Holy Island consists of a few irregular

---

[117] Stovies: a Scottish staple made from potatoes, onions and, for example, leftover roast beef and dripping.

streets and narrow lanes branching off from a small square called the Market Place. In the middle of this and close to the old monastic ruins stood the ancient Church Cross. Not many years back a short piece of its shaft remained, which went by the name of the "petting stone," over which newly-married people were made to leap for good luck.

Modern improvement has however removed this ancient Catholic landmark, and it is now supplanted with a cross which is worthy of no particular notice. The early church history of Lindisfarne is the history of the See Of Durham. The bishopric was founded in AD 634 and this island was the residence of fourteen bishops, among whom was the saintly Cuthbert, a notice of whose life, works and death is recorded faithfully by the Venerable Bede. About the close of the tenth century the see was removed, owing to the cruel incursions of the Danes, to Chester le Street and afterwards to Durham. And in the commencement of the following century Lindisfarne, so long the residence of episcopy, became the seat of the priory of Holy Island.

This priory, so interesting and beautiful in its decay, was erected about AD 1090 and belonged to the monks of the order of St Benedict. After the dissolution of monastic houses the possessions of the priory were granted by Henry VIII to the dean and chapter of Durham, to whom they still belong. The priory is of the Norman style, with some parts of Saxon, which would appear to indicate a building of older date than 1090. The church is in the form of a cross. The tower is said to have been the prototype for Durham cathedral and stood in the centre supported by two large arches, standing diagonally. One of them is yet standing, from its lightness and fine proportions it is the most beautiful object in the ruins. Probably this tower has not formed a lantern, as in most cathedrals, but I would infer from the angle arches crossing diagonally that they formed a canopy roof. The whole has been built in red and white sandstone, much worn and perforated like a net in the most exposed places. I observed in the inside, ranged along the wells, a number of stones with a curiously designed cable ornament. Some of these appeared to me to have been the shafts of crosses and tombstones, but these stones were not decayed, though evidently very ancient, and were a quite different stone from those of the priory.

Before leaving the ruins I could not help noticing the presence of a sea fowl like a dove, which on our entry perched itself above the ancient altar site. This bird was so tame as to remain all the time of our stay, altho we were sometimes close beside it. It was of one uniform white and very pure white — while we were leaving it dropt a feather from its wing, which I went back for and brought away with me.

*

As our time did not admit of a longer stay in this venerable ruin, and feeling besides that I was much in ignorance of its history, which I trust hereafter to read up, we passed into the parish church, in its immediate vicinity. This is only less venerable than the priory, having been founded before 1145, and although it shows a good deal of modern additions, yet much of the ancient Norman structure is still perceived. I understand it has always been served by a curate since the Reformation. Previous to that time its priest was stipendiary and received from the priory £4 per annum for his salary. In passing out of the door I noticed something uncommon about the doorstep and, on closer examination, I found a large old marble slab having indentations at its corners the shape of four shields while in the centre is that of a figure. The outline required no effort to decide that it was the Blessed Virgin and the whole design originally had been in brasses let into the marble.

Dimensions are 7' by 3'

At first sight I was inclined to the belief that this was one of the old altars, till I cleared away the rubbish showing the figure in the centre of the stone. I conclude that it has been a mural tablet in the chapel of the lady altar, and such as may be seen in both old and modern Catholic churches at the present day. On after enquiry I found that it had been removed from the Priory ruins by a late incumbent — to do duty as a doorstep!

I took a survey round the churchyard in the expectation of finding some old stones of Catholic times, but in this I was disappointed — not one could I find of earlier date than 1620. But I had got a glimpse, as I entered the churchyard, of some melancholy records of the *Pegasus* tragedy. There I began to read and copy, when says my companion: "I think it is time to look after our 'corporation' [ie, stomach]. While you are having some time to yourself, I will run over to Mr Wilson's and order some dinner [lunch], and hunt up the old schoolmaster, and an old fisherman I want to see."

Myself: "Quite right, John, do that. But before you go, ask for some information about two things inside the church there. The first is, two candles on the altar; and the other is, a written intimation on the pews which I cannot help thinking may have connection with these candles! The card runs thus: 'The members of this congregation are earnestly requested to join, and that loudly, in the responses.' Curious, isn't it?"

Quoth John: "Well, I noticed that too, and thinks I to myself, some pestering Free Kirk folk have been here putting the simple fisher folk up to some nonsense — and *they are kicking*. But I will soon find out all about it — the fact is, we are all 'high' [church] down hereaway. So much so that I can imagine my vicar coming to school some morning and saying to me, 'John, I have a letter from the bishop saying that the Queen has resigned her prerogative of first bishop in favour of Pius 9.[118] So till further notice, you can put these catechisms in the waste basket.' 'All right,' says I, 'you are my Vicar of Bray, and I am your schoolmaster, only look out about the temporalities ... .'[119] But we can have a talk about it as we cross the sands. Meantime, work quick while I see after dinner."

*

In Memory of	Sacred
Field Flowers	to the Memory of
Son of the Revd Field Flowers	James Richard Elliot
and Francis his wife	of Rochdale Lancashire
of Tealby Vicarage	Attorney at Law
Lincolnshire	who was lost in the wreck of the
aged 13 years	Pegasus Steamer
Who was drowned on 19th July	on the 20th July 1843
1843	and interred here on the 19th of
When the Steamer Pegasus	the following Month
was wrecked off Holy Island	in the 36th year of his age

---

[118] Pope Pius IX, aka Pio Nono, was the longest-reigning elected pope in the history of the Catholic Church, serving from 1846 until his death, a period of nearly 32 years. During his pontificate, he convened the First Vatical Council in 1869, which decreed papal infallibility. He was beatified in 2000.

[119] "Vicar of Bray" is a satirical description of an individual fundamentally changing his principles to remain in ecclesiastical office as external requirements change around him. The religious upheavals in England from 1533 to 1559 and from 1633 to 1715 made it almost impossible for any individual to comply with the successive religious requirements of the state.

Here are other mournful records of that catastrophe of the *Pegasus* on the Goldstone rock, in this churchyard, I wonder if the Revd. Mr Mackenzie is buried here, or in Bamburgh?[120]

Apart from this sad tragedy, I have two associations which connect my own early life with the *Pegasus*. The first is that I sailed in her in 1837 from Leith to London, when my mother (at the time in sea bathing lodgings at Granton) and my sister Henrietta walked from Granton to Leith with me to see me on board, and they were uncommonly amused with "a fleeing [flying] horse on the fore end o' the ship." I believe it used to be a standing joke with them afterwards, my sailing away "in sic a daft-like ship — having a horse wi' wings and web feet."[121]

My other memory of that same voyage was my taking a sketch, when going through the channel where she was wrecked six years after, of these ruins and the Island, as also of others of the Farne group and scraps along the Yorkshire coast. I have another memory of that voyage, of an honest hospitable Jew, who saved me from robbery and acted the good Samaritan at Hull where we had to break our voyage. I believe that was the only night I ever spent in a Jew's house and the hospitable treatment I got from these excellent people, without fee or reward, I have never forgot.

I have only time for another inscription, connected with the ill-fated ship, as follows — there are several others.

> Erected in Memory of
> Mungo Easson
> From Dundee — aged 23 years
> He perished on board the steamer *Pegasus*

---

[120] Just past midnight on 20 July 1843, the paddle steamer *SS Pegasus* of the Hull and Leith Steam Packet Company struck the Goldstone Rock in the Farne Islands. Of the fifty seven people on board, only six survived. The subsequent inquest found that the wreck was the result of "gross carelessness of the master and those on lookout". The Revd. J.M. Mackenzie, editor of the *Congregational Magazine*, was on his way to Bedford, where his parents lived and where he had been due to preach the following Sunday.

[121] The *Pegasus* boasted a magnificent winged-horse figurehead.

When wrecked off Holy Island on the

Morning of the 21st July 1843

His Body

Which is here interred, was found

near the scene of the wreck, and brought

on shore by a French fishing boat, after

having been three weeks in the water

A cross in bronze has a heart on which is the following inscription in French:

GI—GIT

Le Corps de Pierre Petitpont

Epoux de Lizabeth Germe

Decede le 4 Aout 1860

The above is a newly put-up cross in pure statuary marble and is a graceful and neat work and finishes for the present my visit to the churchyard of Holy Island.

*

On the top of Holy Island castle — 1PM.

To the south from here, the ground rises abruptly and rocky, clothed with a bit of the only green grass I see in the island. Here, on the top, the fishermen have some old boats set up on edge with a sort of seat inside. If I may judge from the few hours since I came, they seem to spend a great part of the day lounging there — probably some of them are pilots, and that is their place of look-out. To the east - the Farne Islands - Bamburgh castle on the right and under a mile distance the channel in between this and the castle on our left is the Swadman buoy where the *Pegasus* wreck took place.

"Is there anything remarkable in the history of this little castle, John?"

"Yes — it once stood a siege in 1715 and capitulated on honourable terms, a garrison of ten brave warriors went out with their arms, and the besieging force of two - the gallant Erringtons, father and son - walked in and took possession in the *name of King James* — wasn't it a grand lark? But the best of it was, their own vessel sailed away on seeing a government frigate coming round from Berwick, so they had no support but had to stand a siege in their turn, and of course it did not last long — they were taken prisoner and lodged in the Berwick gaol, but managed to escape out, before they had been 24 hours in. This castle I believe dates from 1530 and, excepting this siege, has nothing remarkable about it. There was another castle of older date just at the west of the little haven on our right hand, but not a vestige remains but yonder mound.[122]

"Observe now that little islet rock further round to west, that is St Cuthbert's isle where he had his little oratory, and the only place where they find these

---

[122] In 1715 the garrison of Bamburgh castle consisted of seven men, five of whom were absent. Lancelot Errington, an ardent North-country Jacobite, master of a small vessel lying in the harbour, discovered this. Accompanied by his nephew, Mark, he overpowered the two men who were left in charge, turning them out of the castle. He then signaled to the mainland for reinforcements, but none were forthcoming. Instead, a company of King's men came and reoccupied the place. The Erringtons were obliged to escape by swimming out to sea, but were shot, wounded and captured. Subsequently they contrived to burrow their way out of their cell in Berwick and, after hiding for nine days in a peat-stack, managed to escape to France.

peculiar fossils called St Cuthbert's beads.[123] I wish we could get some, but our time is getting short, mind, and if we stay all night we spoil tomorrow's programme, which is not to be thought of.

"So, at the moment, the tide is ebb and flowing back again, but we can spare half an hour to have a gossip among the natives — for instance, that group at the boats. What strong tall fellows they are!"

"They are indeed, an interesting study, for I observe a something in their fine manly faces not at all common in our parts."

"I suspect it is owing to their Norse blood, and little if any crossing outside this island."

"Yes, we shall go to them. But first tell me the names of the Farnes group, while we have such a magnificent view from the top of this height of some 80 feet."

"First then, straight before us, is the Longstone — Grace Darling's Island, from where she rescued the crew of the *Forfarshire* in 1838.[124]

"Closer into the shore of the castle is the one called [Inner] Farne from which the group take their name — there it was where St Cuthbert is said to have died. That long dark one to the left is the Brownsman; next, further round the coast, is 'Wide Open' [West Wideopen], 'Ox Sears' [Knoxes Reef], Meggetstone [Megstone], the Staples [Staple] — I have forgot the names of the others, but altogether they are 17 in number. This is one of them and called Lindisfarne, some say from the Lindis, a small stream over yonder which rises about the Cheviots, but best-known by the name of Holy Island. By the way, I often wonder what motive those old saints could have in selecting such a bleak unloveable place as this. Why, there's not a single tree or bush in it, and only one well of fresh water — pronounced first-rate by the natives, but which you and I considered decidedly brackish."

---

[123] St Cuthbert's beads are thick disc-shaped portions of the stems of fossilized marine invertebrates. They were strung together to make rosaries, hence the association with the saint.

[124] Grace Darling was the daughter of a lighthouse keeper. In the early hours of 7 September 1838, during a terrible gale, the 22-year-old Grace spotted the wreck of the *Forfarshire*, which had foundered on the rocks and broken in half. She and her father rowed out to the wreck and rescued nine survivors.

"Perhaps the motives of the saints were self-denial and mortification of pleasures which the world esteems, John, and counts their lives folly. But your remark reminds me of a question I intended to ask you. Yonder is Berwick, where my Henrietta toiled for years in her labour of love — teaching her Catholic school and often, often in her letters to me did she speak of this sacred spot. Pray, did she ever come here?"

"Only once, and long did she wait for 'her father' but *he never came*. So she had two long carts hired and set off with her children to this place, and I am pretty sure that a good deal, if not all, the cost came out of her own pocket. My vicar would not have done the like to me I guess!"

"You don't know what he might do if, instead of a handsome income, he had to descend to Father Connor's position and live on the free-will offerings of the poor, delvers and drainers, and poorer than his own schoolteacher. Few of your priests either would or could do it, John — the nursery they are reared in is incompatible with the fasting and hardships which Father Connor has to put [up] with, and which is done without a murmur, *pro amore dei* [for the love of god]."

"Oh, is that the way of it? Well, although I don't quite go in with that sort of doctrine, and I believe you and I won't agree on church matters, yet I know that we are at one on Henrietta. How devoted and enthusiastic to her faith! How untiring and exemplary in all her duties and, as your people down here often remark, 'her place will never be filled in Berwick'."

"True, most true, John — nor in Barnard Castle, nor in her father's house, will there ever be another who will accomplish the work of a long life in such a short one, as she did. No, spring will succeed the storms of winter, and the flowers will blossom on the Magdalen Fields where she loved to walk and gather them for the altar, but centuries may run their course ere they see another Henrietta L. Currie."[125]

"How she would have enjoyed this day among the old ruins of Holy Isle she was so fond of talking about, and the old saints of the church, in company with you

---

[125] Having married Francis Xavier Greiner, a Galashiels watchmaker in 1871, AC's second daughter, Henrietta Lang Currie, died in childbirth the following year.

her father whom she had such a veneration for. And by the way, before we drop our ecclesiastical talk - I know you don't care about it with a chap like I - but before doing so, inform me on a subject I used to hear Henrietta sometimes speak on. Of course I laughed the thing over, but since that time I find our own parsons have got hold of it: 'St Edwards Prayer and Prophesy about England' — is it true fact, or a monkish legend?"[126]

"I believe the fact of the dying king's prophesy is *true* John — that 'England, after departing for three furlongs from the unity of the Holy Catholic Faith, would then return and ever after be the brightest jewel in the church's crown.' I have watched the fulfillment of this prophecy in the last ten years, and I am sanguine enough to believe that in your side of the house, John, the signs are so significant, that if things go on as they are doing the time can't be long. The case, if true, will be all the more remarkable in as much as there has been no other instance since the days of the apostles of any country once losing Holy Catholic Faith, that ever got the grace again of reviving it. At least such was the remark made to me by M. Lemaire, prefect of the Seine, ten or twelve years ago.[127] He both knew of the prophecy and had perfect faith in its fulfillment 'as the time prophesied had commenced then.'"

"Strange! I must admit, perhaps there may be faith in the supernatural after all — what fear and trembling in some quarters about church lands, should that come to pass! Only think of, say, the Duke of Bedford, etc, etc, not forgetting him of

---

[126] The reference is to a deathbed prophesy made by the Anglo-Saxon king Edward the Confessor (1004~1066). In future centuries, God would punish the English for their wickedness by separating the green tree from its parent root, subsequently interpreted as the schism of the English church from its Roman Catholic origin. The distance between green tree and life-giving root was three furlongs, signifying three centuries, at the end of which England would again be reunited with the Catholic church. The prophesy was quoted by Ambrose Lisle Phillipps, an English Catholic convert who worked for to reconcile the Anglican church with Rome, on the occasion of the reorganization of the Catholic hierarchy of bishoprics in England, see note below.
[127] Obscure: Cannot find any reference to a M. Lemaire prefect of the Seine, Seine et Marne, Seine St Denis, or Seine Maritime.

the 'Durham letter' —why, it may as well have been a docken! [ie, something of no significance] for any good it ever did.[128]

"Oh, I had forgot to tell you I found out all about the candles, we are not altogether right in our surmises about them. The fact is this, the present incumbent is a new man, a son of the Bishop of ___. The last one was well-liked by the fishermen, and was always among them, humble and ever-ready to advise with them in all their troubles. This one on the contrary is very aristocratic and proud — never meets the people but on Sunday, never speaks to them at any other time. Of course he is as unpopular as a man can be, both are ritualists, and the congregation are taking revenge by keeping silence at the responses, and the choir won't sing. But ritualism has nothing to do with it, it is only the fisher-folk's way of showing him that they care nowt for him.[129]

"And in this grand herring season, how comes it that we have never seen a living creature in this garrison since we came? Perhaps like us they are gone on a holiday. I have a great mind to take the use of their boat, that neat little thing before us. We shall just go across to Bamburgh and back in no time, only they are cunning enough to bring the oars up to the castle. Suppose we look for them in some of their lockers — this door is labelled 'store room.'"

"Why, John, you can't be serious — it's piracy."

---

[128] The home of the Duke of Bedford is Woburn Abbey, originally a Cistercian monastery. Lord John Russell, author of the Durham letter, was a younger son of the Duke. Written in October 1850 and published openly, the letter was to the Bishop of Durham, attacking the Pope for having reorganized the Catholic church hierarchy of bishoprics in England. Russell alleged that the reorganization challenged the established church and its royal leadership by implying that Rome held authority over England. The letter was in part a response to an inflammatory sermon preached in Birmingham a few days earlier by John Henry Newman, the leader of the Tractarian movement, proclaiming that God was leading England back to the true church. Some saw the Tractarian movement as "a dark Jesuitical conspiracy to unprotestantise England, and to ruin us with Rome." A list published in 1878 of "Rome's Recruits", Protestants who had become Catholics since the Tractarian movement, included an entry for "Andrew Currie, sculptor."

[129] Ritualism - aka "bells and smells" - refers to an emphasis on rituals and ceremonies of the church, in particular of communion. In the Anglican church during the mid to late nineteenth century, the role of ritual was a subject of heated debate between low and high church factions. One aspect of ritualism was the use of "lights," especially the practice of putting candles on the high altar.

"Oh, never mind 'piracy', they all know me hereabouts, and my brother Adam better — he is constantly here mending their boats and I am sure that's one of his make. I'll just tell them I wanted to test her sailing qualities.

"No oars here — let's try the room below."

*

Crossing the Sands

"How changed since we waded mid-leg in the morning under a drizzling rain. Now the level sand is hard and caking under a bright sun, so we will keep shoes on till we reach the Lowe. Meantime, to add to our pleasant walk of three miles, let us have a bit of Sir Walter on this road: I brought away *Marmion* in my pocket, I sometimes practice my boys in school with some of the passages:

> The tide did now its flood-mark gain,
> And girdled in the saint's domain;
> For, with the flow and ebb, its style
> Varies from continent to isle;
> Dry-shod, o'er sands, twice every day,
> The pilgrims to the shrine find way;
> Twice every day, the waves efface
> Of staves and sandalled feet the trace.

"But before I read you more, let's settle tomorrow's program: shall it be St Abbs Head, or my schoolhouse, and another review of Flodden? Why, we have not seen the 'wishing well,' where the English host drank before the battle, nor St Paulinus's burn, where he baptised no end of painted savages. You can't go home tomorrow, neither can you finish your article, not to speak of drawings of these interesting places and the Twizel brig, too."[130]

"I fully understand, and am touched by your kindness, John. No doubt these places are most interesting, but I can come back and have another day on them. My first act early tomorrow is to walk along the Magdalen Fields, in the footsteps of my noble daughter, to pluck another flower to put in Margaret's wreath and then to take a sketch of your mother's upper window, with its little box of marigolds - Henrietta's room and window - then home, where, alas! there is *no Margaret now* to read my notes to."[131]

* * *

---

[130] St Abbs Head is a rocky promontory, the location of a lighthouse; St Paulinus was the first Christian missionary to the kingdom of Northumbria. Lady's Well, Holystone, is where in 627 Paulinus is said to have baptised the heathen English King Edwin, his son Osfrid and 3,000 of his people. It was formerly a pilgrimage site for Catholics; Twizel bridge was strategically important as the English army used it to transport their artillery across the river Till for the battle of Flodden. Andrew Currie returned the following year (1876) to make drawings of Twizel bridge and Twizel castle.

[131] Magdalene Fields is situated between the old city walls and the sea cliffs. Now a golf club. AC's eldest daughter, Margaret King Currie, had died just a few weeks earlier, in June 1875, of tuberculosis, aged 32.

WRITINGS FOUR

MISCELLANEOUS

[The following stories are all taken from the *Tales and Traits of the Borders* section of the *Border Counties Magazine*, 1880~1881.]

THE SPECTRE SEEN AT THE BISHOP'S STONE

One Saturday in November 1831, I had a day's leave from my employer at Denholm to go home to Ettrick; and the day being clear and shiny, with a touch of frost, I enjoyed the long tramp of fifteen miles very much. My communings on the long road were of no particular consequence. I jogged on cheerily by Woolrig, and, once past this and on to the moorland, I considered the journey as good as accomplished.

The Bishop's Stone is an eerie place on a dark night, or even in the moonlight, as I had experienced every time I chanced to pass it under night; and some thoughts about it, as I passed on this particular occasion, suggested that, as I would see old Murray in the evening, I would endeavour to get him to relate the story about the ghost he once saw there. He had told me the story before, but, likely enough, he had forgotten he had done so; and I wanted to hear him tell it over again, in order to see if he varied in the details, and thus, in a manner, test its truth and the belief he entertained as to the reality of the apparition.

Such were my thoughts and they were fortunately realised. My mother had taken a longing for a bit of fish; and she said to me, some time after I had reached home: "I wish ye wad gang doon to the mill, and get ane frae Jamie Murray. He has aye plenty reested [smoked] in the mill-kiln; and if he hasna, he will be sure to get ye ane oot o' the dam."

I found the decent old miller lighting-in at the kiln-logie. I took my seat beside him, and we soon got into conversation on mills, new and old, how they did in his young days, not so particular as they are now, etcetera.

"Ah mind," he said, "o' the fittin' up o' the first barley mill in Ashkirk Mill, whan ah was a young chap and the miller's laidman there. We wroucht weel through the nicht to get her on. There was nae lack o' whusky nor company to see the new performance; and there was amang them ane that was weel kenned in thae days, and whae was aye a welcome visitor aboot the mills, where he howfed [lived], for his droll stories an' news. They caw'd him Andrew Gemmels; nae doot ye'll hae hard o' him. He was an auld sodger, that had foughten at Culloden, an' mony other battles; and queer stories he could tell about them, whan ye gat him in the richt key, an' that was aye when ye gaed him a gude meltith [meal], a nicht's ludgin' an' a pickle [some] meal away wi' him in the mornin'. Andrew's measure, that pleased him best, was his ain neive [fist]; and he could gar [make] that turn oot twice what his awmous [alms] dish [begging bowl] could do, wi the squeezin', ye ken."[132]

After a little more general conversation, I led the old man on to the story of the ghost he once saw at the Bishop's Stone, and nearly word-for-word, and in his own way of telling, as near as I can, it is as follows:

---

[132] Andrew Gemmels was the model for Edie Ochiltree.

"Aweel, ah ne'er was a superstitious man a' ma life, an' ah'm free to say that excep' this ae strange sicht ah never afore nor sin' syne [since then] saw onything supernatural; an ah dinna believe ah ever tell't the story to aboon half-a-dozen folk in ma life, aye, no e'en to Jean Rea, ma ain wife, for twae or three year after we were married. What was the use, considerin' that folk noo-a-days disna believe these things, an' ye only get yersel' lauched at?"

Here ensued a long pause, and I began to fear that I might be included in the category of *unbelievers*, and so miss the story. But I was mistaken — the old man had only been reflecting on the past, as the sequel shows.

"Nae doot," he resumed, "ah *did* get an awfu' fricht that nicht, an ah'll ne'er deny that ah was bedfast for some days. Auld [Doctor] Anderson o' Selkirk - this ane's father - was at me, but couldna make oot ma case, an' ah never made him ony the wiser aboot what began ma trouble. However, ah cam' roond at last; an' atween yow an' mey, ah'll tell ye ae gude thing cam' oot o't - that ah downa tell to every ane - it made mey a better man efter; an' whae kens but, in the mercifu' providence o' the Almichty, it was sent for that purpose? At ony rate, ah hae sometimes thought sae.

"Ma story is this - an' yow that has schule lair [school learning] an' awquant wi' sae muckle new licht [modern] o' things they hae fund oot noo-a-days aboot the sterns [stars] an' sae an' sae, gin [if] ye can gie mey, e'en yet, a feasible explanation to convince a plain auld man that it was explainable frae Nature, than ah'm willin', e'en yet, to believe it micht be a natural delusion on ma pairt, an' naething mair; only, take tent! [pay attention] ah was as sober as ah am enow, in the best o' health and speerits, an' the licht as clear as a full mune can gie it.

"Jean Rea (the gudewife) and mey had kinda drawn up [been going out together] a while afore this. Wey had been schuled thegither, an' oor pawrents belanged to the same wurship; and sae wey had early ta'en a likin' to ane another. Aweel, she gaed to her first service [ie, as a servant] at Headshaw, and' wey had a sair pairtin', ah mind; but wey made it up that ah was to come ower an' see her efter a while, an' whan there was a munelicht nicht.

"Sae, ah daursa [daresay] ah had sent owre word ah was comin' on sic like nicht, an' she had tauld her maister an' mistress - decent folk that gude to Midlem [church?] , too, and was very kind to baith her and mey, baith than an' efter. Ah fand Jean likit them uncommon weel, an' them her; and sae, efter gettin' there, and gettin' some four'-oors [?] an' supper, they made family wurship, and than they tauld Jean an' mey that wey had twae oors till eleeven o'clock to oor ain private cracks in the kitchen by oorsells. The auld folk for ordinar' [normally] gude to bed by ten, but on this nicht there was a cow like to calve, an' they war gaun to sit up a bit.

"Sae we had oor cracks, an' away ah cam' aboot the time, an took the road ower the muir for Ettrick in gran' speerits. Ah was a stout [robust] young chap than, aboot twenty; ah'm gaun seventy-six noo. Comin' alang the parish road on the tap of the hicht [hill], a thocht strak mey a' at aince that ah wad strike off, for a near-cut, past the Bishop's Stane and Outer Huntly ground; an' sae ah did sae, whustlin' vera cheery, ah mind, as ah gaed ower the bent in the clear munelicht, and takin' a look roond at times. Ah had nae thocht o' ghaists, an' didna even ken that ah was on a place that gat an ill name wi' some murder aince committed there. Ah hae hard sin' syne [since then] that it was a Papish priest or bishop, and that that was the beginnin' o' the fitba' played there till no mony years back atween Alewater and Ettrick folk. But, bey that as it may, ah had just looted [stooped] doon to take a birn [burr] oot o' ma shoe for a minute, an' the neist, when ah lookit up - still whustlin' - to ma amazement, there was a man walkin' on afore mey, wi' a doug at his fit!

"Noo, ah wasnae wey feard — ah only thocht ah hadna seen him while ah was lootin' doon; an' sae ah gaed him a hillo, an' 'to take time, an' ah wad gie him ma company.' But naither him nor his doug took the least notice o' mey, but walkit on in the direction o' a gey [large] but steep knowe, that rises sharp frae the flat o' the muir.

"Still, ah had nae fear, an' considered that this micht be ane o' the gentry folk takin' a munelicht walk we' his greyhoond, an' that didna care to speak to the like o' mey. Sae ah keepit just aboot the same distance frae him, on that account - an' that wasna ower fifty yairds - till he gat to the foot o' the brae, an' began to climb it, wi' the greyhoond or staghoond at his fit. It was noo, when ah saw him aboot as kenspeckle [clearly] as ah sey yow, that ah comprehended that, if this was ane o' oor gentry, he had ta'en a dress that ah ne'er saw, aither afore or sin' syne, an' ah wull confess that than, as he strided slowly up the brae, did there come ower me a kind o' eerie feelin'. What was his dress, d'ye say? Weel, ah wull tell ye, as near as ah can, for it has been impressed on ma memory sin' that day, ye may be sure, and e'en the particulars, for it was aboot as licht as noonday.

"He was a big man, and had on what ah took at first for a mantle or greatcoat; but as ah stood still at the brae fit, when he was gaun up, ah saw verra distink it was a minister's cloak, wi' somethin' white, that gaed a flaff [flapped] noo and than frae aneth [beneath] it; an' he had a kind o' bonnet turned up at the edges, an' somethin' in his hand like a walking stick, wi' a big turned heed that the mune glanced on. Just as he stood on the tap, ah gat a glimpse o' his face, an' it was *wan*, an' he was readin' a buik that he keepit lookin' doon on, as he slowly sank on the other side o' the brae. In less than three minutes efter his heed disappeared, ah made the tap mysel', and lookit a' roond. Naethin' was to be seen! There was nae sae muckle as a thresh bush [clump of rushes] to hide him! Ma hair raised the bonnet on ma head, an ah ran back, in mortal terror, a' the road hame!"

Here the old man relapsed into silence, and after an interval, I ventured to remark: "That's an extraordinary story, James! I cannot tell what to make of it by any lair of mine. But first, let me ask you a few questions, to try for a natural explanation. In the first place, were Jean and you not talking over some ghost stories before you left her that night?"

"Never sic a thing in oor heeds," he replied.

"Well, we shall say that's settled. Let me ask you next, might it not have been the moon throwing your own shadow, or a cloud casting a shadow?"

"Na! The mune was high in the lift [sky], on ma left hand. Ah was gaun westward, an' this was strecht afore mey. Forbye, there was naither a bus [bush] nor a clud in the lift to make a shadow. Sae that'll nae do. Of course, there wad be ma ain shadow, but that wad be on ma richt hand side."

"Next, and I am done. Had you not too much whiskey, or might not your stomach have been out of order?"

"Nane o' them!" he answered decisively. "Ah ne'er was better than aboot that time; an' as for the other - the whusky - ah darsa, ah gat ae glass at pairtin' whan ah left Headshaw, and that's just aye been ma extent in drinkin' till this day. That wadna effect ony man. Na, na! Had ah been drinkin', ah wad efterwards hae laid that to that, and thocht nae mair aboot it; but ah was perfectly sober, an' thinkin' on onything but ghaists, and this ane was sae near, that ah saw every wrinkle in his dress."

Such, then, is the story of the spectre seen at the Bishop's Stone, the reality of which was firmly believed in, as we have seen, by the person who related the narrative. As I venture no explanation of my own, and have met with nothing tending to elucidate the matter, I leave it to those who, in the old man's own words, have "schule lair an' awquant wi' sae muckle new licht o' things they hae fund oot noo-a-days aboot the sterns an' sae and sae."

* * *

WILLIAM MURRAY'S SECRET

Whenever I climb Oakwood Mill Brae I take a seat and look across the level meadow, which in my young days was a peat moss, with deep holes filled with water. The prospect always recalls to my mind a very interesting incident connected with this moss which came to pass some fifty years ago. I shall endeavour to relate the salient points of this curious circumstance as they linger in my memory.

William Murray was the son of James Murray, in those days the tenant of Howford Mill, in Ettrick; and at the time I am speaking of he might be thirteen years of age or thereabouts. Well, one day his father sent him to Oakwood Mill to assist his aunt, Jenny White, in casting peats in the moss referred to. Jenny set William above with the "flaughter" [flat] spade, to cut the peat downwards in the ordinary way, she herself going below to take delivery, and lay them on the peat barrow. In this way they went on for some time, till a pretty large stone slab appeared near the surface, which stopped their labour for a while. At last they got it unearthed and turned over, and again resumed their respective places and employments. At the second or third cut, however, William send down into his aunt's lap a mass of glittering silver coins, in number about 300. Of this treasure Jenny took instant possession, and no doubt considered her fortune made. But ere long came a command from the Sheriff to deliver the coins up; and accordingly she had to hand them over to the Lord of the Manor, Lord Polwarth — minus, however, a good few that were purloined by one and another, before that came to pass. The deposit had evidently been in the grave of a Roman soldier, some fragments of Roman armour, much rusted and decayed, having been found near the same place, as well as some human bones in good preservation.

Young William Murray was much chagrined at not getting a farthing of the treasure which he had been so instrumental in discovering. In the hope of finding more treasure, therefore, he went in the evenings, unknown to anyone, all over the moss, probing it with an iron rod. At length he discovered another slab, about fifty yards to the west of the previous one. William, who was a secretive lad, told no one of this second discovery, but went at night to the spot, and with a spade unearthed the slab, which was much larger than the first discovered — so much so, that he was unable by himself to move it from the spot and, not having any lever appliances, he was reluctantly obliged to cover it up again, and leave it as it was. Before he did this, however, he took note of the stone as being deep cut with some inscriptions on the surface; and he also took exact bearings of its position, observing that it was in a line between two old trees, the one on the south and other on the north of the moss. I think the youth had in his mind all sorts of plans as to how he might accomplish the process of exhuming by himself; but at last he gave the task up as too difficult, and some years after made up his mind to impart the secret to me and get my assistance.

I think William was serving at Howford when he revealed the secret to me. I mind of an errand on which he was sent to Selkirk with the pony, and I along with him; and it was then I was shown the spot in the moss, with no end of exhortations not to tell a living creature, and with many inquiries as to when and how we two should set about the task of gaining possession of the treasure. That was not easily done, as a huge stone such as he described could not be lifted at will by two raw youths under cover of night. So the project was delayed by me from month to month, in spite of Murray's urging; and at last I had to go to my apprenticeship, fifteen miles away. Even then William used to press on me to get leave for a Saturday when there was moonlight, that in the evening we might go down to the moss and unearth our silver treasure.

To this I would assent, and many a time I came home mainly for this purpose; but by the time I got there I was usually too tired with my walk of fifteen miles to feel inclined to go another four miles to the moss and back. So it came to pass that at last William Murray - poor fellow! - went off to Australia with my brother John, and shortly after landing there he died. I recollect of his speaking to me on the subject of the treasure not long before he went away. Thus the secret was left with me; although, at this distance of time, and owing to the changes which have taken place on the ground, I am uncertain now of the exact spot pointed out to me when I was a lad.

According to William's minute and I believe truthful account, the stone was a hewn one and inscribed, and may have been a tombstone over human remains; but of course, because there were 300 silver coins below the first stone near it, there was no warrant for there being the same or similar below the second one. Be that as it may, the late Lord Polwarth and I had once a conversation on the subject at Mertoun House; and he surmised that it was probably the tomb of a distinguished soldier, whose treasure might or might not have been buried with him. His Lordship offered to send labourers with me to the spot, to excavate the ground, whenever I gave him notice of being ready to set them to work. But, somehow, I never found a suitable time to go, and ere long his Lordship died, and, of course, there was an end to the matter. Had I set about it, however, I would just have taken Murray's method when he made the discovery — that is, by careful probing with a pointed iron rod all along the line of search.

Often since then I have had grave reflections on what a singularly dilatory character I am! I am old now, then I was young; yet the whole looks, when the mazy years are bridged over, like a tale of yesterday, so fresh and vivid does our first appearance on the stage of life seem, when we cast a backward glance. Yet what a curious thing it would be, if some future generation, amid the changes which are sure to take place in Ettrick as elsewhere, should have revealed to them the silver treasure that so haunted the day and night dreams of my early companion and friend, William Murray.[133]

* * *

---

[133] The underlying chronology of this story is as follows: The initial events must have taken place in the late 1820s, when Andrew was still at Howford, before he began his apprenticeship in 1830. John Lang Currie left for Australia in 1841. Andrew encountered Lord Polwarth (Henry Francis Hepburne-Scott, 1800~1867) in 1855. The story was published in 1880, as Andrew writes, "some fifty years" after the events it describes.

THE PACKMAN AND THE RAM

Oakwood, at one time, had a tenant named Ebenezer Beattie, a man of bold and speculative turn of mind, who also leased a number of other farms, and for many years did a large trade in in sheep and in Highland cattle and ponies with the southern markets. Mr Beattie was a bachelor, and, in lieu of more tender companionship, indulged some strange pets. One of these was a magnificent ram, which generally dined with him. This brute was of a combative disposition, and found pleasure in boxing every living thing that came within its reach, to the great delight of its master, who much enjoyed this sort of fun, particularly if the sufferer chanced to be some gangrel body [ie, a tramp], on which occasion the ram would be let loose, to chase the intruder down to the public road and there capsize him. This practice came at last to be regarded as a grievance by the women and children of the neighbourhood, who were often injured by these frolics of the ram; and a public complaint would probably have been made against it, had it not happened that the pugnacious animal met with an accident which rendered it unfit ever afterwards of engaging in its dangerous pastime.

One day a bold little packman [pedlar] knocked at the kitchen entrance of Oakwood and, getting no reply, opened the door to venture in, when lo! out stalked the ram, looking very grave and majestic, and with its head lowered on a line with the pedlar's legs. But the man, realising the danger, walked backwards till he got to the head of the brae, when he turned sharply round and fled full speed down to the highway, the ram close at his heels all the while. The packman, out of breath, had just gained the public road, when he found himself suddenly lifted into mid air, and the next moment he fell, splash, pack and all, into a deep ditch full of water on the other side of the hedge. When he managed to right himself somewhat, with the water up to his chin, he saw the ram within reach, overlooking him very gravely, and evidently studying the altered situation, in order most effectually to assail the man of odds and ends in his imprisoned position in the deep ditch. The ram seemed at length to have made up its mind as to its line of tactics, for it began to move backward, in order that its charge at the pedlar - or what of him was to be seen - should have the greater force and momentum. But the odds were not, after all, so much against the packman, as the end will show. In the little time left to him, his wit, sharpened by contact with many a hard customer, had improvised a plan of defense suited to the circumstances. When the animal made its charge, the pedlar skilfully swept his ellwand [measuring stick] with full force across its legs, while he immediately afterwards ducked his own head to avoid its blow. This plan succeeded so well that at last - though at the cost of the ellwand - he broke one of the brute's fore legs, which disabled his antagonist, and allowed himself to escape from his unpleasant and dangerous predicament.

Mr Beattie was, of course, furious at the maiming of his favourite pet, and threatened the terrors of the law. He could not get up a case, however, as the occurrence took place on the public road, and the pedlar was only defending dear life — or such of it as was left him in the ditch. One good public result followed the pedlar's sacrifice: the women and children of the neighbourhood, as well as gangrel bodies in general, ever afterwards enjoyed immunity from the rough gambols of the animal. The ram, however, was carefully tended by its master in its misfortune, and was in future granted the *odium cum dignitate* [leisure with dignity] accorded only to tried and faithful service.

* * *

HENRY SCOTT RIDDELL IN MINTO KIRK,

FIRST SUNDAY OF APRIL 1832

I have seen and heard Mr H.S. Riddell for the first time today.[134] On the whole, I may say I have been disappointed. He seemed to labour under some constraint, as if he dared not let himself out — a putting on of the brake, as it were, on the poetic fire, lest it should burst out and extinguish the ordinary placid and narrow stream of pulpit oratory. Only in his last prayer, after he had warmed up with his subject, did he give forth sublime and noble utterances, worthy of the author of "Songs of the Ark." In person, Mr Riddell resembles a homely farmer or shepherd, with an aspect of heaviness and massiveness about him such as recalls Sir Walter Scott, till he gets animated with his subject, and then his aspect becomes wonderfully transformed into a man of bright and poetic fervour. As the kirk was skailing [breaking up], something like the following was overheard:

A: "Hoo d'ye like 'im, Gibbie?"

B: "Very fair. Ah think he's soond."

C: "Whae is he? He's mair like a herd than a minister."

D: "Oh! That's him o' T'iothead — Mr Riddell."

---

[134] Minto is near Denholm. Andrew was evidently attending church there in the third year of his apprenticeship. Henry Scott Riddell (1798~1870) was a minor Scottish poet, the son of a shepherd who as a boy himself also worked as a shepherd. At Eskdalemuir the family were visited by James Hogg. On the death of his father, Riddell attended the parish school of Biggar, Lanarkshire, where he wrote *The Crook and the Plaid*, one of his best-known songs. Riddell entered Edinburgh University, where he was befriended by Professor John Wilson. He eventually became a licentiate of the Church of Scotland, settling at Teviothead. In 1831 he published *Songs of the Ark*, "sacred pieces which are not of much account." At the invitation of his friend Charles Rogers, Riddell attended and spoke at the inauguration of Andrew Currie's monument to the Ettrick Shepherd in 1860.

E: "Gie mey a minister that gi'es us a screed o' soond doctrine, an' nane o' yer cauld stuff o' gude warks, as we gat frae — —. Ah judge this ane's soond."

F: "An' that's the man that poeted 'The Cruik an' Plaid;' an' him a minister!"

* * *

TIMELINE

1812, 6 November - Andew Currie born at Howford, Yarrow, Selkirkshire, eldest son of William Currie & Henrietta Lang

1814 - Publication of *Waverley*, first novel by Sir Walter Scott

1820~1826 - AC attends Selkirk Grammar School

1825 - AC's younger brother William dies, aged 5

1830, June - AC apprenticed to Robert Moody, millwright of Denholm [until 1835]

1831 - AC's father, William, dies, aged 59

1832, 21 September - Sir Walter Scott dies, aged 62

1835 - James Hogg, Ettrick Shepherd, dies, aged 65

1835- AC sails from Leith to London

c1835 - AC shows sketches and carvings to William Allan, subsequently president of Royal Scottish Academy, who advises him to concentrate on sculpture

c1835~39 works as millwright at HM Dockyard Chatham, Kent

1837 - AC sails from Leith to London aboard steamer *SS Pegasus*

1839 September - AC witnesses departure of *HMS Erebus* & *Terror* from Chatham

1839, 22 September - AC marries Isabella "Belle" Hardie, daughter of George Hardie, hosier of Denholm, and Margaret King, in Cavers, Roxburgh

1841 - AC "millwright employing one apprentice" [1841 census]

1841 - AC's younger brother, John Lang Currie, emigrates to Australia, aged 23

1841, September - AC's first child, William, born in Earlston, Berwickshire

1843, 11 March - AC's second child, Margaret King, born in Earlston

1843 - AC renews Rhymer's (water) Mill, Earlston

1845, 1 February - AC's first child, William, dies, aged 4

1845, 25 August - AC's third child, Henrietta Lang, born in Earlston

1847, AC's fourth child, George Hardie, born in Earlston

1848 - AC's mother, Henrietta, dies, aged 73

1848 - AC's youngest brother, George, & sister Henrietta emigrate to Australia

1848 - AC begins work on first commission, "symbolically-carved" bookcase for library at Cowdenknowes (final part finished in 1883)

1848 - Assists Sir John Murray in designing and erecting cairn monument commemorating Covenanters who fought at battle of Philiphaugh

1849, 18 September - AC's fifth child, Helen, born in Earlston

1851- 10 May - AC's sixth child, William John, born in Earlston

1851 - AC "millwright employing 3 men" in Earlston [1851 census]

1854 - AC's seventh child, Andrew Lang, born in Earlston

1855 - AC exhibits at Royal Scottish Academy for first time, aged 43; sells carving of partridge to James Hope-Scott
"Fairy flower stand" won in raffle by Lord/Lady Polworth of Mertoun House

c1857 - AC moves to Fisher's Tower, Darnick, sets up studio

1859 - AC executes bust of Burns to commemorate the centenary of the poet's birth + makes plaster copies

1859, 2 March - Mungo Park statue inaugurated, Selkirk

1860, 13 February - Becomes Fellow of Society of Antiquaries of Scotland

1860, 28 June - James Hogg [the Ettrick Shepherd] statue inaugurated, St Mary's Loch

1860, October - Sudden death of assistant, John Henderson

1861 - AC "sculptor employing 2 men" in Darnick [1861 census]

[Date unknown, but after 1861] - AC sculpts figure for Sir Frederick Graham of Netherby Hall

1863 - AC sculpts "Angel Figures" on Drummond Tract Depot, King Street, Stirling

1864, 18 December - AC confirmed as a Catholic

1866 - AC sculpts altar of St Patrick, Church of Our Lady & St Andrew, Galashiels

1867 - AC photographed working at studio in Darnick

1867, August - AC sculpts "couchant deerhounds" for the Hope-Scotts' door at Abbotsford in time for visit of Queen Victoria

1870 - AC sculpts pulpit & altar rails, Church of Our Lady & St Andrew, Galashiels

1871 - AC sculpts Old Mortality and Edie Ochiltree for upper tier of NE buttress, Scott Monument, Edinburgh

1872, 8 July - daughter Henrietta Lang Currie (Greiner) dies in childbirth, aged 27

1874 - AC sculpts replacement figure for [Charles] Marjoribanks Monument, Coldstream

1875, 5 June, daughter Margaret King Currie dies of tuberculosis, aged 32

1875, September - AC visits Flodden, Holy Isle on holiday

1875, 1 November - Helen Currie marries James Hume Nisbet at St Patrick's Roman Catholic Chapel, Edinburgh

1876, 7 July, birth of first grandchild, Margaret Henrietta Nisbet, in Edinburgh

1876, 27 September, AC elected member of Berwickshire Naturalists' Club

1876 - AC commissioned to carve statue of Robert the Bruce ["the Bruce sheathing his sword after victory"] for the esplanade of Stirling Castle

1876 - AC sculpts large medallion of Sir Walter Scott to mark the writer's birthplace

1877 - AC commissioned to carve statue of Sacred Heart for St John's Roman Catholic Church, Portobello

1877, 8 - AC exhibits at RSA

1878 - "Rome's Recruits" list published, "of Protestants who have become Catholics since the Tractarian movement," including "Andrew Currie, sculptor"

1880 - Oak mantlepiece commissioned by AC's brother John Lang for his mansion in St Kilda, shown at International Exhibition in Melbourne

1881 - Restores Maxton Cross for Sir William Ramsay Fairfax

1882 - AC sculpts "Girl Holding Flowers", marble bust, Edinburgh [City Art Centre]

1887, 30 December, grand-daughter Noel Ruth Laura Helen Nisbet born in Wealdstone, Middlesex

1888, 7 July, death of wife Belle of heart failure, aged 72

1889, 29 April, AC marries Agnes Miller Greig at Church of Sacred Heart, Lauriston Street, Edinburgh

1891, 28 February - AC dies, of heart disease, aged 78, in Melville Drive, Edinburgh; buried in Weirhill Cemetery, Melrose

APPENDIX ONE

- MISSING WORKS -

- Fairy Flower Stand, exhibited at RSA [1855]

- Goat's Head, exhibited at RSA [1855]

- Carved bookcase, including figures of Neptune, Moses & Burns, Geelong College

- Bust of Robert Burns [1859], executed for Royal Caledonian Society of London

- Angel Figures on Drummond Tract Depot at Stirling [1863]

- Bust of bearded male, photographed at AC's workshop in Darnick [1867]

- Figure of a Ram, Buckholmside Skin & Tan Works, Galashiels [c 1874]

- Medallions of Sir Walter Scott & Christopher North, Abbotsford [c 1876]

- Arthur Dalrymple Forbes Gordon, model for a marble bust, exhibited at RSA [1877]

- Statue of Sacred Heart, St John's Church, Portobello [1877]

Anyone who knows the whereabouts of the above works, or any other works by Andrew Currie, please contact the author: bejaystone@gmail.com

APPENDIX TWO

- NINETEENTH-CENTURY SCOTTISH SCULPTORS –

Thomas Campbell	1790 ~ 1858
John Greenshields	1792 ~ 1835
Robert Forrest	1798 ~ 1852
Laurence Macdonald	1799 ~ 1878
James Thom	1802 ~ 1850
Alexander Handyside Ritchie	1804 ~ 1870
(Sir) John Steell	1804 ~ 1891
Peter Slater	1809 ~ 1860
Patrick Park	1811 ~ 1855
Andrew Currie	**1812 ~ 1891**
William Calder Marshall	1813 ~ 1894
William Brodie	1815 ~ 1881
John Currie	1816 ~ 1879
John Mossman	1817 ~ 1890
Amelia Paton Hill	1820 ~ 1904
George Edwin Ewing	1828 ~ 1884
(George) Clark Stanton	1832 ~ 1894
George (Anderson) Lawson	1832 ~ 1904
John Hutchinson	1832 ~ 1910
David (D.W.) Stevenson	1842 ~ 1904
Thomas Clapperton	1879 ~ 1962

SOURCES

One

Inauguration of the Ettrick Shepherd's Monument, The Scotsman, 29 June 1860, page number unknown (taken from *The Scotsman Digital Archive*)

Hogg Monument Inauguration, The Daily Courant, 30 June 1860 (reprinted in *The Border Telegraph*, 27 August 1935

Inauguration of Hogg's Monument at St Mary's Loch, London Review, 14 July 1860, pp 33&34

Leaves From My Autobiography, Charles Rogers, Grampian Club, London, 1876, pp 270~278

Byways of the Scottish Border, George Eyre-Todd, Lewis, Selkirk, 1893, p 16

Proposed Monument to the Ettrick Shepherd, Caledonian Mercury & Daily Express, 7 December 1859

Extempore Effusion upon the Death of James Hogg, Poetical Works of William Wordsworth, Vol V, Moxon, London, 1870, p 98

Poets and Poetry of Scotland, James Grant Wilson, Blackie, London, 1876 spenserians.cath.vt.edu/BiographyRecord.php?action=GET&bioid=34904

Queen's Wake, James Hogg, Blackwood, Edinburgh, 1819, p 340

Shepherd's Calendar, James Hogg, Blackwood, 1829, p 57

The Stone & The Statue, Margaret Jackson Young, *Border Life*, [date unknown] p 30

·*A Border Sculptor*, Lillias E. Cotesworth, *Border Magazine*, Vol VII, 1902, pp 38~40

Two

Picture of Scotland, Vol I, Robert Chambers, William Tate, 1828, p 140

www.tchaikovsky-research.org/en/Works/Orchestral/TH049/index.html

www.surnamedb.com/Surname/Curror

Marmion, Canto Second, Sir Walter Scott, 1808, opening lines
www.online-literature.com/walter_scott/marmion/2/

History of Selkirkshire: Chronicles of Ettrick Forest, T. Craig-Brown, David Douglas, Edinburgh, 1884, p 311

Rule Water and Its People, George Tancred, Constable, Edinburgh, 1907
archive.org/stream/rulewaterandits01tancgoog/rulewaterandits01tancgoog_djvu.txt

General View of the Agriculture of the Counties of Roxburgh and Selkirk, Robert Douglas, Sherwood, London, 1813, p 297

The Langs of Selkirk, Patrick Sellar Lang, Mason, Firth & McCutcheon, Melbourne, 1910, pp 13~15

Howford Sale, Kelso Chronicle, 19 May 1848

See Part III, Writings: Reminiscences 1825 & Diary 1830

Centenary Memorial of Sir Walter Scott, Bart, Charles Lockhart, London, 1871, pp 58&59

The Scots Magazine, Vol. 60, Alex Chapman, Edinburgh, 1789, p 362

Letter to *The Scotsman,* J.H.H.T., 25 June 1920, p 6

Three

The articles of indenture are quoted from an 1861 contract between Robert Moodie and George & James Laidlaw. I am assuming that the language was legal boilerplate and that conditions would not have changed much in thirty years.

See Part III, Writings Two: Diary 1830

Treatise on Mills and Millwork, William Fairbairn, Longmans, London, 1871, p ix
archive.org/stream/treatiseonmills01fairgoog

Correspondence of the Right Honourable Sir John Sinclair, Bart, Colburn & Bentley, London, 1831, p 413

www.denholmvillage.co.uk

Biographical Memoirs of Eminent Novelists, Walter Scott, Vol II, Cadell, Edinburgh, 1834, p 139

Andrew Currie: A Gifted Border Sculptor, Geo. Desson, *Border Magazine*, Vol XI, Jan-Dec 1906, pp 4&5

Significant Scots: Sir William Allan, Electric Scotland
www.electricscotland.com/history/other/allan_william.htm

Currie, John Lang, J.Ann Hone, Australian Dictionary of Biography, Vol III, Melbourne University Press, Melbourne, 1969
adb.anu.edu.au/biography/currie-john-lang-3304

Journal of George Currie, State Library of Victoria

Letter from George Currie to Jean Scott, 7 December 1848, State Library of Victoria

Works of Walter Scott, Vol II, Constable, Edinburgh, 1806, pp 178 & 179

Cornhill Magazine, Vol XIII, Smith, Elder, London, 1889, p 303

Full Text of the Romance and Prophecies of Thomas of Erceldoune, James Murray, Trubner, London, 1875, pp v, xliv, l

www.ercildoune.com.au/index.php?page=history

A Border Sculptor, Lillias E. Cotesworth, *Border Magazine*, Vol VII, 1902, pp 38~40

Four

The main source for this chapter is *Virtue and Vision: Sculpture and Scotland 1540~1990*, ed Fiona Pearson, National Galleries of Scotland, 1991. In particular, two essays: *Sir John Steell and the Idea of a Native School of Sculpture*, Fiona Pearson; *Thomas Campbell and Laurence Macdonald: the Roman Solution to the Scottish Sculptor's Dilemma*, Helen E. Smailes.

Complete Works of William Hazlitt, Vol XVIII, ed. P.P. Howe, Dent, London, 1930, p 168

John Steell, father and son, sculptors, Joe Rock's Research Pages sites.google.com/site/joerocksresearchpages/john-steell-father-and-son-sculptors

Edinburgh Literary Journal, Vol IV, Ballantyne, Edinburgh, 1830, p 363

Edinburgh Literary Journal, Vol II, Ballantyne, Edinburgh, 1829, p 212

Tam O'Shanter & Souter Johnny, [classified ad], *The Scotsman*, 26 November 1828

Georgian Era: Memoirs of the Most Eminent Persons, Who Have Flourished in Great Britain, Vol IV, Vizetelly, Branston, London, 1834, pp 180, 182

Complete Works of Sir Walter Scott, Vol VII, Conner & Cooke, 1837, p 537

Scotland's Work & Worth, Vol II, Charles Thompson, Morrison & Gibb, Edinburgh, 1910, p 712

The Scot in America: Artists and Architects

www.electricscotland.com/history/america/scotinamerica_chap6.htm

Patrick Park, Sculptor, Charles Mackay, *Gentleman's Magazine*, date unknown (reprinted in Otago Witness 1885, p 25)

paperspast.natlib.govt.nz/cgi-bin/paperspast?a=d&d=OW18850214.2.55.3

Anecdotes of Chantrey, London Saturday Journal, Vol 1, Brittain, London, 1842, p 235

Letter to *The Scotsman*, W.S. Crockett, 28 June 1920, p 8

Hogg Monument Inauguration, The Daily Courant, 30 June 1860 (reprinted in *The Border Telegraph*, 27 August 1935)

www.edinburghmuseums.org.uk/CMSTemplates/ScottMonumentVirtualTour/pages/hisnovels/statues/friar_tuck.htm

www.glasgowsculpture.com/pg_biography.php?sub=ritchie_ah

Five

A Border Sculptor, Lillias E. Cotesworth, *Border Magazine*, Vol VII, 1902, pp 38~40

Hogg Monument Inauguration, The Daily Courant, 30 June 1860 (reprinted in *The Border Telegraph*, 27 August 1935

Letter from Andrew Currie to Lord Polwarth, National Archives of Scotland, 19 January 1856

Memoirs of the Life of Sir Walter Scott, bart, Vol II, John Gibson Lockhart, Carey, Lea & Blanchard, Philadelphia, 1837, p 174

History & Antiquities of Roxburghshire and Adjacent Districts, Alexander Jeffrey, Seton & Mackenzie, 1864, p 69

Restoration of Darnick Tower, Gentleman's Magazine, Vol 211, 1861, p 32 (reprinted from *Border Advertiser*)

Familiar Anecdotes of Sir Walter Scott, James Hogg, Harper, New York, 1834, p 236

Picture of Scotland, Robert Chambers, Edinburgh, Tait, 1828, p 116

Lay of the Last Minstrel, Poetical Works of Sir Walter Scott, Bart, Appleton, New York, 1864, p 19

Ancient Scottish Monastic and Feudal Remains, The Scotsman, 17 May 1865, p 6

News Notes from Melrose, The Scotsman, 19 March 1865, p 2

Letter to *The Athanaeum,* Geo Huntley Gordon, 25 June 1864, pp 877, 878

Letter to *Freemason's Magazine,* 1868, p 189

Proceedings of Society of Antiquaries of Scotland, Vol 2, 1854-1857, Society of Antiquaries of Scotland, Edinburgh, 11859, p 484

Proceedings of Society of Antiquaries of Scotland, Vol 47, C.G. Cash, Society of Antiquaries of Scotland, Edinburgh, 1913, p 360

Yarrow — Archaeological Discovery, The Scotsman, 6 June 1857 (reprinted from *Border Advertiser*)

Gentleman's Magazine, Vol 208, 1860, p 380

History of Berwickshire Naturalists' Club, Vol 10, Neil, Edinburgh, 1882, p 402

In the Scotch Border, H.C., *New York Times,* 12 February 1882

Bust of Burns (advertisement), *The Scotsman,* 8 January 1859, p 1

Chronicle of the Hundredth Birthday of Robert Burns, James Ballantine, Fullerton, Edinburgh, 1859, p 241

The Scotsman, 27 January 1859

gerald-massey.org.uk/massey/cmc_burns_centenary.htm

Six

The Builder, 1858

Mungo Park African Explorer, Charles Withers, Old Gala Club, 12 November 2003

www.oldgalaclub.org.uk/12-11-03_mungo_park.htm

History of the Berwickshire Naturalists' Club, Vol X, Blair, Edinburgh, 1885, p 390

Leaves From My Autobiography, Charles Rogers, Grampian Club, London, 1876, p 278

Memoirs of the Life of Sir Walter Scott, bart, Vol II, John Gibson Lockhart, Carey, Lea & Blanchard, Philadelphia, 1837, p 236

Life and Travels of Mungo Park in Central Africa, Mungo Park, Echo Library 2006 (reprint), p 213

History of Berwickshire Naturalists' Club, Vol 10, Neil, Edinburgh, 1882, p 399

Mungo Park's Monument, The Scotsman, 14 August 1858, p 3

Monument and Monumental Inscriptions of Scotland, Vol I, Charles Rogers, London, 1871, p 274

Account of the Life of Mr Park, Murray, London, 1815 , p 80

Inauguration of the Monument to Mungo Park at Selkirk, The Scotsman, 4 March 1859

Movement of the Hogg Block from Langholm to Darnick, *Eskdale & Liddesdale Advertiser* 21 December 1859, reprinted from *Border Advertiser*

Proposed Monument to the Ettrick Shepherd, Caledonian Mercury & Daily Express, 7 December 1859

Darnick - Sudden Death, The Scotsman, 24 October 1859

Seven

Border Magazine Advertiser, Vol I, Edinburgh, December 1863, p ii

A Walk About Zion, Elspeth King, 2008

www.scran.ac.uk/database/record.php?usi=000-000-028-993-C

www.oldtowncemetery.co.uk/history/pyramid.html

Stirling Tract Enterprise, Industries of Stirling and District, Stirling Council Libraries, (originally published) 1909

Old Stirling, Elspeth King, Stenlake, Catrine, 2009, p 68

Sir Walter Scott and John Henry Newman, Patrick Kilough, August 2007

www.patrickkillough.com/courses/sirws_jhn.html

Memoirs of the Life of Sir Walter Scott, bart, Vol VII, John Gibson Lockhart, Cadell, Edinburgh, 1838, p 180

Memoirs of James Robert Hope-Scott of Abbotsford, Robert Ornsby, James Robert Hope-Scott, Murray Edinburgh, 1884, p 150

Letter to *The Athanaeum,* Geo Huntley Gordon, 25 June 1864, pp 877, 878

Centenary Memorial of Sir Walter Scott, Bart., Charles Stewart Montgomerie Lockhart, London, Virtue & Co., 1871, pp 41, p 124

Address to the Berwickshire Naturalists' Club, Sir George Douglas, Proceedings of the Berwickshire Naturalists' Club, Vol XVII, October 1901, pp 11 & 12

www.ourladyandstandrew.org/founders.html

Rome's Recruits, Whitehall Review, Parker, London, 1878

See Part III, Writings Two: Diary 1830

Oblate Communications Historical Directory: Galashiels, Scotland, 1852~1859
www.omiworld.org/dictionary.asp?v=5&vol=2&let=G

Centenary Memorial of Sir Walter Scott, Bart., Charles Stewart Montgomerie Lockhart, Virtue & Co., London, 1871, p 125

St John's Roman Catholic Church, Portobello, The Scotsman, 22 August 1877, p 4

Eight

The Scott Monument, N. M. McQ. Holmes & Lyn M. Stubs, City of Edinburgh Museums & Art Galleries, Edinburgh, 1979

Scott Monument Completion, Building News and Engineering Journal, Vol 23, 1872, p 268

Scott Monument Statues, The Scotsman, 23 January 1872, p 3

A Border Sculptor, Lillias E. Cotesworth, *Border Magazine*, Vol VII, 1902, pp 38~40

The Waverley Anecdotes, Vol I, J. Cochrane & J McCrone, Schulze, London 1833, p 180

The Antiquary, Sir Walter Scott, Oxford World Classics, OUP, Oxford 2002, p 43

History of the Scott Monument, James Colston, Colston & Son, Edinburgh 1881, pp 100 & 101

Address to the Berwickshire Naturalists' Club, Sir George Douglas, Proceedings of the Berwickshire Naturalists' Club, Vol XVII, October 1901, pp 11 & 12

The Scott Originals, W.S. Crockett, Foulis, Edinburgh, 1912, pp 33~40

Notices & Anecdotes Illustrative of the Incidents, Characters, and Scenery Described in the Novels and Romances of Sir Walter Scott, Baudry's European Library, Paris 1833, pp 102~111

Tales of My Landlord, Sir Walter Scott, Baudry's European Library, Paris, 1831, p 124

See Part III, Writings One: Reminiscences 1825

www.ecclesmachan.org.uk/oindust.htm

Nine

George Cruikshank's Life, Times & Art, Vol II, Robert L. Patten, Rutgers University Press, New Jersey, 1996, pp 469~476
Monument to King Robert the Bruce, The Scotsman, 11 March 1872, p 4

Letter from Andrew Currie to Charles Rogers, 14 December 1877, George Cruikshank Collection, Princeton University Library

Monument to King Robert the Bruce, The British Architect and Northern Engineer, 29 September 1876, p 205

Unveiling of the Bruce Statue at Sterling, The Scotsman, 26 November p 6

Inauguration of the Bruce Statue, Aberdeen Weekly Journal, 26 November 1877

Inauguration of the Bruce Monument, Stirling Observer and Midland Counties Advertiser, 29 November 1877

Statue of King Robert the Bruce, Dundee Courier & Argus and Northern Warder, 7 December 1877

Ten

See Part III, Writings Three: Reminiscences 1875

en.wikipedia.org/wiki/Flowers_of_the_Forest

Border Counties Magazine, Vol I, October 1880, pp 85 & 86

Complete Works of Walter Scott, Conner & Cooke, New York, 1833, p 430

Nesbitt & Nisbet Artists, Raymond Nisbet Rolinson, Nesbitt/Nisbet Society, London, 2008, pp 10~13

The Artists of Queensland Avenue, Judith Goodman, Merton Historical Society Bulletin 137, March 2001, p 14

Ashes: A Tale of Two Spheres, Hume Nesbitt, Authors' Cooperative Publishing, London, 1890, pp 63~65

The Langs of Selkirk, Patrick Sellar Lang, Mason, Firth & McCutcheon, Melbourne, 1910, pp 13~15

Currie, John Lang, J.Ann Hone, Australian Dictionary of Biography, Vol III, Melbourne University Press, Melbourne, 1969
adb.anu.edu.au/biography/currie-john-lang-3304

The [Melbourne] *Age*, 25 July 1939

Maxton Cross, Border Counties Magazine, Vol I, October 1880, p 131

Eleven

History of the Berwickshire Naturalists' Club, Vol VIII, Blair, Edinburgh, 1879, p32

History of the Berwickshire Naturalists' Club, Vol X, Blair, Edinburgh, 1885, pp 268, 274, 396~405
archive.org/stream/historyofberwick10berw#page/n3/mode/2up

William Murray's Secret [letter], Francis Lynn, *The Border Magazine*, Vol IX, Menzies, Edinburgh, 1904, p 226

Border Counties Magazine, Vol 1, Litster, Galashiels, 1880/1

North and South of the Tweed, Jean Lang, Jack, Edinburgh, 1913, pp 212~218; pp 245~248

A Border Sculptor, Lillias E. Cotesworth, *The Border Magazine*, Vol VII, 1902, pp 38~40

Obituary and Funeral Notice of Andrew Currie, *The Scotsman*, 2 March 1891

Address to the Berwickshire Naturalists' Club, Sir George Douglas, Proceedings of the Berwickshire Naturalists' Club, Vol XVII, October 1901, pp 11 & 12

Andrew Currie: A Gifted Border Sculptor, Geo. Desson, *Border Magazine*, Vol XI, Jan-Dec 1906, pp 4&5

History of St Mary's Abbey, Melrose, James Wade, Jack, Edinburgh, 1861, p 103

* * *

ACKNOWLEDGEMENTS

I have enjoyed all my books, but I can honestly say that this one has been the most fun to research and write. In large part the pleasure derived from the many interactions I had with "the team" — the friends and relatives old and new who have contributed their time, skills and much else in helping me gather the materials that make up this book.

Above all I am deeply grateful to my good friend Angus McDonald for many things, but in particular his tenacity in tracking down long-lost works by Andrew Currie, for which he earned the title of "number-one sculpture detective." Angus made countless phone calls, chased entire flocks of wild geese, and never took no for an answer from anyone.

My original idea was to publish high-quality images of all of Andrew Currie's known works. Given that I had essentially no budget, I wasn't sure whether this would be possible. Happily Walter McLaren and my old friend John Reiach, both professional photographers, rallied round and generously donated their services. They poured themselves into the project, in some cases returning repeatedly to photograph works, with the remarkable results for all to see. I cannot thank them enough. Another old friend, Lee Noel, kindly volunteered his talent and time to produce the beautiful cover design.

My cousin Alison Clark's visit to Australia helped stimulate my interest in Andrew Currie. Alison's consummate librarian's skills were invaluable in retrieving items from the darkest depths of databases. My brother and sister-in-law Bill & Mara laid the groundwork for Border researches and laid on fine hospitality for the team. My other brother John also contributed by digging up vital reference materials. And my son Scott turned out to have unsuspected but vital book formatting skills.

A happy by-product of this project is that I have discovered several previously-unknown cousins. They include Jenny Kahn and John Emond. Jenny drew on her formidable genealogical nous to point me in the right direction. She also read first drafts and made useful suggestions and comments. John, among other kindnesses, introduced me to Walter, who turned out to be not just a fine photographer but also a master of the dark arts of Photoshop.

Various museums and institutions generously contributed advice and images. Dr Helen Smailes, doyenne of nineteenth-century Scottish sculpture and Senior Curator at the National Gallery of Scotland, gently walked me through the arcana of mallet and chisel. Thanks also to David Patterson, Curator of Fine Art at the City

Art Centre Edinburgh; Paul McCauley, Conservation Office at the City of Edinburgh's Museum Collections Centre; David Mitchell, Director of Conservation of Historic Scotland; Matthew Withey of the Abbotsford Trust; Dr Elspeth King, Director of the Stirling Smith Art Gallery and Museum; Dr Margaret Collin, President of the Melrose Historical Ass ociation; and Aileen Wilson of the Clapperton Trust.

Niel Redpath and Catherine Brumwell were kindness itself in letting a stranger into their homes to photograph Andrew Currie's first commissions. Above all, many thanks to Chris & Val Lang, without whom this book would never have happened. Also to Tom & Monica Dennis, for their invaluable cooperation. And, as ever, to my wife Setsuko, for her support and for putting up with me for the duration of yet another obsession.

Melbourne September 2012

Made in the USA
Charleston, SC
17 October 2012